Re-*de*-sign

fb

Re-*de*-sign

New Directions for Your Interior Design Career

C a t h y   W h i t l o c k

ASID

Fairchild Books
New York

Executive Editor: Olga T. Kontzias
Editorial Development Director: Jennifer Crane
Senior Development Editor: Joseph Miranda
Associate Art Director: Erin Fitzsimmons
Production Director: Ginger Hillman
Production Editor: Jessica Rozler
Cover Design: Erin Fitzsimmons
Cover Art: © Fernando Bengoechea/Beateworks/Corbis
Text Design: Renato Stanisic
Page Composition: SR Desktop Services

Library of Congress Catalog Card Number: 2008934255

ISBN: 978-1-56367-639-0

GST R 133004424

Printed in China

TP15

Extended Contents

Foreword

By Sherri Donghia

The role of an interior designer today is as diverse and chameleon-like as the spaces and products and moods they are commissioned to create. Being a citizen of the world and immersing oneself into foreign cultures through travel, film, and books is key to developing relevance and believability as a taste-maker. Having an insatiable appetite for what is best in art, architecture, and fashion, from the past and present, will nourish and enrich your work, and inspire and educate your clients and associates. A consistent refresher program of continuing education in subjects from materials and finishes to sustainable product standards and building codes is necessary to be a professional designer in the twenty-first century. Learning by exposure through reading international publications on all related disciplines is a never ending flow of information and inspiration. Attending lectures, trade shows, antique markets, show houses,

auctions, and estate sales keeps your eye sharp and your mind agile.

Looking forward and backward simultaneously is a skill that when mastered enables a designer to create interiors that are timely and timeless, comfortable and functional. Knowledge of the historical past woven into the best of contemporary design and technology will result in rooms and products enjoyed for decades.

We are in a constant climate of change that demands us to stay open-minded and informed and able to collaborate with people of diverse backgrounds and areas of expertise.

Each commission and design brief is a unique problem to be solved and should reflect a signature style that speaks volumes about the people occupying the space. Custom couture interiors and products should be the highest quality work available through professionally trained designers and their trade sources and workrooms, so do not disappoint!

Contrasts and contradictions should live side by side to create positive energy and a seductive environment. This design tension when successfully achieved is an artful balance of antique and modern, handmade and high tech, refined and primitive, precious antique and found object. There should be a special place for arrangements of highly personal memorabilia and photographs in a carefully ordered display for the enjoyment of family and friends. These very private vignettes, along with the all important well stocked library are the heart and soul of every thinking person's home—a repository of the intellectual adventures of the owners.

Human beings crave spaces to call their own whether grand or modest, and the designer must listen and learn in order to create living collages that eloquently reflect their inhabitants. In the best of these environments there is an air about the arrangement of furniture and objects that suggests everything came together in an unplanned accidental fashion. Nothing too studied or forced, just an illusion that it all happened with a sweep of the hand. This is the sign of memorable design for me.

The Japanese concept of Wabi Sabi rooted in Zen Buddhism, celebrates the impermanence of the natural world. It teaches that true contentment begins with the acceptance of imperfections, both our own and everyone else's. As an aesthetic theory, Wabi Sabi asserts that imperfection is what gives an object its beauty and soul. I strongly believe that design is now more in sync with this ancient philosophy. A good example is the importance and acceptance of PATINA in the mix of furnishings, accessories, wall, ceiling, and floor treatments. These elements do not have a specific color, but instead posses a multi-layered patina that is the result of its age, history, and circumstance. They have an interesting story to tell that gives depth and character to the room.

Being fluent in using the basic elements of design to their best advantage is paramount to successful interiors. Form, light, texture, and color seem simple enough as the basic tools of the trade, but are complex concepts worth exploring and experimenting with throughout one's career.

Form provides the foundation for innovative beauty; it is the designer's interpretation that gives a piece its soul. The Golden Mean, also known as the Divine Proportion, is the ultimate formula for a proportional ratio that is universally pleasing and comforting. Artists and architects through the ages have either consciously or unconsciously used the concept in their designs. An in-depth study of the Golden Mean is a worthwhile endeavor that will have positive lasting results.

Texture is a designer's aphrodisiac. It seduces and ensnares, offering endless visual and tactile pleasures. We associate texture with warmth, protection, and love on an emotional level, and on a physical level with hand, drape, and weave structure. A mix of textures in a room creates a pleasing cornucopia of dissonant sensations, so important to feeling authenticity and character in a space.

Color, of all the design elements is perhaps the most intimately linked to emotional experiences and moods. I think that layers of complex colors found in nature work gracefully with each other, and their reaction to light is more compelling as each layer creates its own luminous palette. Your clients are ready for more sophisticated use of color in the many choices of materials and finishes currently available. Unique color combinations and surface techniques provide the first step in creating personal collages that are becoming the wave of the future.

Light is to a home as optimism is to a person. Everything else, great space, quality furnishings, brilliant artwork, feels somewhat uninspired without it. Lighting specialists are more in demand than ever for indoor and outdoor design solutions. Research and experiment with mixing traditional and contemporary lighting sources. There is nothing more enchanting for me than a combination of Venetian glass lighting, candlelight, and mirrors. Try this if you want to be transported to another place and time.

Good design is also good business. The designer-as-artist model has kept the creative professional from being more strategically involved as a knowledgeable collaborator. Today's professional should have the ability to traverse boundaries into the world of business, which requires them to be engaged in multiple disciplines. Employ someone to focus on the business of design if this specialty is not your strength.

Decoration and design are both elements that can elevate a space above the commonplace. It's one thing to furnish a house and quite another to imbue it with unique style. Have fun and enjoy the challenge, opportunity, and responsibility of your well chosen career.

Preface

Hailed as the quintessential interior decorators of yesteryear, Elsie de Wolfe and Sybil Colefax might not recognize the world of today's interior designer.

Primarily born out of a need to modernize the homes of the wealthy at the turn of the century, the concept of hiring a professional to transform the look of an interior space was introduced and the interior decorator was born. Armed with good taste, design skills, and social status—and replacing the work that once fell under the domain of architects, cabinet makers and upholsterers—these pioneering men and women primarily focused on the decorative and ornamental design of the interior. Their groundbreaking work (along with the contributions of other professionals from a century before) paved the way for the interior design profession of today.

And while both past and present professional roles remain the same (think of the proverbial "Jack and Jill of All Trades" as designer, psychologist, mediator, shopper, floor and space planner, etc.) today's designers have added product and furniture designer, writer, retailer, and even radio and television star to their resumes.

From a constantly evolving global marketplace fueled by savvy design consumers, an increase in mass marketed furnishings, demand for specialty services and new technologies permanently dotting the business landscape, it's a brave new world of design. Add to the mix the factors of an uncertain economy, the greening of the environment, changes in society and lifestyles, and the advent of do it yourself television and retailing and you have a recipe for a revolution in how we do business.

While the age-old choice for designers has always been residential and/or contract, modern students and designers are venturing into numerous avenues uncharted by their predecessors. As we face a world of catalogues, cyberspace, and cable television, specialization and diversification will become our mantra.

As a self-professed "Jill-of-All-Trades" myself, the idea for this book came to me while standing at the intersection of my own career crossroad. I primarily practiced as a residential interior designer for almost twenty-two years and noticed massive changes in the business. After attending Parsons School of Design, I was fortunate enough to live and work in New York during what I called the *Bonfire of the Vanities* period— a time where tony well-heeled Wall Street clients thought nothing of dropping a month's salary on bullion fringe. It was a booming time of over-the-top abundance, lavish excess . . . and designers charging retail.

Over the years, the terrain has changed. Clients are now able to find furnishings once available to the trade only, surprisingly on their own. The newsstands are stocked with shelter publications giving all sorts of advice to the novice. The Internet provides a wealth of upholstery styles at the touch of a button and basic cable channels tell all you need to know on how to choose a paint color. The residential Renaissance has begun.

Don't get me wrong—there will always be a need for products and services only provided by an interior designer. A skilled eye, talent, and years of experience coupled with customer service and quality workmanship will trump the "do-it-yourselfer" anytime. There is also an increasing need for talented contract designers to meet the demands of the burgeoning market of commercial offices, hotels, restaurants, and retail shops. But competition remains fierce and the need for specialization and diversification becomes even more appealing if not a downright necessity.

Perhaps it is my own self-diagnosed attention-deficit-disorder, desire to try all the items in the buffet line, coupled with an insatiable curiosity that led my career to a new arena—design journalism. Soon I began to write magazine articles, made guest appearances on Home and Garden Television and the Fine Living channel, and subsequent book deals followed.

My natural inquisitiveness led me to the inner workings of the design industry. I became curious as to how an architectural icon transformed the way we look at simple everyday household items or how a successful interior designer expanded her business with a line of products and retail shops. And how a fellow colleague took a page from Martha Stewart and built an empire on the lifestyle concept with a magazine, television show, line of books, and furniture. How did these professionals enter the business? What areas did they train in? What motivated them to advance to the top of their field and how did they get there?

And so a book was born.

Re-de-sign: New Directions for Your Interior Design Career will shine a much needed spotlight on an array of career alternatives in the interior design field from the tried-and-true areas of residential and contract to specialty design. It will also serve as a guide for those considering a career in design and the interior design student as well as the established designer who wants to take their professional practice to new heights.

Part One will focus on the interior design industry, providing an overview of the profession and the role of the interior designer of the past, present, and future. Just like the principles of designing a room, there are no simple formulas for designing a career and certainly no set rules for success. Education, career planning, the job search and outlook, salaries, and an overview of portfolio preparation will assist and advise students in developing their academic careers.

Parts Two through Four will focus on the roles of "The Residential and Contract Designer" as well as the various specialty areas of "The Diversified Designer" as retailer, showroom and catalogue owner, and marketer. The newly crowned term of "The Lifestyle Designer" will be profiled along with "The Product and Furniture Designer." I will also feature a number of various specialties from yacht and airplane design to home staging for "The Specialty Designer."

The "Designer in the Media"—my favorite area—will highlight design journalists from book publishing and magazines to television personalities. Our design counterparts in Tinseltown, production designers and set decorators, will be profiled in "The Designer in Hollywood."

I use the six P's to detail the different design professions: Profession overview; Process of the roles and responsibilities; Preparation of your career including education, training, and extracurricular activities; Pay (I know, designers are not just in it for the money!); and the Path (which covers the journey to that goal).

Each chapter will end with Profiles of leading interior designers and professionals from adjacent careers. Many of these designers have come from all walks of life; some have design degrees and others are self-taught and their backgrounds are as diverse as their styles. While some may appear to have been given "a leg up" so to speak or be at the right place at the right time, hard work, perseverance, talent, and an ability to think outside the box are the secrets to their success. What these designers have in common is a multi-dimensional career and that their achievements can easily fit in any one of the various chapters. For example, Jonathan Adler has retail shops, a multi-category line of home furnishings, books, and has most recently become a television star. And they have all taken diversification to new heights.

Interior design can truly be a wonderful profession. There is nothing like the thrill of a satisfied client when they first walk into a finished installation, the sense of accomplishment when you solve the insurmountable space problem, or seeing your designs splashed in full color splendor on the glossy pages of a magazine.

But it is also hard work, long hours, and quite often the pay, experience, and time is not equal. And it is also far from glamorous. I can recall one too many times facing bad fabric dye lots, orders gone awry, and indecisive clients searching through a grueling fourteen shades of red paint for the perfect color for their dining room. I even had a client call me late one night and request that I go to Harry's Bar in Manhattan and match up a paint color to a Bellini cocktail (apparently he was looking for the perfect shade of peach!). Every designer has their own war stories to tell.

It is my sincere wish that you find this book informative and educational, as well as inspirational and enjoyable, and that your design career be a rewarding one. May your travels be well planned yet spontaneous. Above all, be sure to savor the journey.

And if Elsie or Sybil were alive today, no doubt they would have plans for their own television show or a product line at Target . . . and be making the world a more beautiful place in the process.

Acknowledgments

They say life is a series of synchronistic moments where one experience leads to another. Such was the case in 2005 when Inge Heckel, President of the New York School of Interior Design, asked me to speak at their lecture series on my favorite topic, design in the cinema.

As luck would have it Joseph Miranda, an editor at Fairchild Books, was in the audience. After a subsequent meeting, one book idea led to another, and while I hate to use yet a second cliché in the same paragraph, the rest was history.

I am so grateful to Joseph and Olga Kontzias, executive editor, for understanding the concept, seeing the possibilities, believing in me, and most importantly, making this book a reality. A special thank you also to Jennifer Crane, senior development editor, for walking me through the basics and to Jessica Rozler, production editor, and Erin Fitzsimmons, associate art director, for all of their wonderful help.

A very special heartfelt thank you to Sherri Donghia for writing the Foreword. She is truly a shining example of the multifaceted creative designer of modern times and I thank her for sharing both her wisdom and story.

A book of this magnitude could not be written without the guidance, advice, and support from all facets of the interior design industry. Thanks to the many architects, designers, decorators, teachers, media, journalists, public relations firms, and all of the many assistants who literally opened up their doors, journals, businesses, and rolodexes in helping me write this book. I am truly indebted to you all.

I would like to thank Jonathan Adler (your interview was hilarious as expected), Scott Ageloff of the New York School of Design, Victoria Amado, Ann Black of the University of Cincinnati, Monique Backross of Susan Magrino Public Relations, Andrew Baseman (set decorator extraordinaire), Fred Berns,

Linda Berry of Bella Linea (thank you for all your encouragement), John Black, Elizabeth Butzer at Susan Becher P.R., Tracy Bross, Nina Campbell, Jean Chene at California Closets, Clodagh, Korenna Cline of ASID, Susie Coelho (your energy is amazing!), Adrienne Cullen of Dorothy Draper, Zane Curry, Laura Daily of Ballard Designs, Andrea Danese of Harry N. Abrams, Ann Davis of Travis and Company, Ashley Dennison at Susan Magrino P.R., Margaret Evans at Veranda, Lynn Davis of Home and Garden Television, Vanessa Gallant of Callison, Suzan Globus of ASID, Mitchell Gold and Eloise Goldman of Mitchell Gold, Denise Guerin of the University of Texas at Austin, Keith Granet, and the extraordinary Michael Graves.

A special thank you also goes to Nina Griscom, Cheryl Gulley of the Watkins School of Art & Design, Penny Guyon of Firefly Media, Jacqui Hall-Handeman of Michael Graves, Inc., Alexa Hampton, Thom Hauser of the University of Georgia, Inge Heckel (you played a pivotal part of my career), Phillip Hilgersom at Holland America, Laura Holland at Hickory Chair, Martin Horner, Donna Hysmith of Designer's Gallery, Karen Figilis (your Rolodex is incredible!), Alison Julius of Vicente Wolf, Margo Jones of Savannah College of Art and Design, Celerie Kemble, Sheryl King at Laneventure, Sue Fisher King, Max Konig of Nina Campbell, Mary Knackstedt (your books were such an inspiration and your work on the industry is groundbreaking), Nancy Kwallek at the University of Texas, Thomas Lavin, Sally Sirkin Lewis, Ryan London at Susie Coelho Enterprises, Angela Luedke at Haworth, and Ron Mandelbaum at Photofest (your patience and photographic library are second to none).

The participation of Brent Martin of Primevista TV, Deb McCain, Martha McCully from HGTV's *Design Star*, Bob Mitchell, Jeannie Moonery at Donghia, Lemore Moses of Hirsch/Bedner Associates, Mary Kate Murray of Michael Graves, Inc., Chris Casson Madden, Tori Mannes, Candace Manroe of *Traditional Home* (one of my favorite editors ever), Jaime Marland at Rhode Island School of Design, Mark Meagher, Cathy Mitchell at Hickory Chair, Laura Monk of Dogwood, Lisa Newsom of *Veranda*, Steve Nobel, Joan Perniconi at Crate & Barrel, James Pope of Ballard Designs, and Jocelyn Pysarchuk at IIDA is most appreciated.

Many thanks go to Constance Ramos, Jay Reardon at Hickory Chair, Cloudia Rebar, Sarah Richardson, Joel Rizor at Screen Door Entertainment, Mary Beth Robinson, Rick Roseman, Glenda Rovello, Ben Saltzman of Michael Graves Design Studio, Mike Sands at Tui Pranich, Emily Shirden at Todd Oldham, Rita Sue Siegel, Whitney Sisler of the Pacific Design Center, Ruthie Sommers of Chapman-Radcliffe, Martha Stewart, Leslie Stevens of LaForce-Stevens (your friendship is invaluable), Alexandra Stoddard, Hal Tine of Savannah College of Art and Design, Page Thorgersen of California Closets, Amy Tessler at Wilson Associates, Dotty Travis, June Triolo of J. Robert Scott, Allison Uljee at Vicente Wolf, Lauren Urband at kwid design, Bryan Scott Venegas, Kelly Wearstler, Brandon Wells at Valtekz, Marilyn White of Brunschwig and Fils, Jan Whitson of Hickory Chair, Deb Willis at Jonathan Adler, Trisha Wilson, Vicente Wolf, and Donna May Woods at Brunschwig and Fils.

A personal thanks goes to Elizabeth Betts Hickman who helped to expand my horizons and ultimately add the title of journalist to my resume. She has always been there with the right answer and her insights and wisdom far exceed her years. A special thanks to Ellen Rolfes, Brenda Welch, Shannon Eldredge, Cheryl Henry, and Mary Cordell who have literally been with me from the very beginning of this journey, and are such amazing cheerleaders.

Thank you to all of my many friends who are too numerous to mention (you know who you are) and have been there to support me, cheer me on, and understand the meaning of deadlines and all nighters.

And special gratitude to the support of my mother (who once had the classic comment, "I would take on ironing before I would do what you do for a living!") and late father who also published a book for academia. I am sorry he didn't live to see me published.

PART 1

The Interior Design Industry

"Interior design: a multifaceted profession in which creative and technical solutions are applied within a structure to achieve a built-in interior environment. These solutions are functional, enhance the quality of life and culture of the occupants, and are aesthetically attractive."

—AMERICAN SOCIETY OF INTERIOR DESIGNERS

The Domicile of Design

OVERVIEW OF THE INTERIOR DESIGN PROFESSION

Technically speaking, this definition of interior design sums it up best.

Simply speaking, interior design is a business. It is a multi-million dollar industry that employs over 66,500 people in interior design and architectural firms, wholesale and government and a host of other specialty areas. It is a global industry where some $57 billion worth of products and services are specified, contributing greatly to the economy as a whole. It is a professional practice that has grown considerably in numbers, salaries, billing, and opportunities.

And it is perhaps one of the most complex and misunderstood. Anyone can tell you what a lawyer or doctor does, but ask them about the role of an interior designer and they will respond with a variety of answers. Interior design is not only a profession, it is a lifestyle and not just the task of selecting the fabric on a sofa.

First let's look at the facts. Three in ten designers are self-employed, two in ten work in interior design firms, and one in ten are employed in architecture or landscape firms. Sixty percent of the profession is female (architectural firms tend to be more male dominated). Once considered a suitable profession for women while waiting for the proverbial "Mr. Right," today's designer is serious, dedicated, and educated, and at least half of all practicing designers have completed two or more years of college or vocational training. The majority of designers are nationally licensed and belong to professional associations such as the American Society of Interior Designers (ASID), International Interior Design Association (IIDA), and the National Kitchen and Bath Association (NKBA).

Cultural generation groups known as "baby boomers" and "generation X" comprise the majority of the profession with the ages of practicing designers falling between 35 to 54. (ASID studies show there is a lack of talent due to the fact nearly half of practicing designers are 45 and older.) Affluent areas such as California (Los Angeles and San Francisco), New York (New York City), Illinois (Chicago), Georgia (Atlanta) and Florida (West Palm Beach) rank among the highest in the employment of interior designers—just look

at any city with a "to the trade only" design center as an indicator. Residential interior design remains one of the most perennially popular areas where two-thirds of the practice specialize in single-family homes along with remodeling and kitchen and bath projects. Office and hospitality design run a close second and third choice respectively followed by health care, retail, education, government, and institutional design as common career choices.

Salaries will vary from state to state and are naturally dependent on economic conditions, the housing market, and other factors. Starting salaries range from the mid-thirties to the low forties and are higher in metropolitan areas. Designers in large commercial firms tend to make more money. While studies show that self-employed designers make anywhere from $20,000 to $120,000, the sky can be the limit depending on their level of success and expertise. They will bill anywhere from $75 to $225 an hour and up and vary by market and specialty. Studies also show

TOP TWENTY INTERIOR DESIGN REGIONS

1. Chicago	11. San Francisco
2. New York	12. West Palm Beach/Boca Raton
3. Los Angeles/Long Beach	13. Detroit
4. Atlanta	14. Phoenix/Mesa
5. Dallas	15. Denver
6. Washington, DC	16. San Diego
7. Houston	17. Boston
8. Seattle	18. Nassau/Suffolk County, NY
9. Orange County, CA	19. Oakland
10. Philadelphia	20. Minneapolis-St. Paul

Source: Dun and Bradstreet 9/2006

that the majority of income may come from the traditional billing method of markup on products and furnishings and hourly fees as part of the design process.

ASID studies also report that an increased growth in the industry will continue through the year 2010 with a particular need for design services in the office, health care, and hospitality industries. A healthy housing market and commercial business expansion coupled with increasing consumer wealth will dictate a demand for design services. The need for specialization and niche marketing will be of the utmost importance as keen competition for jobs, the changing complexity and spending habits of consumers, and a variety of economic, social, cultural, and environmental trends continue to have an impact on the industry.

The visibility of interior design is on the rise and the field is enjoying its time in the spotlight like never before. With the proliferation of shelter magazines, lavishly illustrated design books, and home improvement television channels, the profession has become a popular, if not inadvertently (and somewhat misleading) glamorous profession. In a society obsessed by celebrity, style, and sophistication, interior design has become the profession of the moment, heralded in *Architectural Digest*'s famed "AD 100" list, *Interior Design*'s Hall of Fame, and *House Beautiful*'s annual list of the 100 best decorators in America. Designers have been hilariously portrayed on the television screen as flaky

FIGURE 1.1
Designers' home away from home: The Pacific Design Center in Los Angeles is "To the trade only."

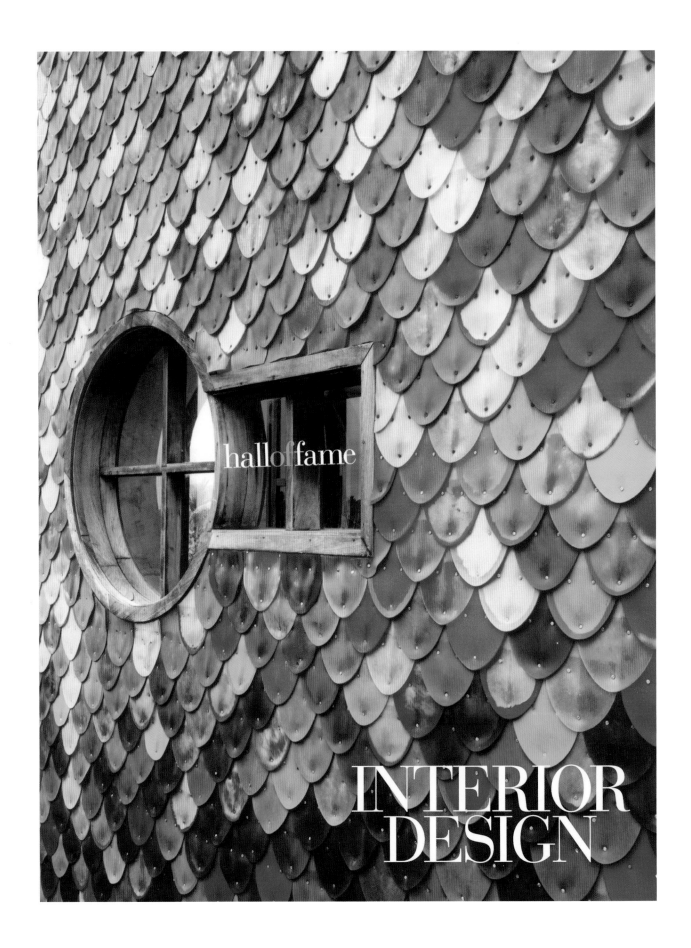

halloffame

INTERIOR
DESIGN

and food obsessed in *Will and Grace* to a quartet of ditzy southern socialite/professionals in *Designing Women*. The silver screen has not been any kinder—Doris Day played the ubiquitous interior decorator in search of a husband in *Pillow Talk* and Patricia Neal as the first predatory decorator a.k.a. "Mrs. Robinson" in *Breakfast at Tiffany's*.

We are also seeing a time of the celebrity interior designer as witnessed by reality television shows such as *Top Design* and *Extreme Makeover: Home Edition*, and the Home and Garden Television network. Also in vogue is the marriage of high-end designers and mass market retailers such as Michael Graves and Victoria Hagan for Target as well as the crossover of fashion designers and furniture design such as Todd Oldham and La-Z-Boy and Armani with his Armani Casa line.

Interior design will continue to be an important service, one that provides a vital contribution to society, enriching and improving the quality of our daily lives. While producing both a functional and attractive environment is an important factor, design is also a major force, addressing social problems such as those caused by natural disasters or offering alternatives with ergonomic, universal, and sustainable design. As noted by Suzan Globus, President of ASID, "The profession is so exciting today because we (interior designers) are beginning to document the results of the change in behaviors of the people

FIGURE 1.2
Interior Design magazine's annual "Hall of Fame" issue.

FIGURE 1.3
Designing Women was one of the first television shows to feature the interior design business.

"PILLOW TALK" An Arwin Production A Universal-International Release

Printed in U.S.A. © 1959, Universal Pictures Company, Inc. ● Permission granted for newspaper and magazine reproduction ● Any other use, including television, prohibited.

FIGURE 1.4
Doris Day as decorator Jan Morris in the film *Pillow Talk* (Universal, 1959).

FIGURE 1.5
Actress Debra Messing as interior designer Grace Adler in the Emmy Award–winning television series *Will and Grace.*

inhabiting the spaces we design. For example, increased productivity and faster rates of healing are a few of the behaviors being studied."

All of these changes—both bad and good—have come at a price as designers are reevaluating how they do business. "The widespread interest in interior design has prompted interior designers to move from charging product-based fees to hourly or project fees for services," notes Globus. "This has opened up a dialogue about the true value of interior design services, which extends far beyond product specification, to providing outcome based solutions."

FIGURE 1.6
Interior design joins the ranks of reality television with the Bravo Network's show *Top Design*.

FIGURE 1.7
Todd Oldham's Snap sofa design in Circus Cerise for La-Z-Boy furniture.

FIGURE 1.8
Fashion turned furniture designer and television star Todd Oldham.

CHANGING CONSUMERS, CHANGING MARKETPLACE

While it's doubtful that Bob Dylan had business on his mind when he penned the then radical sixties hit "The Times They Are A Changin'," it's pretty indicative of the state of affairs today.

Blame it on the Internet, terrorism and the events of September 11, 2001, increased national wealth, the proliferation of mass-marketed products, and instant gratification—

the face of consumers and the way we do business have dramatically changed.

Socially, people are living longer, healthier, and leading more productive lives. The baby boomers are maturing and moving into their senior years, representing a very large consumer base. Traditionally the "boomers" use the services of interior designers and as they mature, so will the marketplace. Conversely, "Generation Y" consumers (think twenty-somethings) are more prone to decorating by way of catalogues, mass retailers, and the Internet depending on their level of wealth and time.

Interior design is often seen as a luxury and as a result, subject to the ups and downs of the economy. And as the

economy grows, more consumers and businesses will require design services. Fortunately, there will always be those who hire designers to save time and energy and for their professionalism and peace of mind.

Globally, increased anxiety over crime, planetary changes, overcrowding, stress, and the increasing demands of everyday life gave birth to a new way of living known as "cocooning." The term was coined by futurist trend guru Faith Popcorn who aptly predicted a segment of the population would feel the "need to protect oneself from the unpredictable realities of the outside world." As a result, entertaining and working from the home and creating a safe haven of creature comforts became more and more important.

The age-old concept of home and hearth is nothing new. Home will forever be considered our castle as well as one of our most expensive possessions. Lifestyles, clothing, and home furnishings have become more relaxed as consumers take the concept of comfort to new heights. The desire to stay home often translates into the addition of a home gym, yoga, meditation, and media rooms as people are rediscovering the need to live in a self-contained environment. A rise in self-employment requires the addition of home offices while affluence brings travel that trickles down to luxury hotels and an increase in hospitality design.

The complexity of the consumer has changed as well. A recent research study by kitchen cabinet maker Merillat divided consumers into four purchasing groups:

FIGURE 1.9
Young designer in studio.

- Luxury Leaders—They are generally affluent and have large homes (coined McMansions) and are highly educated, affluent and style conscious in their clothing and furnishings. Their well-appointed homes will most likely have a wine cellar, media center, home office, and a great room.
- Domestic Dwellers—This segment represents a more traditional group of homeowners who live comfortably, but are not ostentatious. They tend to be homebodies and prefer a more conventional mainstream decor.
- Busy Bees—They are made up of busy families as both parents work. They are similar to domestic dwellers in many ways but are slightly younger and have a higher income.
- Career Builders—Career builders are most likely first-time home buyers. They are well educated and spend a great deal of time working, as career success is quite important. They bought their home primarily as an investment, and quite often chose the house based on resale. They are the youngest segment and may have lower incomes than the other homeowners.

TRENDS AND TECHNOLOGY

The following represents a list of some of the most important trends impacting the design industry in the past decade as well as a crystal ball glimpse of things to come.

Aging Marketplace

The Census Bureau and the National Institute on Aging project that by 2030,

FIGURE 1.10
Interior designer Clodagh's spa designs for Kohler.

close to 20 percent of all Americans will be over the age of 65 with the average life expectancy of working adults rising to the low 80s. "Boomers" will be caring for aging parents and relatives as well as facing concerns over their own retirement. Senior living communities will be commonplace, especially those that offer hospitality and amenities.

This consumer group offers unique marketing challenges as homes and products will need to be elderly-friendly. With more than $2 trillion in spending power, affluent boomers will have money for travel and expect the hospitality, hotel, and resort industries to follow suit with design features in mind. From low-maintenance homes to user-friendly furnishings, the ergonomic needs of a growing elderly population will also need to be addressed.

Baby boomers currently in their mid-fifties to mid-sixties are building and/or buying their second homes predominantly located on the beach, mountains, or golf course. These homes need to be designed as boomers redecorate or recycle existing furnishings.

FIGURE 1.11
Baby boomers represent a market with more than $2 trillion in annual spending power.

Home Building Market

Home sales will fluctuate with the economy as falling prices can indicate the need for remodeling and staying put (and of course good for residential design). Commercial construction is expected to increase as approximately $200 billion in hospital construction is anticipated in the coming decade.

Home interiors will also change dramatically as living rooms and family rooms morph into the "great room" and media and home gyms often replace a guest room. Rooms will be multifunctional with organization and technology playing key factors in their design. There is also a trend towards more open-plan space and furniture designers will have to meet the challenge with more freestanding furniture. Work, hobbies, entertainment, and day-to-day living will be incorporated into the design of a room as never before. Indoor living moves outdoors and look for the continuation of "his and hers" closets and bathroom. Thanks to an increased interest in fine food and cooking, kitchens will remain one of the most popular, decorated, and expensive areas of the house as the primary place to gather.

Home size will also change, as the average home will consist of 7.5 rooms (according to the International Furnishings and Design Association). Raymond Chevallier, former executive vice president of F. Schumacher & Co., New York, says he sees two divergent trends in overall home design: "I think you will continue to see larger homes built, as long as the economy stays strong and people have money to spend. At the same time, however, I think there will be a trend towards smaller homes as people get older and want to simplify their lives." Thomas Ward, past New York–based president of West-Point Stevens, comments, "Homes have gotten very large, and this trend will continue, because people want a greater variety of personal amenities in their homes. For example, people want a home spa, a fitness center, a Jacuzzi tub, and all of these take up a lot of space."

Media and Entertainment Rooms

Why go to the local Cineplex when you can have a multimedia room at home? Industry experts believe that one out of every four U.S. households has some sort of home theater with eight percent of new homes being built with a media room. While these rooms constitute an expensive luxury for some, they are most likely to be incorporated into new home design. There will also be a great deal of attention paid to areas for media, computers and the Internet as technology becomes a permanent part of our lives.

The "Smart Home" automation trend of the last century will continue to be a force with light and climate control, control of doors, window shutters, and security and surveillance systems incorporated into our design plans.

Mass Marketing of Interior Design

High-end style furnishings at low-end prices are being mass marketed at record levels. From paint to pillow and everything in between, consumers are now able to go into national retailers such as Pottery Barn, Mitchell Gold/ Bob Williams, West Elm, Crate & Barrel, and Williams Sonoma Home and general merchants such as Target, JCPenney, and Kmart for instant decor. Well known high-end fashion and interior designers have been tapped to collaborate with retailers on furnishings, lighting, accessories, and even candles.

Available through retail store, catalogue, or Internet and often known as "design in a box," the concept is attractive to consumers who want instant gratification, have a second home, budget constraints, or design a room without the help of a professional.

FIGURE 1.12
Media rooms are becoming a popular addition in 21st century home design.

Do-It-Yourself

Growth in discount furniture stores and home improvement mega-centers has spurred a trend in the do-it-yourself design craze. The phenomenon even inspired Home and Garden Television to spin off a do-it-yourself channel (DIY Network) that reaches 45 million homes. Older homes in need of repair created the niche for the PBS show *This Old House* and style maven Martha Stewart turned a one-woman show into a mega-corporation with her gracious living concept (rooted in do-it-yourself) through television, a magazine, merchandising, and even a line of Martha-inspired homes.

Notes interior design business consultant Fred Berns, "There is less full service design work coming out of initial meetings with clients. Many clients hire designers now to do small projects and piecemeal work. HGTV may have something to do with this, since it's opened the gates to a whole new generation of do-it-yourselfers."

Green/Sustainability Design

Also referred to as "green design" and "eco-design," sustainability is the art of designing furnishings, buildings, and products that are made with renewable resources that do not harm the environment. The year 2006 marked the year of the green, adding the word to our cultural lexicon thanks to the endeavors of socially conscious individuals and in reaction to the environmental crisis.

According to Suzann Globus, "Sustainability is a huge growth opportunity for interior designers" as designers meet the needs of a demanding environmentally responsible public. A *Furniture Today* magazine study shows it's the fastest growing design segment and the home furnishings industry has incorporated the concept into ozone friendly, non-carcinogenic materials shipped in totally recyclable cartons.

Specialty Crossover

Noting the vague lines between interior design disciplines, ASID came up with the term "specialty crossover." For example, the hospitality industry looked to residential practices with the design of luxury boutique hotels that spawned a whole new trend in home furnishings and linens. Residential designers look to office and commercial design for home offices and to hospitality for home spas. The popularity of luxury boutique hotels has caused the hospitality industry to rely on the residential market for advice.

Curated Consumption

The website www.trendwatching.com predicts the emerging trend of millions of consumers following style gurus (they credit Martha Stewart as the Rosetta Stone). Curators of style dictate how we dress, eat, decorate, and essentially live through Internet blogs, magazine columns, television, and radio shows. As consumers with short attention spans seek the latest and the greatest, needy audiences will require experts on an even bigger scale. Designers who specialize in a particular niche can capitalize on this trend by becoming a leading expert or "curator" in their field.

FIGURE 1.13
Storefront for Mitchell Gold + Bob Williams.

FIGURE 1.14
Eco-friendly Santo Paul dining table by Environment Furniture.

FIGURE 1.15
Luxury boutique hotel designs influence the residential market. Shown here is a bedroom in the W Hotel.

FIGURE 1.16
Uber-designer Martha Stewart put the concept of lifestyle living and branding on the map.

With the Click of a Mouse

The new consumer is more savvy, smart, better educated, and often turns to the Internet for research and purchasing. Studies show that nearly nine out of ten households use the World Wide Web to research a product's price and nearly two-fifths of online researchers belong to Generation X or Y, i.e. the twenty-something and thirty-something groups respectively. Technology has enabled us to keep up like never before and has virtually changed the landscape of shopping. Interior designer Kelly Wearstler comments that "access to the world via technology" represents one of the biggest changes in the industry today. As a result, consumers are more demanding, knowledgeable and in control than ever.

The Internet (as well as catalogue shopping) has in some cases replaced traditional brick and mortar storefronts.

Consumers have an incredible array of choices when it comes to buying home furnishings: department stores, catalogues and mail order, furniture showrooms, specialty furniture stores, manufacturer's outlets, and, of course, interior designers are all popular sources. Thousands of sites help consumers literally do anything, from selecting and purchasing wallpaper to actual do-it-yourself installation.

And an educated consumer is a good thing according to interior designer Jonathan Adler. "Savvy consumers are good consumers! The more consumers understand design, style, quality—even the basic principles of manufacturing— the better they can appreciate and demand good design," he says.

Designers can benefit greatly from the Internet as it provides a wonderful tool for research and the majority of vendors have virtual online showrooms.

FIGURE 1.17
The Internet is a major business tool for the interior designer.

According to Berns, the Internet represents a new frontier for the designer and the way they do marketing and promotion as well as the sourcing of new products. "Websites have emerged as the key marketing tool for most design firms," says Berns. "Print promotion is less prevalent than in the past. It's never been easier to buy elsewhere the design services and products that local residential and commercial design pros sell. The Web has provided end users with a whole new range of buying options. Customers are more choosy and demanding than they used to be, not to mention more knowledgeable (thanks again, to the Web)."

In short, the Internet will affect not only the way consumers do business but the way designers work, advertise, communicate, and grow. Virtually an integral part of our lives, technology will continue to grow and knowledge will be key.

We must adapt with the sophisticated changes in order to thrive and survive.

REFERENCES

American Society of Interior Designers. (2007). *The Interior Design Profession: Facts and Figures*. Washington, D.C.: American Society of Interior Designers.

Berns, Fred. Website: www.fredberns.com.

Bureau of Labor Statistics, U.S. Department of Labor, *Occupational Outlook Handbook, 2006-07 Edition*. Retrieved December 7, 2007, from website: www.bls.gov/oco/ocos293.htm.

Curated Consumption. Retrieved October, 2007, from website: www.trendwatching.com.

Dampierre, Florence. (1989). *The Decorator*. New York: Rizzoli.

Forest, Sara D. (2006). *Vault Guide to Interior Design Careers*. New York: Vault, Inc.

Knackstedt, Mary V. (1995) *Interior Design and Beyond: Art, Science and Industry*. New York: John Wiley & Sons.

————. (2005). *The Interior Design Business Handbook*. New York: John Wiley & Sons.

Market Probe International. (2006). *2006 Universe Study of the Interior Design Profession*.

Merillat's Third Phase of Research Uncovers Four Distinct Consumer Segments. Retrieved May 10, 2007, from website: www.merillat.com.

Popcorn, Faith and Marigold, Lys. (1996). *Clicking: 16 Trends to Future Fit Your Life, Your Work, and Your Business*. New York: HarperCollins.

Viewing a Crystal Ball of Home Design: Survey by IFDA Predicts Changes in Home and Lifestyles by the Year 2020 (November, 2001). Retrieved December 5, 2007, from website: www.ifda.com/news.

"It is a fearful mistake to leave the entire planning of your home to a person whose social experience may be limited, for instance, for they can impose on their conception of our tastes with a damning permanency and emphasis."
— ELSIE DE WOLFE, *THE HOUSE IN GOOD TASTE*

The Role of the Interior Designer

HISTORY OVERVIEW OF THE PROFESSION

What do the lair of the caveman, the mummy's tomb, and a thatched hut have in common? They all vie for a place in history as some of the earliest domiciles to be designed on record. Ancient societies devised all sorts of practical ways to escape the elements in the form of simple teepees, caves, and igloos using materials available at the time. Soon round huts of baked bricks and palm leaves evolved into box-like shelters with four walls and a roof. Residential dwellings from cottages, lodges, ranch and tract houses, apartments, townhouses, and even houseboats, to villas, mansions, dachas, estates, and the aptly named great house subsequently followed—all in need of decoration.

While the exact moment of the birth of interior decoration and design is not known, the practice no doubt corresponded with the need for practicality and the traditions and lifestyle of its occupants, a tenet that still holds true today. History has told the tale of architectural triumphs in Egypt and ancient Greece and the opulence and decadent design of the Roman Empire, while some historians point out the profession began to take shape during the Italian Renaissance (1450–1600). Known as a time of literal rebirth, as Europe emerged from the shadow of the dark ages, the period was also a time of aristocracy and all the trappings of great wealth were on full display. Grand palaces were the home of magnificent works of art, heavily ornamented furnishings, and intricate interior architecture. As design became a symbol of wealth and power, the profession began to take shape and the die was cast.

INTERIOR DECORATORS OF THE PAST

While much has been written on the history of decorative arts, historical architecture and interiors, the underpinnings of the profession itself are not quite as vast. The job of interior decoration usually fell under the jurisdiction of architects, upholsterers, cabinet makers, or other skilled artisans, mostly from Western Europe.

While the primary role of architects at the time was the design of a building, many did double duty such as the famed neoclassical Scottish architect Robert Adam (1728–1792) who designed everything from "doorknobs to watch fobs." As early as 1758, he was designing complete decorative schemes for country houses. William Kent, a noted painter, furniture designer, and central architect of the Palladian style of the early 18th century was also cited as one of the first to take charge of an entire interior. Each European country varied—in London this role fell into the hands of the upholsterer while the *marchand-mercier* (translation: merchant of goods) took the honors in France.

How Would You Like to Have Napoleon as a Client?

Two of the very first decorators were the French architects Charles Basant-Percier (1764–1838) and Pierre-

Francois-Léonard Fontaine (1752–1853). Considered the founders and leading proponents of the Neoclassical Empire style that we know today, their designs blended both the old and new elements of an interior. Both men began their design careers at the Academie des Beaux-Arts and success followed; Percier became the director of set design at the Paris Opera and was soon joined by Fontaine. The pair spent four years designing classical backdrops.

The duo's work garnered attention from the rich and influential citizens of Paris. Soon they were designing furniture and restoring private residences, providing everything from Sevres porcelain to the state bed. One such installation was the residence of Monsieur Chauvelain who happened to be

FIGURE 2.2
Architect Charles Percier's design at the Throne Room of the Tuillerie Palace in France.

the neighbor of Josephine Bonaparte. As luck would have it, she soon hired them to renovate her home with Napoleon, the famous Malmaison. Napoleon also hired them as his personal architects and their official "commercial design" career began with the Hotel des Invalides. More contracts in the City of Lights ensued—the layout of Rue de Rivoli, planning of the Seine River bridges, renovation of the Louvre, and the designs for the Arc de Triomphe du Carrousel.

Napoleon, perhaps the one of the first difficult clients of note, hired the pair to build a palace for his son.

FIGURE 2.4
Artist Pierre Joseph
Petit's rendering of
Malmaison.

FIGURE 2.5
Napoleon's bedroom
at Chateau de
Malmaison.

Over a four-year period, numerous designs were submitted to the persnickety emperor who eventually bailed on the project due to insufficient funds! To add insult to injury, Napoleon fired Percier yet retained Fontaine for "official state duties."

Percier's later years were spent teaching and designing furniture, clocks, and Sevres vases. Fontaine worked on the restoration of the Palais Royal, the Elyse Palace, and the Theatre-Francais. He eventually held the position as architect of the Louvre and Tuillerie Palaces until the amazing age of 86.

DESIGNING WOMEN

The actual term of interior decorator became a part of the language in the late nineteenth and early twentieth centuries, designated for those who specialized in furnishing interiors. Many were also dealers of furniture, antiquities, and rugs. Their design approach was innovative, modern, and a backlash to the overcrowded, overdone, and oppressive Victorian interiors of the early part of the century.

While many talented, pioneering, and revolutionary architects, decorators, and designers contributed greatly to the formation of the profession, several designing women placed the term decorator on the map beginning in the early part of the century. The interior design movement was in full swing by the 1920s and the practice became a suitable career choice for society women to make use of their innate skills for wealthy friends and clients (often one in the same).

Nicknamed "society decorators," Syrie Maugham (1879–1955), Sybil Colefax (1874–1954), and Nancy Lancaster (1897–1994) created fashionable interiors across the pond. Maugham began with a successful shop in London that grew into a design career that included British royalty and American clients. Colefax formed a partnership with John Fowler (1906–1977) and their fabrics and wallpapers live on with the firm Colefax and Fowler. Virginia-bred Lancaster later formed a firm with Fowler in England where they specialized in the English Country Style made popular in the 90s.

The United States had its own version of the society decorator, the colorful Elsie de Wolfe.

Elsie de Wolfe, America's First Interior Decorator

"I believe in plenty of optimism and white paint."
—Elsie de Wolfe

Ironically one of the first—and self-proclaimed—American interior decorators began her career as an actress (and according to the critics, a mediocre yet well dressed one at that). Talented, social, eccentric, and fame-seeking Elsie de Wolfe (1865–1950), a.k.a. Lady Mendl, was one of the most infamous professionals of the early 1900s. She became interested in interior decorating as a result of stage design and left the Empire Stock Theatre Company to launch her design career in 1903. Her timing was perfect as the period signaled a renewed interest in home interiors.

Her big break came when longtime friend and architect Stanford White referred her to The Colony Club, a commission he was working on at the time. Her revolutionary beige designs were a huge success, placing her on the social radar of Manhattan as a bona fide decorator in demand.

Elsie de Wolfe's lifestyle gave her all the ingredients needed for a successful society decorator. A permanent fixture on the New York, Paris, and London social circuits, her client list grew with such social luminaries as Anne Morgan and the Duke and Duchess of Windsor. Client Henry Clay Frick gave her ten percent of all his purchases, making him one of the largest art and antiques collectors in America and propelling the socialite into millionaire status.

Clients loved de Wolfe's use of light colors and fresh new interiors, freeing wealthy households of the dark floors and drab velvet draperies of Victorian styles of the past. She was also known as one of the first to use antique reproductions and favored eighteenth century French and English furnishings. Her design philosophy of the early 1900s still holds up today as she believed in simple, harmonious, and uncluttered designs and the edict of the home as a reflection of the owner's personality.

In a career move reminiscent of the twenty-first century, de Wolfe produced articles on home decoration for the magazines *The Delineator* (subtitled *A Journal of Fashion, Culture, and Fine Arts*) and *Ladies Home Journal.* This led to the publication of her landmark book, *A House in Good Taste* (1913 and reissued by Rizzoli International Publications, 2004) which is still printed today. Creating yet another first, the book became

a "how-to" decorating manual for the homemaker with limited money.

Truly the Martha Stewart of her time, she was well versed in the art of entertaining, great food and couture fashion. She also introduced the concept of small intimate dinners and the cocktail party to society and can be credited with the concept of lifestyle design. Ever the eccentric style maker, de Wolfe was perhaps one of the first women of her time to dye her hair with a blue rinse, perform daily handstands, and was immortalized in song by Cole Porter ("Anything Goes" and "That Black and White Baby of Mine") and Irving Berlin ("Harlem on My Mind").

FIGURE 2.6
Elsie de Wolfe (a.k.a "Lady Mendl"), noted American society hostess and interior decorator.

FIGURE 2.7
A flamboyant figure
for the times,
de Wolfe's daily
regimen included
headstands.

While she has been dead for almost sixty years, her influences can still be felt today. One of her most important contributions was paving the way for women to make a respectable living and for that, we thank her.

Dorothy Draper, America's First True Interior Designer

"If it looks right, it is right."
—Dorothy Draper

While Lady Mendl laid her claim on the title of first interior decorator, history credits Dorothy Draper as the first interior designer.

Born to a wealthy family in affluent Tuxedo Park, New York, Draper became a true pioneer by establishing the first interior design company in 1923 at a time when women were not recognized as business owners. Draper was known for the design of commercial interiors such as the restaurant at New York's Metropolitan Museum of Art (coined the "Dorotheum"), the Packard car, and airplane interiors.

She designed dozens of offices, restaurants, and hospitals throughout her illustrious career. Draper's successful interiors were the result of breaking away from the characteristic historical period interiors of the day and her trademark "Modern Baroque" style was applicable to large commercial spaces.

The Draper hallmark was the use of vibrant color combinations such as aubergine and pink with chartreuse and a touch of turquoise. Other design touches included black and white checkered floors, signature cabbage rose chintz, paneled lacquered doors, and intricate mirrors.

Also known for her lifestyle concept, Draper wrote a number of books on entertaining, etiquette, and design (many are reprinted today). She dispensed design advice in her regular column in *Good Housekeeping* magazine, designed her own line of fabrics, created packaging for a cosmetic company and decorated prominent residences across the world. Known as "The Draper Touch," her style was ever encompassing. The multi-talented designer was involved in all aspects of a commission from the menus, matchbook covers, and staff uniforms to the rooms and lobbies of a hotel.

Draper's work lives on today as seen in New York's Carlyle Hotel and The Greenbrier in West Virginia (Draper's design of the Victorian Writing Room remains one of the most photographed in the United States). Designer and Draper protégée Carleton Varney summed it up best in his book *The Draper Touch: The High Life and High Style of Dorothy Draper* (Simon and Schuster, 1988), "That any of her work remains . . . speaks volumes about her talent. Her touch has survived in a time that does not value the past. She was truly the last grande dame."

FIGURE 2.8
Interior designer Dorothy Draper in the 1930s.

FIGURE 2.9
Draper's eye-popping designs for the black and white dining room at the Arrowhead Springs Hotel in California.

THE INTERIOR DESIGNER OF THE 1960S TO THE PRESENT

FIGURE 2.10
Considered one of Draper's most inspired works is the restaurant for New York's Metropolitan Museum of Art. Coined the "Dorotheum," it was built around a huge pool with gigantic birdcage style chandeliers.

After the industrial revolution, America experienced a cultural and economic emergence of the middle class, creating another group of clients decorating their homes and in need of furnishings. Benefiting from the post war building boom, mass furniture production and mail order catalogues were filled with iconic three piece matching "suites" and the latest technological inventions. Magazines dispensed design advice and began to focus on products and furnishings which in turn created consumer interest and the creation of the interior design industry.

While the profession flourished, the 1950s and 1960s were a time of important change as people with architectural and design training entered the field and many interior decorators became interior designers. While the designation of interior decorator gained popularity in the late nineteenth and early twentieth centuries, the classification of interior designer as one who is formally educated and trained made the industry a much more professional one (see sidebar).

It was also a time of mentoring as many of the great mid-century decorators and designers learned at the feet of their masters. The stylish and eloquent Billy Baldwin (1903–1984) who decorated the apartment of Brooke Astor and author of two highly acclaimed books got his start with New York decorator Ruby Ross Wood (1881–1950). Parsons School of Design alumna Eleanor Brown McMillen (1890–1991) opened the first "full service" interior design firm McMillen, Inc. and gave interior designer and lifestyle author Alexandra Stoddard and chairman Betty Sherrill their start.

Formed in 1962 by Albert Hadley and Sister Parish (1910–1994), Parish-Hadley designed some of the most important interiors of the century such as the Kennedy White House and employed another design legend, Mark Hampton (1940–1998). A former student at the London School of Economics, the diversified designer also worked for David Hicks in London and McMillen Inc. before starting his own company. In addition to designing interiors, offices, boats, and airplanes, his projects also included the design of Christmas decorations for Presidents Carter and Reagan.

FIGURE 2.11
Interior designer Albert Hadley.

A designer in her own right, Hampton's daughter Alexa carries on the design practice in addition to her own line of fabrics, furniture and lighting. (Her illustrious career is profiled in Chapter 5).

David Hicks (1928–1998), John Saladino, Angelo Donghia (1935–1985), Van Day Truex (1904–1979), Mario Buatta (and others to numerous to mention) are just a few of the many trend-setting innovators to leave their mark on the development of the industry in

FIGURE 2.12
Interior designer Mrs. Henry Parish II (a.k.a. "Sister Parish") seated in Parish-Hadley, her New York firm, in a room full of patterned fabrics.

the twentieth century. Known for his contemporary sixties style settings, Hicks hated florals while Buatta was crowned "The Prince of Chintz." Saladino made historic references in contemporary settings his personal trademark while Donghia became one of the first designers to license his products. As head of the Parsons School of Design, Truex was one of the most influential design educators of the century and eventually became director of design at Tiffany & Co.

The traditions of innovation, creativity, and excellence in design are

thankfully carried on in this century by Clodagh, Sherri Donghia, Sally Sirkin Lewis, Nina Campbell, Vicente Wolf, Michael Graves, Kelly Wearstler, and many others (profiled in future chapters).

While possessing an innate sense of style, color, space, and proportion are a few of the many attributes needed to be an interior designer, the profession today requires education from an accredited school, training, and many must pass national competency examinations (NCIDQ—National

FIGURE 2.16
The multi-talented
Kelly Wearstler is
an interior designer,
author, product
designer, and
television star.

Council for Interior Design Qualification). Not only should a designer have talent and creativity, but a head for business, organization, and marketing is a must. The successful designer must also keep up with new products, new technological advances, and rapidly changing building and safety codes. The ability to know CAD (computer-aided design) is also beneficial. And above all, today's designer is a multi-tasker with unlimited amounts of energy as the job is often twenty-four hours a day, seven days a week.

THE DIVERSE DESIGNER OF THE FUTURE

Change is occurring at the speed of light in the design industry. For many interior designers, gone are the days of charging retail and exclusively selling items available to the trade only. Many professionals in the new millennium will need to look past specializing only in residential and contract areas if they are to survive.

The interior designer of the future will branch out and diversify, utilizing their talents and expertise in several areas of the field. They may have a thriving residential practice and expand with a line of home furnishings or pen a monthly magazine column. They might venture into the hot area of the moment, home staging, or specialize in elder design for senior communities. In this time of increasing media exposure, professionals will benefit greatly from press and public appearances. Those

with name recognition will have the greatest chance at landing their own television show, licensing deal, or simply attracting new clients.

As today's world expands and opportunities arise on a global level, designers will specialize in areas never even considered before. Interior designers will be wise to keep a vigilant eye on the future by paying attention to trends and being ready to position themselves and/or their business in the marketplace. (See Chapter 11: The Specialty Designer for detailed analysis and further look at the variety of options available.)

According to Tama Duffy Day, ASID, IDA, LEED, and principal of

FIGURE 2.17
Designs of the future: Kelly Wearstler's interiors for Viceroy Hotel in Los Angeles.

INTERIOR DECORATOR VERSUS INTERIOR DESIGNER

It's usually best not to call an interior designer an interior decorator.

While there is certainly nothing wrong with the title interior decorator, many in the profession tend to give the term an amateur connotation. And while both terms are mistakenly synonymous to the general public, there is a marked difference in both disciplines.

By definition, interior decorators are involved primarily in planning all decorative and ornamental aspects of a room's décor—furniture, wallpaper, fabric, draperies, light fixtures, painting, accessories, and layout. Mostly specializing in residential design, interior decorators are often self-taught or have limited schooling in interior design courses.

Interior designers are educated and professionally trained in all facets of the design process. They plan interiors, work with clients, contractors, architects, and a variety of artisans and specialists. They have a working knowledge of safety and building codes, business practices, as well as art and design history, and ergonomics. Experts in creative problem solving, they are formally trained in drafting, drawing (and often CAD), and select and specify all areas of furnishings, products, lighting, and materials. Performing many of the aesthetic tasks of an interior decorator, the role of the interior designer also focuses on the function, efficiency, and safety of a space in a variety of areas from residential homes to restaurants, hotels, offices, and government buildings.

the design firm Perkins+Wil, "The future interior designers will be socially conscious leaders, inspirational creators, savvy business people. They will be licensed to practice. They will be artful communicators, and critical thinkers. They will be highly skilled and highly personal. They will understand the importance of how broadly we touch everyone's lives. And they will continue to shape intimate spaces that promote learning, thinking, playing, eating, healing, working, and relaxing."

REFERENCES

Blakemore, Robbie G. (1997). *The History of Interior Design and Furniture: From Ancient Egypt to Nineteenth-Century Europe*. New York: John Wiley & Sons.

Brown, Erica. (1980). *Interior Views: Design at Its Best*. New York: Viking Studio.

————. (1982). *Sixty Years of Interior Design: The World Of McMillen*. New York: Viking Studio.

de Wolfe, Elsie (2004). *The House in Good Taste*. New York: Rizzoli. Originally published in 1913.

Diamonstein, Barbara Lee. (1982). *Interior Design*. New York: Rizzoli.

Fisher, Jeannette J. (2006). *The History of Interior Design*. Retrieved May, 2007, from website www.jeannettefisher.com.

Forest, Sara D. *Vault Guide to Interior Design Careers* (2006). New York: Vault, Inc.

Hampton, Mark (1992). *Legendary Decorators of the 20th Century*. London: Robert Hale.

Jones, Chester (1989). *Colefax and Fowler*. New York: Bulfinch.

Knackstedt, Mary V. (1995) *Interior Design and Beyond: Art, Science and Industry*. New York: John Wiley & Sons.

_____. (2005). *The Interior Design Business Handbook*. New York: John Wiley & Sons.

Lewis, Adam. (2004) *Albert Hadley: The Story of America's Preeminent Interior Designer*. New York: Rizzoli.

Parish, Sister, Hadley, Albert and Petankas, Christopher. (1995). *Parish Hadley: Sixty Years of American Design*. Boston: Little, Brown.

Pile, John (2000). *A History of Interior Design*. New York: John Wiley & Sons.

_____. (2003). *Interior Design (3rd Edition)*. New York: Prentice Hall.

Rapp, Linda (2002). Percier and Fontaine. From glbtq: An Encyclopedia of Gay, Lesbian, Bisexual, Transgender and Queer Culture. Website: http://glbtq.com/arts/percier_fontaine.html.

Sparke, Penny (1998). *A Century of Design: Design Pioneers of the 20th Century*. New York: Barron's.

Tappert, Annette and Edkins, Diana (1994). *The Power of Style*. New York: Crown.

Varney, Carleton (1988). *The Draper Touch: The High Life and High Style of Dorothy Draper*. New York: Simon and Schuster.

_____. (2006). *In the Pink: Dorothy Draper, America's Most Fabulous Decorator*. New York: Pointed Leaf Press.

Webster, Katherine (2007). *Legendary Women*. Retrieved November, 2007, from website: http://canadian interiordesign.com.

Wilssens, Ken. (2007). *The History of Interior Design*. Retrieved August, 2007, from website: www.ezine articles.com.

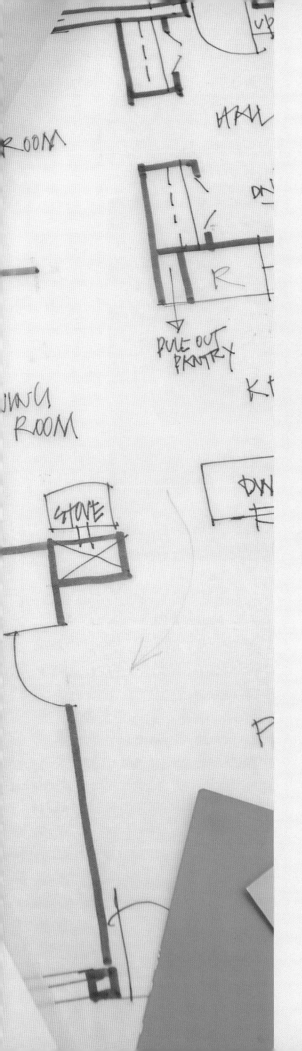

"Education is of the utmost importance. Competition is fierce, and the better prepared one is, the more successful one will be. Education is another ticket in the lottery. The more tickets you have, the better your chances are to win."

—CHARLES GANDY, INTERIOR DESIGNER, FASID, FISA

The Design Education

OVERVIEW OF THE INTERIOR DESIGN EDUCATION

So you have a good eye, innate sense of style, and the ability to sketch a drapery treatment? Not enough. Have a flair for furnishings, love to shop for antiques, and can even rewire a lamp? Still not enough. While these are all excellent traits, design today must start with the proper education.

Interior design is a serious business, one that involves not only the knowledge of color, scale, and decoration, but construction, codes, and plumbing. It's a business where thousands of dollars can be spent on hotel carpeting or custom upholstery—mistakes and miscalculations can be costly. With so much money on the line, this is not a job for the novice. As new technology and products in the marketplace develop and increasingly complicated building codes and standards change, clients will expect more and designers will have to keep up.

The self-taught designer (or decorator as the case may be) will be a remnant of the past—they undermine the credibility of the field as a whole and muddy the waters between bona fide interior designers and the public. To become a design professional, your career should be built on five platforms—formal education (two- to four-year programs), work experi-

FIGURE 3.1
Interior design
students at the
University of
Cincinnati.

FIGURE 3.2
Interior designer
with carpet and
fabric samples.

ence, passing the National Council for Interior Design Qualification (NCIDQ) exam, licensing approval, and joining professional organization(s).

American Society of Interior Designers (ASID) reports that at least 50 percent of all practicing designers in the United States have completed two or more years of college or vocational training and 45 percent have completed a four-year college program. Of these numbers, 40 percent obtained an interior design degree and the remainder received degrees in fine arts, liberal arts, and architecture. There are presently 161 accredited interior design programs in the United States and Canada.

While residential design is certainly an area one can practice without a formal education, contract (also known as commercial or business) design and other specialty areas will always require and demand the proper schooling. In addition, education will definitely be a huge advantage as many employers will consider the level of education in reviewing your qualifications. In general, it is always best to be educated and informed. Period.

THE DESIGN SCHOOL

An interior design degree from an interior design school, program, or university will certainly be one of the most beneficial building blocks for a career in this field. Besides the obvi-

ous educational benefits, the design degree is often vital as an entrée to an entry level position with a design firm and will distinguish an individual as an interior designer over the term interior decorator.

University Program or Design School?

Perhaps one of the most important decisions in a design career is the choice of school. There are as many types of programs and degrees as there are chair and sofa styles— two-year or four-year program, large university, private design, or art school? Or a combination thereof? The choice can be a daunting one.

If you are looking for the traditional college experience, the interior design program housed within a university is

FIGURE 3.3
The interior design program at the University of Cincinnati is currently ranked number two. Shown here are students in the design lab.

a good choice. Nancy Kwallek, director of the interior design program at the University of Texas, notes that attending a college of interior design within a university can give you the "guarantee of a liberal arts/general education program by having to satisfy forty or more hours of liberal arts outside of a design education." There is also the chance to have "more opportunities to interact with interdisciplinary majors across campus," she states.

Design schools offer a more tailored environment as the focus is primarily on design. Cheryl Gulley, Associate professor of interior design at Watkins College of Art & Design feels these types of schools offer "a much more integrated approach with electives available in other disciplines that are somewhat allied." Class sizes might be smaller, your contemporaries would be primarily design majors (as opposed to those taking classes as an elective), and in some cases, more appropriate and/or additional facilities and equipment are available.

Before choosing a school, first consider the area within the field of design you would like to specialize in and where you would like to work (both in terms of industry and geographical location). For example, if your goal is to become a production designer or set decorator, selecting a reputable and accredited design school or college that specializes in or has a strong course emphasis in these areas is naturally a good idea. Since these jobs are primarily located in New York, Los Angeles, and

FIGURE 3.4
Fleet library at the Rhode Island School of Design, a private arts and design school in Providence, Rhode Island.

Chicago, you could tailor your search to schools in those cities as well.

Also check to see if the school is accredited. The Council for Interior Design Accreditation (CIDA, formerly known as FIDER) is a non-profit agency that sets very specific standards for the education of interior designers. They address and evaluate curriculum, faculty, and facilities, and accredit college and university interior design programs accordingly. (A list of these schools can be found at www.accredit-id.org.)

Curriculum is also a very important consideration (see the following section) as well as costs, location, alumni, and career placement options within the school. Zane Curry, associate professor and associate chair of interior design at Texas Tech University advises students to "seriously consider the industry success of alumni, background and design experience of faculty, and "fit"

of curriculum (more pragmatic versus more theoretical), and area in which the student wishes to work."

Location of the school can be important as those in or near a big city offer a wealth of exposure to design centers, museums, and all things design related. Look at the size of the school—how large are the classes and the student body? Talking with faculty members is another important item on the list. What are their interests, backgrounds, and design and teaching philosophy? Visit several schools and talk with students about their experiences. Investigate the career placement department and inquire about internship and "study abroad" opportunities. See if you are comfortable with the facilities and campus and if possible, sit in on a class.

Many schools offer an interior design internship program which helps both students and employers get the

FIGURE 3.5
Student at work at the University of Cincinnati.

FIGURE 3.6
DesignIntelligence's book *America's Best Architecture & Design Schools* ranks the top interior design schools in the country.

most out of their internships and thus provide a smooth transition from classroom to workplace. Also, inquire about the graduation and employment rate and extracurricular activities such as guest lecturers and field trips.

Both the bookstore and Internet offer a wide array of information on choosing an interior design school. The top fifteen interior design schools in the country are ranked by DesignIntelligence and the Design Features Council (in conjunction with the *Almanac of Architecture and Design*) and proves to be a valuable tool. Their yearly findings are published in the book *America's Best Architecture and Interior Design Schools* (Greenway Communications, 2008) that covers industrial design and landscape architecture as well as interior design and traditional architecture schools. They also profile schools that offer the best value for your money and/or have the most prestigious educators.

Everything from *U.S. News & World Report* ("America's Best Colleges") to *The Princeton Review* yearly ranks the top institutions in the country and *Business-Week* lists the top schools that combine both design and business in their "D-Schools: The Global List" report as well.

Enjoying top billing are schools such as the University of Cincinnati (ranked number one for eight years in a row), Cornell University, Pratt Institute, Kansas State University, and Arizona State University. Traditional design schools such as Harrington Institute, New York School of Design, Fashion Institute of Technology, Rhode Island School of Design, and Savannah College of Art and Design are also popular choices among art and design schools.

There are many wonderful institutions to choose from and ranking plays just one of the many guidelines in selecting a school. (While the numbers game is useful, top rankings do not always mean a perfect fit for the student.)

In the end, trust your intuition. It will guide you to the most appropriate career choice and school.

The Design Degree

Interior design programs can be found in a variety of academic schools and departments. While interior design disciplines may typically fall in the school of interior design, programs may also be located in home economics/human ecology, fine arts, architecture, environmental design, industrial design, and applied art/commercial design.

There are several different types of degrees available in interior design programs. Your selection will naturally depend on the chosen area of specialty. Industry experts and employers recommend a full interior design program (four-year bachelor's degree is the norm) to be the most beneficial for a design career.

While the types of degrees often vary in scope from school to school, the following are the most common degrees available:

- Bachelor Degree: This is the most common path and is comprised of an intensive four-year course of study that includes both professional and educational courses as well as fundamentals and theory. Students can obtain this degree through Bachelor of Arts, Bachelor of Science, and Bachelor of Fine Arts. A student can

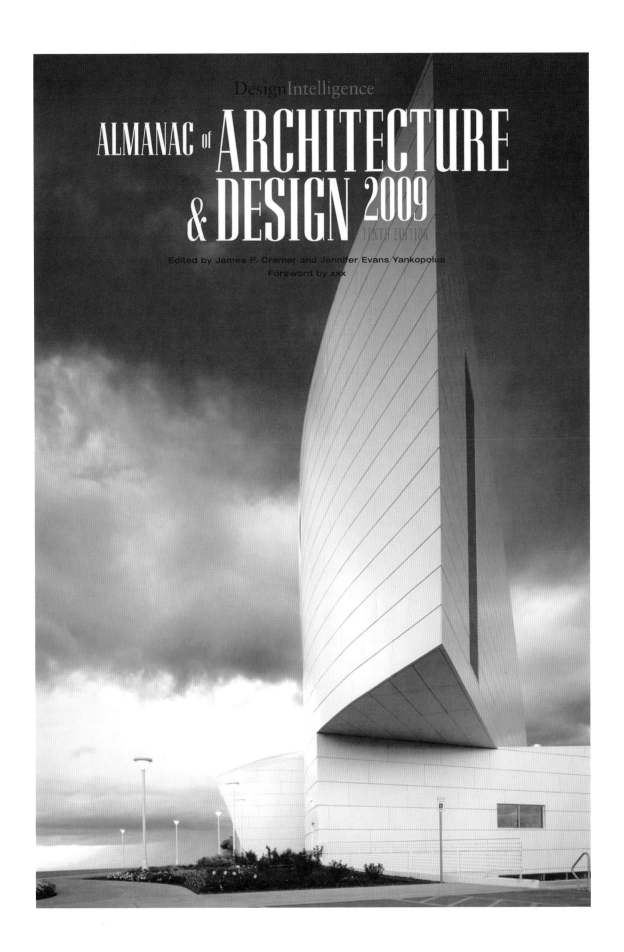

DesignIntelligence

ALMANAC of ARCHITECTURE & DESIGN 2009

Tenth Edition

Edited by James P. Cramer and Jennifer Evans Yankopolus

Foreword by xxx

meet the obligations for membership in national professional organizations by combining education requirements with internships and work experience. A bachelor's also allows students to take the NCIDQ exam.

- Associate Degree: Associate of Arts, Associate of Science, and Associate of Applied Science are the most common versions and this degree is generally obtained in a one- to two-year program. Students can also continue this program and apply their credits to a Bachelors Degree.

- Certificate: This is a one- to two-year course of study that covers the introductory aspects of interior design and in some cases includes advanced level courses in specialty areas. It is also one of the most popular choices for those who want to become residential interior designers or specialize in

FIGURE 3.7
Interior design educator.

sales or other allied areas of the field such as kitchen and bath designers. (It is important to note that this will not meet the criteria needed for certification, however, it may meet the need for kitchen and bath designer certification.)

Graduates may also continue their education with a master's degree (generally two-year program of study) or more specialized certification in areas such as kitchen and bath design. This degree will focus on advanced studies consisting of research and special projects. Some interior design students move into the master of architecture program as well.

In and Out of the Classroom

The successful design career begins with a combination of both education and experience, in and out of the classroom. While there is no substitute for a thorough blend of classes and technical instruction tailored to a specific specialty, the practical hands-on extra-curricular experience often provides the finishing touch.

Course Curriculum and Extra Curricular Activities

When choosing a school "there is not a one size fits all solution," says Scott Ageloff, vice president for academic affairs at the New York School of Interior Design. "A student should try and determine their goals and objectives and find the CIDA-accredited school whose curriculum in the best fit in term of its focus," he explains.

Curriculum naturally plays a major role in school selection and while

introductory courses are necessary, more specialized classes tailored to a student's career goals will follow. The basic interior design curriculum should include a mixture of fundamental and educational courses and studio experience. Courses will focus on interior, color and design theory, drafting (both manual and CAD) and rendering, decorative arts, and architectural history. Further studies will incorporate textiles, kitchen and bath design, space planning, furniture design, environmental design, construction and building, mechanical systems, codes, lighting, global design, and other specialized areas of study in the curriculum.

The majority of interior design educators agree that business courses are a must. Accounting, marketing, business ethics, advertising, public relations, sales, and even website design would all be beneficial electives to take. In the future, look for schools to make these subjects a required part of the curriculum.

FIGURE 3.8
"Yellow Crabapple" textile design project by Rhode Island School of Design student Alice Engel.

FIGURE 3.9
One chair design, three different materials. Rhode Island School of Design student project by Tatiana Maino-Lledo.

FIGURE 3.10
Innovative composite fabric by designer Celerie Kemble for Valtekz.

Learning must not stop with graduation or holiday recess. Sherri Donghia, former executive vice president/creative director of the renowned fabric and furniture firm Donghia, is a lifelong traveler. She advises students to carry journals with them wherever they go, jotting down sketches, watercolors, ideas, and take photographs. Donghia also notes "Olympic class shopping is a great educator, especially when you are traveling," as many of her flea market treasures found in distant lands have led to the inspiration of many a textile design.

Donghia also urges students to "continue your education through books, newspapers, trade journals, and every sort of magazine—the more obscure the better." Visit museums, art galleries and go to the cinema. Study the decorative arts, as history has much to teach us

Students are also encouraged to take courses that will help them excel professionally. "A good interior design program will require a professional practice course that will prepare students to understand the business of interior design as well as assist them in cover letter and resume writing, portfolio preparation and job interviewing," explains Mary Beth Robinson, former associate professor of interior design at the University of Tennessee-Knoxville. The interior design degree should be well rounded and balanced with courses in liberal arts or humanities. Psychology is another important subject as so much of interior design has its roots in human interaction and society.

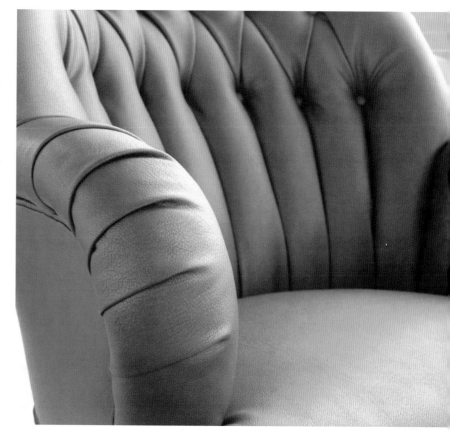

and books are free at the local library. Attend workshops, lectures, designer showhouses, and keep your senses and mind open. Inspiration is everywhere.

And most importantly, give back. Gulley notes that students at Watkins are encouraged to "participate in community service projects such as Habitat for Humanity." Design students at Texas Tech University are involved in Lifeworks, a local charity organization that designs apartment interiors for foster children who are making a life on their own.

INTERPRETING THE INITIALS: NCIDQ, CERTIFICATION AND LICENSURE

As with many professions, interior design is subject to government rules and regulations and certification, registration or licensing by individual state

boards is required in order to practice in the field. Graduates must first pass the National Council for Interior Design Qualification (NCIDQ) exam that requires six years of combined education and experience in interior design. For eligibility requirements visit the agency's website www.ncidq.org.

Secondly, you must register in the state you plan to practice after passing the examination. While this will entail registration fees and the need to take continuing education classes (CEU's), it will also result in higher standards and more regulation. Certification and licensing is very important to the overall profession as noted by former president of NCIDQ, Linda Elliott Smith. She explains that the process is "critical to the protection of the public health, safety and welfare. This ensures that the public can rely on those individuals with certification and licensure as having

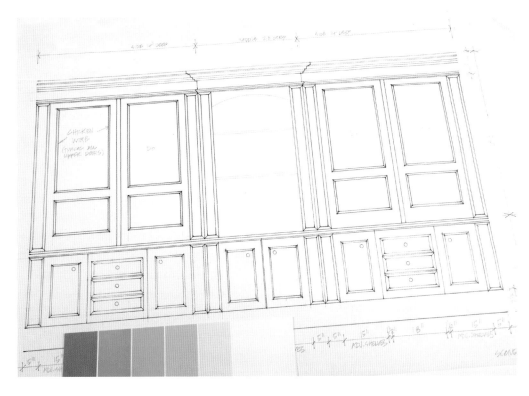

FIGURE 3.11
Blueprints are a part of daily life for the interior design student.

obtained a certain standard of education and professional experience."

With licensing comes a peace of mind for the consumer as they can rest assured the person they hire has the proper training and credentials to do a professional job. Suzan Globus agrees, "Licensing helps those who value professional interior design services to identify those who are qualified to provide services for their project." Most importantly, the process will erase the public stigma that the industry is frivolous and give it a deserved legitimacy.

Another important reason to become licensed is the ability to practice in other states should the business need arise. Given our global and mobile marketplace today, designers may have the chance to work in other states and licensing will make this possible.

To date, twenty-six U.S. states have enacted interior design legislation that dictates who can use the term interior designer. (It is estimated that within the next decade the entire country will require all interior designers to be licensed). Generally, there are two types of interior design legislation: title acts (registration or certification), which set standards for the use of a certain title but do not prevent anyone from practicing interior design; and practice acts (licensure), which require that professionals obtain a state license to offer interior design services.

TYPES OF INTERIOR DESIGN LEGISLATION

- Title Act: Regulates the use of a title, such as "registered interior designer"

and is enacted in order to raise public awareness of the qualifications of professional interior designers in that particular state. Title acts do not require individuals to become licensed in order to practice interior design, nor do they restrict an individual from providing the service of interior design. A person cannot, however, advertise or represent themselves as a "registered" interior designer unless he or she meets the minimum education, experience and examination requirements established in that state/province, and he or she fully applies for use of the state-regulated title with the proper state board or provincial association.

- Practice Act: A type of law that requires an individual to have a license in order to practice a profession. Practice acts prohibit the performance of professional services by anyone not licensed by the state agency charged with the duty of regulating that profession. Practice acts also regulate a designated title (e.g., "registered interior designer," "licensed interior designer," "interior designer") and often regulate other terminology as well (e.g., "interior design" and "interior design services").

- Self-Certification: Self-certification is like a title act because it regulates the use of a title. The difference between a title act and self-certification is the entity in control of the title. In title acts, the state controls the use of the title through a state board typically appointed by the governor. In self-certification, however, the title is controlled by an independent professional organization whose board members are appointed by interior design professionals. The state has very little oversight over self-certification. California is the only jurisdiction with a self-certification law.

CLASSIFICATIONS FOR INTERIOR DESIGNERS

- Certified Interior Designer: A person who has met certain education, experience, and examination requirements and is registered with locations with title acts.
- Registered Interior Designer: A person who has met certain educa- tion, experience and examination requirements and is registered with the interior design board in his or her state or province. This title can be used with either a title act or a practice act.
- Licensed Interior Designer: A person who has met certain education, experience and examination requirements and is registered with the interior design board in his or her state or province. Usually this designation is reserved for locations with practice acts.

Reprinted from *The Interior Design Profession: Facts and Figures.* (2007). Washington, D.C.: American Society of Interior Designers.

FIGURE 3.12 ASID Map of Registration.

Interior Design Registration Laws

Title

Practice

Self-Certification

Permitting Statute

PROFESSIONAL ORGANIZATIONS

As the interior design profession continued to grow in the early part of the twentieth century, decorators met in major cities all over the country to network and share ideas that led to the formation of decorators clubs. In 1931, the first national group known as the American Institute of Interior Decorators (AID) was born. Decades later, AID and the National Society of Interior Designers merged in 1975 to form the largest professional organization, American Society of Interior Designers.

ASID (38,000 members) and the International Interior Design Association (IIDA) (13,000 members) represent the two largest professional design organizations and there is a wide array of more specialized organizations as well. Many of these organizations promote high standards through education and legislation, raise awareness, and assist in the professional development of its members. Design professionals must meet rigorous standards to join (see ASID sidebar on page 54) and the benefits are many.

By meeting these stringent standards and gaining acceptance, the designer

FIGURE 3.13
ASID is the largest professional organization for interior designers.

||I|D|A

INTERNATIONAL
INTERIOR DESIGN
ASSOCIATION

enjoys credibility and prestige. They can network with like-minded individuals from the sole practitioner to those in large firms. Chapter meetings are periodically held and further career development is obtained through educational seminars, newsletters, websites, and conventions. Many associations offer continuing education, publications, design competitions, workshops for the NCIDQ exam (known in ASID as "STEP"), insurance plans, marketing tools, and designer referral services.

ASID President Suzan Globus feels that her organization "has served me by providing jobs, employees, information, and business support throughout my design career and I find it to be an indispensable resource." In addition, professional organizations work tirelessly on behalf of the designer in matters of government regulations that affect public health, safety, and welfare as well as the business of the profession.

Students can benefit greatly and jump-start their career by joining a professional organization. Membership can provide both learning and access to professionals that results in networking and employment through access to a job bank, student mentoring programs, and

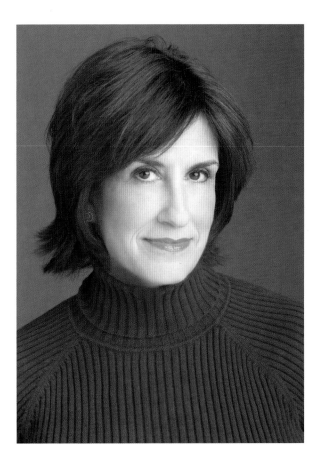

portfolio and resume reviews. There is also a student newsletter, scholarship competition, chapter events, seminars, and workshops. And by joining as a student, they can obtain an Allied membership after graduation.

In addition to ASID's student category (which boasts more than 12,000 students nationally), The University of Texas developed a student organization known as "Ampersand" that combines both ASID and IIDA membership. Students are encouraged to join professional associations, and as Gulley notes, "It's a great opportunity to meet the professional designers and make relations which may contribute to a future internship or potential position with a design firm."

There is power, knowledge, and camaraderie in numbers. Both students and interior design professionals are encouraged to join forces with one or many of the professional resources and organizations at their disposal. A number of specialty organizations that support career activities such as the American Society of Furniture Designers, International Society of Lighting Designers, and American Academy of Healthcare Interior Designers are also available for membership. (See appendix at the end of the book for information).

ASID LEVELS OF MEMBERSHIP

- **Professional Membership:** The highest level of ASID membership is reserved for practitioners who have completed a course of accredited education and equivalent work experience in interior design, and have successfully passed the NCIDQ examination.
- **Educator Membership (Professional):** This level is for educators who are actively engaged as department chairs or full-time instructors in a post-secondary program of interior design education at any university or accredited school of interior design that requires completion of forty semester credit hours in interior design-related courses, and who have successfully passed the NCIDQ exam.
- **Allied Membership:** This level is for practicing interior designers who fulfill the following requirements: a four- or five-year Bachelor's degree with a major in interior design or architecture; or a two- or three-year degree or certificate in interior design.
- **Educator Membership (Allied):** Educators who are actively engaged as department chairs or full-time instructors in a post-secondary program of interior design education at any university or accredited school of interior design that requires completion of forty semester credit hours in interior design-related courses are eligible.
- **Student Membership:** Membership is available to students currently enrolled in an interior design or interior architecture program that requires at least 40 credit hours of design related class work to graduate. Students at schools where an ASID student chapter exists may join as a student chapter member; students at other schools may join as an independent student member. Eligible ASID student members may advance to allied membership upon graduation.
- **Industry Partner Membership:** Members include interior design industry manufacturers and their representatives, related trade associations and market centers. Industry partners provide opportunities for interaction between interior designers and the interior furnishings industry that supplies services and manufactured products.

Courtesy of ASID.

REFERENCES

American Society of Interior Designers. (2007). *The Interior Design Profession: Facts and Figures.* Washington, D.C.: American Society of Interior Designers.

Bureau of Labor Statistics, U.S. Department of Labor, *Occupational Outlook Handbook, 2006–07 Edition.* Retrieved December 7, 2007, from website: www.bls.gov/oco/ocos293.htm.

Cramer, James P. *America's Best Architecture & Design Schools.* (2007). Greenway Communications.

Forest, Sara D. *Vault Guide to Interior Design Careers* (2006). New York: Vault, Inc.

Piotrowski, Christine M. (2003). *Becoming an Interior Designer (A Guide to Careers in Design).* New York: Wiley.

Znoy, Jason A. and ASID Illinois. *Professional Interior Design: A Career Guide.* iUniverse, Inc., New York, 2004.

Designing Your Career

OVERVIEW OF THE INTERIOR DESIGN CAREER

Designing an interior involves the fundamentals of research, problem solving, knowledge, intuition, and most importantly, careful planning. Just as the building and design of a space requires a blueprint, the design career needs a road map in order to be successful.

A career in the interior design industry is not a job, it's a lifestyle. It should be one that you love as you will live and breathe this business every day of the year. Perhaps the late interior designer David Hicks said it best, "I think, eat, and sleep design in all aspects of my daily life; driving down a street, I criticize the way a woman's skirt hangs, the typography of a pub sign, the new local housing; I question the way a friend has lit a room. How a restaurateur has presented his food. I live with design when I go to the cinema, watch television, arrange flowers, visit a store or an old house, when I help my children in choosing between alternatives—hopefully moulding their sense of design and their taste."

It all begins with a passion deep down in our soul. Design is complete creativity, constant curiosity, freedom of expression, and located in virtually every fiber of our being. As designers, you will see beauty, style, and form in everything

FIGURE 4.1
A career plan is just
as important as a
dynamite portfolio.

THE CAREER BLUEPRINT

The journey begins by deciding where you are in life, who you want to be, where you want to go, and what you want to do. Moreover, what is your purpose? It can be something as simple as the need to create beauty and order or the desire to invent a multi-functional item never thought of before. From a plethora of business books to self–assessment inventory tests, there are many ways to arrive at your destination and numerous tools to assist you on your voyage.

Mind Mapping

One of the most popular and creative ways is the concept of "mind mapping" and tailor made to the creative sensibilities of the interior designer. Developed by author Tony Buzan, Mind Maps™ is a terrific brainstorming tool and learning technique that visually connects concepts, ideas, and interconnections. It begins with a main theme in the center of the page and works outward in all directions, producing an amoeba-like structure composed of key phrases and pictures connected to the central issue by lines. The map can be as creative and colorful as you like and effectively stimulates imagination and creativity.

and it will naturally translate to the work at hand. The designing life will incorporate a multitude of interests as today's accomplished designer is not pigeonholed in any one single area of the profession.

Given these factors, it is ironic that many of us will spend more time planning a vacation or the color scheme of an interior than the direction of our career. Whether you are a student deciding on a major or an interior designer seeking a mid-career change within the profession, career planning should be a constant. Oprah Winfrey once said that "Luck is a matter of preparation meeting opportunity" and with today's world changing so rapidly, those with a clear career plan already have a better shot at success. It's never too late to change and the following tips will help you redesign, renovate and/or jumpstart your career.

For career planning purposes, mind mapping provides a vital road map to where you want to go and how to get there. For example, let's say you are a designer seeking ways to expand your current practice or career. Begin by positioning yourself (keyword designer) in the center and let the ideas flow, grouping them in a radial fashion around the center. Look for themes and relationships to these ideas and create subtopics

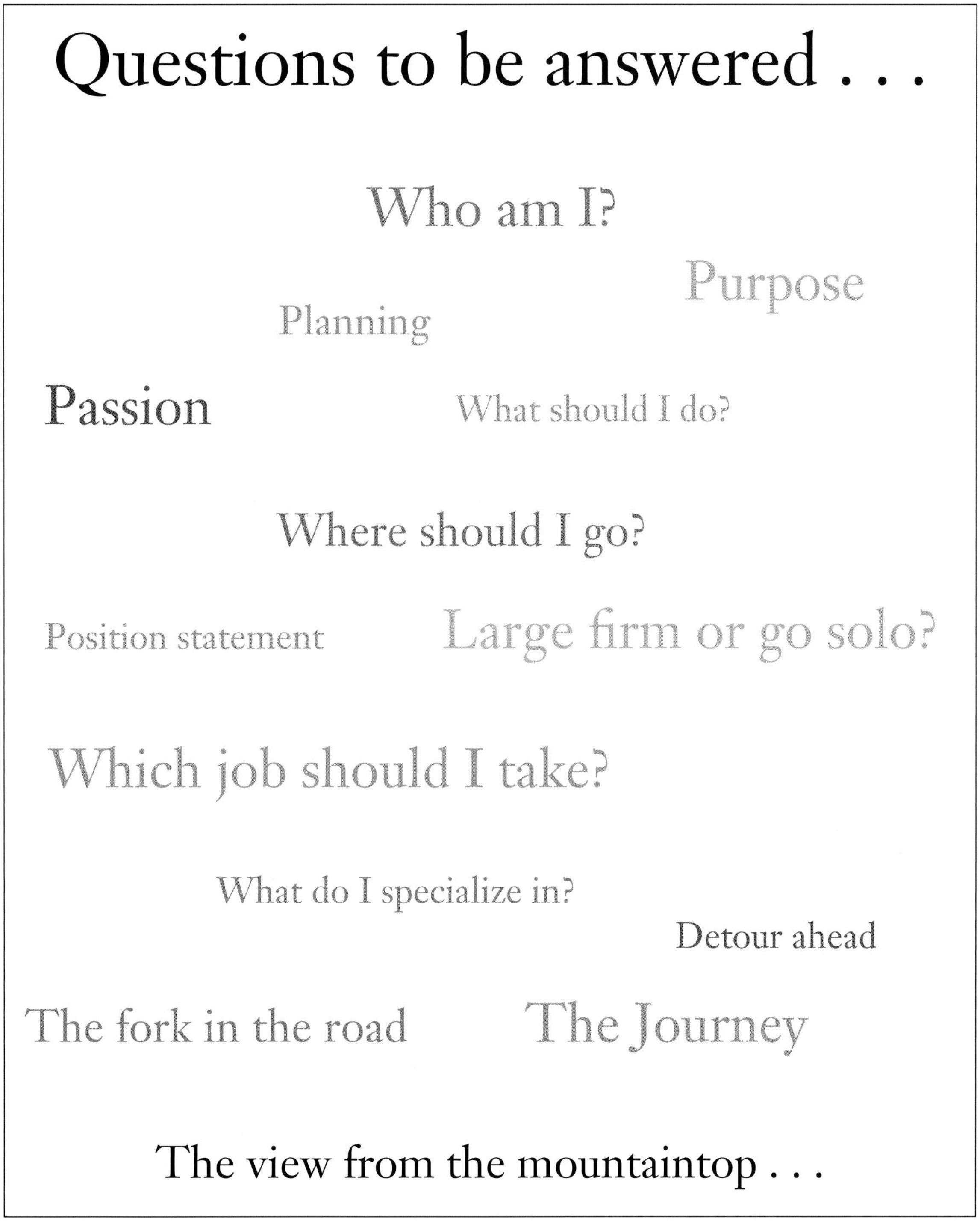

Questions to be answered . . .

Who am I?

Purpose

Planning

Passion

What should I do?

Where should I go?

Position statement

Large firm or go solo?

Which job should I take?

What do I specialize in?

Detour ahead

The fork in the road

The Journey

The view from the mountaintop . . .

where useful. You might make product designer a theme and the various options of fabric, furniture, accessory, and wallpaper designer sub-themes. You can add other characteristics to these as well such as pros and cons, attributes needed, future outlook, etc. Typically, this is a one-page map and you can be as broad as you like or as specific as need be. Leave lots of space, make it visually more interesting with color, shapes, and images and above all, have fun.

FIGURE 4.2
Word Association

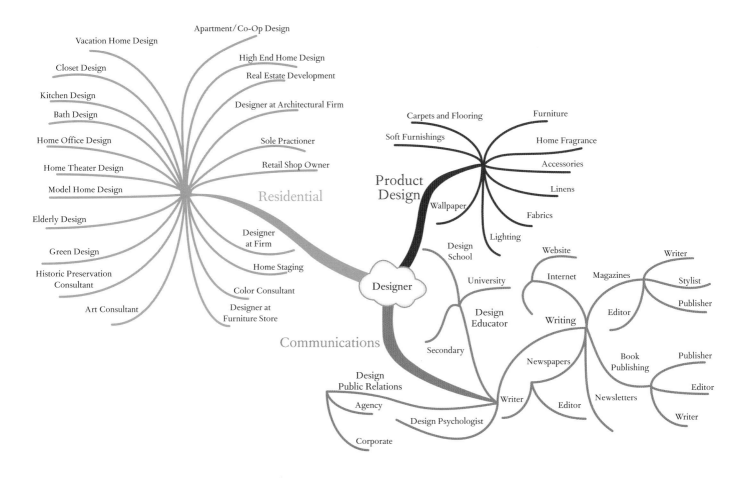

Vacation Home Design
Apartment/Co-Op Design
Closet Design
High End Home Design
Real Estate Development
Kitchen Design
Bath Design
Designer at Architectural Firm
Home Office Design
Home Theater Design
Sole Practioner
Model Home Design
Retail Shop Owner
Residential
Elderly Design
Green Design
Historic Preservation Consultant
Art Consultant
Designer at Firm
Home Staging
Color Consultant
Designer at Furniture Store

Product Design
Carpets and Flooring
Furniture
Soft Furnishings
Home Fragrance
Accessories
Linens
Wallpaper
Fabrics
Lighting

Designer

Design School
University
Website
Internet
Magazines
Writer
Stylist
Publisher
Design Educator
Editor
Writing
Secondary
Communications
Newspapers
Book Publishing
Publisher
Design Public Relations
Agency
Writer
Editor
Newsletters
Editor
Corporate
Design Psychologist
Writer

FIGURE 4.3
Mind Map

Mind mapping is also a terrific aid in problem solving, writing, planning an initial house scheme, and organizing your thoughts and ideas for a presentation. For the computer literate, there are several excellent mind mapping software programs on the market. A sketchpad and an assortment of colored pens will do the task just as well.

Envision your life. Dream about the perfect job. What would you like to design, accomplish, develop? Who would you like to work with and in what type of work environment? Where would you like to live? How do you wish to be known and what would you like

your obituary to ultimately say? What does it take to satisfy you—money, accomplishment, travel, or all of the above? Do you want to work solo and strike out on your own or be part of a team or corporation? Answering all of these questions truthfully will help you with your blueprint.

Know yourself. Take the Myers-Briggs™ personality inventory test described by noted psychologist C.G. Jung. The test determines your personality from sixteen personality types and is useful in career planning at every stage, from the choice of design major to advancing in a corporation. Take a hard look at your skills and interests. In what areas do you excel? What do you dislike? The goal is to maximize your strengths and play down your weaknesses.

Once you decide on a career goal(s), develop a plan. Do you need more skills, training, and education? Do you need to relocate? For instance, a residential designer who sees the need to specialize in design for the elderly and disabled would be wise to take classes in interior space planning and study up on handicap codes and specifications. One, five, and ten year plans are always beneficial, just be sure to make contingencies for various life situations—marriage, family, divorce, relocation, the economy, etc.

Your career blueprint does not have to be set in stone. If the road leads down a dead end, backup, and take a detour. At least you will be armed with a strategy of options.

Position Statement

It is also useful to create a position or mission statement. Simply put, this is your statement of purpose and should be no more than a paragraph stating who you are, where you are going, how you plan to position yourself in the marketplace, and how you will fit in the industry. Your statement might read "I am both a commercial and residential interior designer and plan to open a chain of retail home furnishing stores in the next five years. These stores will offer my own unique line of sustainable furnishings, wallpapers, and accessories and fulfill the needs for more environmentally friendly furnishings in the interior design industry."

Make your position statement clear, concise, and current yet filled with a vision for the future (many career advisors recommend focusing on a five-year span). And most importantly, write it down. A statement of your goals on paper makes it concrete and can be reviewed regularly.

THE JOB SEARCH STRATEGY

The age-old adage is true—it's work just finding a job—and perhaps nothing is more daunting, time consuming, and stressful. With so many areas to consider—from commercial and residential to retail, government, health care, etc.—it's no wonder the task appears monumental. Now that you know what you want to do for the next year or two, you need to identify the tactics for your plan of action. These might include research, talking to experts in your industry, and mirroring people who are already successful at doing what you plan to do. Perhaps the most difficult part is dissecting your plan of attack into a manageable "things to do" list.

Whether you are seeking work at a company or as an entrepreneur, an action plan is vital. Gail Blanke, founder of Lifedesigns and author of *My Wildest Dreams: Living the Life You Long For* developed a useful planning tool for breaking down goals into small steps. Known as "The Mountaintop," Blanke takes a triangular graph and plots out the various tasks required in reaching a goal. For example, let's say you are an interior designer and wish to open a home furnishings store. Beginning at the bottom, list your first step

Open a Home Furnishings Store

Hire employees, set up offices,
adjust schedules as store
construction dictates

Complete a three month marketing,
advertising and Grand Opening plan

Write and place orders three months
prior to being shipped. Place ads for
new employees.

Attend to the trade markets and adjust/
fine tune inventory levels.

Complete a build-out plan for fixtures and
computer equipment. Place orders.

Upon bank approval, financing, commit to a lease
approved by the Attorney of your corporation.

With the accountant, determine administrative
systems and job specifics.

Explore and finalize locations. Set a target opening date.

Formulate a business plan.

Bring an accountant, banker and attorney on board, in that order.

Visualize your concept!

FIGURE 4.4
Mountaintop Graph

(Visualize your concept) and the next step and so on as you go up the pyramid (or climb up the mountaintop). The ultimate goal is naturally located at the apex of the triangle.

Whether you are pursuing design studies, venturing out into the work world, or a seasoned veteran, many of the following strategies will apply.

Never Too Early to Plan: Advice for the Student

If you are an undergraduate studying design, narrow your majors of interest and work with an academic adviser to develop a curriculum of study as soon as possible. Realize no decision is permanent and one area of expertise could easily lead you down the path of another. You might graduate in commercial interiors with a specialty towards restaurant design and eventually become a commercial product designer. Many students find a double major assists in their marketability as well. Try to target areas in the country where building and the economy are prosperous and match your specialization.

Design schools and colleges are filled with career information and assistance; be sure to utilize them. Talk to faculty members and professionals in the field. Network and join professional organizations as a student. Use the career resource library and check out extracurricular events. According to Thom Hauser, interior design area chair at the University of Georgia's Lamar Dodd School of Art, "Many schools will bring in diverse practitioners to make presentations in a number of courses and sit on project review panels. We visit a variety of firms during our annual

fall field trips and rotate among New York City, San Francisco, and Chicago. About 50 percent of our students go each year and about 90 to 95 percent go on at least one of the three while they are in the program."

Also, take advantage of the schools' invaluable assistance with the preparation of resumes, cover letters, and portfolio preparation. As Hauser notes, "Students take a one-hour course on preparing resumes, letters of introduction, portfolios, and interview skills. This is in preparation for internships for the spring or summer before their final

FIGURE 4.5
While design talent is key, employers are also looking for designers with passion, drive, and communication skills.

year in the curriculum. All students submit personal design philosophy statements, resumes, and digital portfolios as part of their senior exit class."

Specialization starts early, as noted by Zane Curry, associate professor and associate chair of interior design at Texas Tech University, "Firms expect a higher entry level of knowledge and skill than in the past . . . and also seem to be more concerned with the knowledge of CAD skills, sustainability, and green design, and a high level of basic interior design skills in the areas of space planning and quick sketch."

Other valuable tips include:

- Join professional organization(s) as a student. This will allow you access to professionals and useful networking experience that could lead to a potential job.
- Begin to develop your resume, cover letters and portfolio while in school. Fine tune these upon graduation and tailor all three to specific areas of your search. (See resume writing for further information).
- Enter your work in competitions, magazines, professional conferences and designer show houses when possible.
- Attend workshops, exhibitions and conferences related to your major.
- Consider "shadowing" an interior design professional for a day. It's an excellent way to see and experience the actual job up close and personal.
- Try to land an internship (see sidebar at the end of the chapter).
- Mary Ellen Robinson, former interior design professor at the University of Tennessee-Knoxville advises

to "research the firm before you interview. Even if a company does not have a position, a student can request a tour of the firm and be introduced to the company in their process of researching businesses."
- Network whenever possible and above all keep learning!

Never Too Late to Change: Advice for the Interior Designer

So you are a graduate, passed the NCIDQ test, and perfected your portfolio. Now what? Or perhaps you have been working for several years and want to change careers within the field, expand your area of expertise or simply need a change of scenery. What is the next step?

First, take an assessment of the marketplace. Based on your self-discovery knowledge discovered during the mind mapping process, try to match up your skills and personality and the type of work environment. If you don't think your creativity or personality can survive a large corporate structure, consider a more relaxed small design office with less than ten people if possible. Do you want to eventually work on high-profile jobs in a fast-paced atmosphere? Consider design firms in larger cities.

Next, do your homework. Research the various occupations within the field and note the educational requirements, salary, working conditions, outlook, and any other intangibles. See which industries will continue to grow in the upcoming decade and what skills you have to offer them. Information is at your fingertips—conduct your research through the Internet, shelter publications, and *Interior Design* magazine's Top 100 List. Hit the local library and look at Dun and Bradstreet's reference books on businesses in the United States.

Make a target list of potential employers. You can locate contact information on local architectural and interior design firms (most importantly, the decision maker to whom you should direct a resume). You can also find out company particulars through the local chamber of commerce, local chapter of your professional organization, and newspaper and magazine archives. Check out the company's website as well. If possible, find out their salary ranges before the first interview and think about what you want from the job in terms of pay, benefits, and opportunities for advancement.

Recruiters advise writing two or more versions of your resume, each tailored to the type of design work you are interested in obtaining. If you apply for a position with a company that primarily specializes in residential design, tailor your resume accordingly and highlight that you are seeking residential work in the objective portion of the resume. The same goes for your portfolio—showing a residential firm your commercial projects could be a waste of time for both parties.

Your resume should never be longer than two pages, one in particular if you are a new graduate. The most important information should be listed at the top (name, address, city and state, phone numbers, and in this day and age of cyberspace, be sure to include your email

FIGURE 4.6
Before the interview, do your homework and thoroughly research the company.

PREPARING THE RESUME

Just as an entrance hall gives the first impression of a house, the resume and cover letter are generally your first introduction to a potential employer or headhunter. This traditional business vitae is composed of the standard contact information, location, work experience, education, and extra-curricular information and is usually accompanied by a brief cover letter stating your intentions and requesting an interview. There are literally dozens of books and information at your disposal on resume and cover letter writing. Crafting these documents for the design industry is no different and the basic principles apply—clarity and brevity are as important as organization, writing style, and correct spelling and grammar.

address). Only provide phone numbers at which you wish to be contacted.

You may want to list a title or label such as product designer after your name so that you are immediately identified. And since interior design and creativity go hand in hand, you can also add a logo to the top of the page.

Components of the Resume

Summary and/or Objective

This includes your interests, skills, experience, and most significantly, your career objective. The primary trick in crafting a resume is being noticed and this is the perfect area to customize and tailor your skills for the job for which you are applying. Be sure to have a different summary for different resumes—if you state you are looking for a textile design position in your objective, it might eliminate one in furniture design.

Professional Experience

This lists your work experience in reverse chronological order. Be sure to include dates of employment, name of the company, a brief description of the position, as well as the location. This is an excellent spot to expand on your experience by listing job details such as *specified purchases, managed a staff of three junior designers,* etc. Naturally, recent positions will be more descriptive than those held decades ago. Also, remember to state if a position was full time or freelance.

Education

Be sure to list degrees and dates in reverse chronological order as well as awards, honors, major, and specialization. If you are a recent graduate you may include any thesis subjects or special projects that support your career objective. This area can also include computer skills, professional affiliations, published articles, panels, and conferences you have attended, showhouses and exhibitions you have participated in, and any professional licenses you may have. (You can also list the latter under

FIGURE 4.7
Tailor your resume to the type of design work you are interested in obtaining.

FIGURE 4.8
Sample Resume 1

DANIELLE GROMOSAIK

2900 Kensington Ave • Apt • 704
Xxxxxxxx • XX 55553
555•555•5507
danielle_smith@yahoo.com

EDUCATION

Xxxxxxxx Xxxxxxxxxxxxx UNIVERSITY, Xxxxxxxx, XX
Bachelor of Fine Arts, December 2003 GPA: 3.8/4.0 Major: Interior Design
• Virginia Tech Summer Study Abroad, (Switzerland, Italy & Germany)
  Architecture Program, June–July 2002

Xxxxxxx COLLEGE, Xxxxx, XX
Bachelor of Arts, May 1998 GPA: 3.6/4.0 Major: French Minor: Elementary Education
• Intensive French Study, *University of Angers*, Angers, France, Sept. 1996-Jan. 1997
• Teacher Licensure, Elementary Ed. NK-8, Secondary Ed. French, Dec. 1998

WORK EXPERIENCE

Baskervill & Son, Xxxxxxxx, XX, June 2003 – Present
Interior Design Intern
• Assisted Senior Designers in the   • Draw architectural details in CAD
  Corporate and Hospitality divisions in a   • Finish / Furniture Selection
  firm of over 100 employees   • Site measurements
• Assisted with spec books by researching   • Constructed complete set of CDs including
  all finishes and materials according to   elevations, casework elevations,
  floor plans,
  project guidelines   finish plans, and finish schedules
• Red lines of CAD drawings
• Assisted with move coordination of our firm

Hummel Associates, Xxxxxxxx, XX, Sept. 2002 – May 2003
Interior Design Intern
• Assisted design director in a small firm   • Maintained sample and architectural library
  focusing on healthcare & corporate design   • Finish / Furniture Selection
• Red lines of CAD drawings   • Site measurements taken to input base
• Constructed presentation and   plans into CAD
  contractor's boards

Gromosaik Design, Xxxxxxxx, XX, May 2002 – Aug. 2002
Assistant to XXX professor
• Conducted on-site building measurements.
• Recreated building floor plans using AutoCAD software.

Riggs Ward Design, L.C, Xxxxxxxx, XX, Aug. 2000 – Aug. 2002
Design Assistant
• Assembled all necessary components to respond to Requests for Qualifications (RFQs)
  Requests for Proposals (RFPs), including identifying qualified subcontractors.
• Assisted with on-site installation of exhibit displays
• Created comprehensive vendor and graphic samples reference databases
• Compiled project spec books and created standard procedures for future jobs
• Wrote and distributed press releases to announce project completions
• Edited copy and assisted with format and layout for print collaterals

Franklin County Schools, Xxxxx Xxxxx, XX, August 1999 - June 2000
Second Grade Teacher
• Managed a group of 18 individuals with varying personalities and abilities

HONORS AND DISTINCTIONS

• The XXX IIDA/Chasen's Scholarship, 2002, 2003
• The XXX Rozanne Epps Scholarship, 2002
• The Pellegrini Scholarship from the Swiss Benevolent Society, 2002, 2003
• The XXX Affinity License Plate Scholarship, 2002, 2003
• Induction into the National Society of Collegiate Scholars, 2002
• Dean's List every semester, 2000-Present
• Participated in the Annual XXX Student Design Exhibition, April 2002

KEY SKILLS

• Strong communication skills   • Adobe Photoshop 7.0
• Strong problem solving abilities   • Block and space planning
• AutoCAD 2002/ADT 3.3   • Graphic computer renderings (StudioViz)
• Manually draft plans, elevations,   • Fluent in French, Conversational
  perspectives, and axon drawings   German (U.S.-Switzerland dual citizen)

Extra-Curricular Activities in a separate section.)

Rita Sue Siegel of Rita Sue Siegel Resources, a global design search firm based in New York City, advises to "Check your resume and cover letter to make sure they are flawless. Keep the resume [to] one page and consider what you might do to improve it and make it stand out among others, without overdoing it. Perhaps the paper or a logo design might be enough to grab

Grace MacDonald

2709 Valley Road
Atlanta, GA 30305
Tel: 404-555-1212 Cell 515-555-1213

gmacdonald@resume.com

Objective

A position as an interior designer with a firm that will utilize my unique skills and creative abilities in both commercial and residential interior design.

Summary

I have more than ten years of successful experience in the interior design industry including specialized experience in law office and high-end residential design and sales.

Experience

Senior Designer, Metropolis Designs, Atlanta, GA 2004-Present
Design and execute interior design projects for commercial and residential interiors. Manage all phases of the interior design process from conception to completion and oversee three junior designers. Liaison with clients and architects.

Junior Designer, Caroline Blakeford Interiors, Atlanta, GA 2000-2004
Assisted Senior Designer on interior design projects for private settings in the southeast and east coasts. Created interior design schemes for clients; coordinated fabrics and furnishings, estimates, purchasing, space planning, and vendor contracts. Implemented and expedited installations as point person for contractors and vendors.

Showroom Sales, Scalamandre, Atlanta, GA 1998-2000
Sales and customer service for high-end fabric showroom. Worked with architects and interior designers. Made sales calls, set up presentations and placed and tracked orders.

Showroom Sample Library, Atlanta, GA 1997-1998
Managed library of fabric, wallpaper, and trim samples and assisted showroom sales persons and designers. Responsible for coordination of fabric color schemes.

Education

Savannah College of Art and Design
Masters, Fine Arts, May, 1997

University of Georgia, Athens, GA
B.A., Interior Design, May, 1995

Achievements

Featured in *House Beautiful* magazine's Top 25 Young Designers of the 2004.
Participated in Southern Living Show house 2003
Habitat for Humanity 2001

Computer Skills

AutoCAD, Adobe Photoshop, Word, Power Point, Excel

Memberships

Professional Member, American Society of Interior Designers, Atlanta, GA chapter
Attend meetings, conferences, and continuing education courses

References available upon request

FIGURE 4.9
Sample Resume 2

attention. Maybe instead of folding and inserting into a standard envelope, you prepare it in a special presentation package. Send resumes to ALL the firms near you, directed to the owner, whether or not they have an opening."

Resumes and cover letters go hand in hand. The cover letter has two main functions—it serves as a letter of introduction and seeks to secure an interview. Be sure to address this to a specific person in the company, primarily the decision maker who is in charge of hiring, stating the resume is enclosed and you would like to schedule an interview. Briefly describe how your specific skills could benefit the employer and make a positive impression.

PREPARING THE PORTFOLIO

If the resume and cover letter are your calling cards, the design portfolio is you, the designer.

Composed of the best representative samples of your body of work, your portfolio should demonstrate your creativity and abilities as an interior designer and be updated and tailored to what the prospective employer is looking for. When selecting your projects, look at the narrative theme of the work as to how you approach the design process. Siegel explains, "Think of a portfolio as a showcase of your experiences, your design ability, and your technical skills. A successful one depends upon planning, a well-organized archive, and good design. It should always be a 'work in progress' with content that evolves as you get more experience and learn what you want to do more of. Like a resume, the portfolio should contain core information but have elements that are customizable for interviews for a particular position or with a particular company."

Denise Guerin, Morse-Alumni Distinguished Professor Interior Design at the University of Minnesota recommends "Tailor projects in the portfolio to suit the profile of the firm you are interviewing with. Some firms prefer to see actual boards and construction drawings as they can evaluate crafts-

manship, color, and texture more accurately. Most employers would rather see fewer well-rounded projects that show your understanding of the design process from preliminary concepts to working drawings."

Showcasing your portfolio gives you a chance to shine and show off your presentation skills, a necessary communication tool for a career in interior design. Walk the prospective employer through the story of the project from conception to completion. Describe the initial objectives and challenges and how you solved any problems. Detail your concepts on the floor plans, color schemes, material choices, and emphasize any unique concepts.

"Take the viewer through the complete process starting with a statement of the problem to be solved and the criteria for success." Guerin notes. "Each employer may be reviewing your portfolio with the need for different skills and abilities and the ability to do CAD and or manual drafting, visual organization, communication both visually and verbally."

Robinson believes that "Preference as to chronological order of work varies, but students need to be consistent in how they order their work. I personally

FIGURE 4.10
Introducing your portfolio gives you an excellent opportunity to show off your presentation skills.

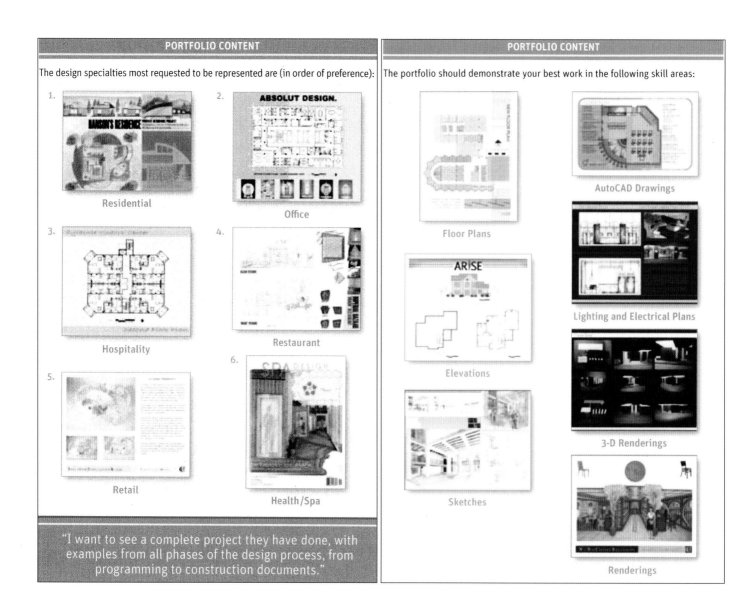

The design specialties most requested to be represented are (in order of preference):

1. Residential
2. Office
3. Hospitality
4. Restaurant
5. Retail
6. Health/Spa

"I want to see a complete project they have done, with examples from all phases of the design process, from programming to construction documents."

The portfolio should demonstrate your best work in the following skill areas:

Floor Plans

AutoCAD Drawings

Elevations

Lighting and Electrical Plans

3-D Renderings

Sketches

Renderings

**FIGURE 4.11
Portfolio of Design
Specialties.**

prefer starting with the most recent to ending with their earliest work. Others prefer starting with where the student began and work up to the present. I feel the best impression—the most developed and impressive work—needs to be shown first."

You can also use a laptop for product, graphic, and environmental design material that is easier to show in digital media. Other display ideas include creating a PowerPoint presentation (expensive and not always available), a CD to accompany the resume, or an online version of your work in a website (which also allows the world to view your resume).

Portfolio Basics 101:
- The basic portfolio will include:
  - Resume
  - Process drawings, concept sketches
  - Set of blueprints/floor plans, hand drafting okay
  - AutoCAD drawing sample(s)
  - Sample board
  - 2- and 3-D drawings and renderings
  - Engineering/construction drawings
  - Lighting and electrical plans
  - Photos of a model(s)
- Sample projects can include the specialties:

- Residential
- Office
- Hospitality
- Restaurant
- Retail
- Health care
- Include five to seven projects if possible.
- Show one example of your work from each stage of the design process.
- Include work that demonstrates color sense and material application.
- Show only real samples and boards, no photocopies.
- The portfolio should be either plastic or leather holding a spiral binder of acetate pages or an attaché case containing boards, design planning books, or sketchbooks. Average size is 11.0 inches × 17.0 inches and no smaller than 11.0 inches × 14.0 inches.
- The image size must be 5.0 inches × 7.0 inches or larger.
- Portfolios are usually presented in a notebook fashion. Use a larger format to show both horizontal and vertical images without having to rotate the portfolio.
- Try to keep the presentation 15–20 minutes.

Robinson concludes, "A portfolio is about content and craftsmanship. Make it handsome, diverse, and convey the message of versatility." Most importantly, make your portfolio images dynamic!

NETWORKING AND HEADHUNTERS

The interior design industry is very close knit and many jobs are found through word of mouth. High-end firms rarely advertise and it's unusual to find jobs through the classifieds. As a result, networking and the use of headhunters are paramount.

Numerous headhunting firms specialize in all aspects of the design industry from fabric librarians to sales and management. You can find a roster of these firms through the Internet (check www.dezignare.com for an extensive list) and the local library. Another added bonus—many employment agency websites offer information on how to format a resume, conduct yourself on a job interview, etc. Always check first to see if a fee is involved.

Make the most of design organizations and all that they have to offer. ASID and IIDA have job banks and career centers respectively that post resumes for job seekers and employers seeking talent. If you are not already a member, you might consider joining ASID, IIDA, or other associations that specialize in your chosen area of interest. Ask to be included on their mailing list.

Attend industry events. The furniture mart in High Point, North Carolina, is held every spring and fall and an excellent opportunity to investigate companies. The National Exposition of Contract Furnishings (NeoCon) is an annual event held in Chicago for the contract industry and provides workshops, education, and networking. To the trade only design centers in major metropolitan areas offer design events as well. (Check the resources for listings.)

As with the practice of interior design, so much of the business is the process of selling—services, products, and ultimately, yourself.

THE INTERVIEW

You sent a resume, followed up with a phone call to introduce yourself, and landed the interview. Now it's show time. Before you head out the door, be sure to do your homework on the company and anticipate the following potential questions:

- Why would you like to work for our company?
- What do you have to offer?
- Why should we hire you? What is your method of working?
- Why are you in interior design?
- What are your strengths and weaknesses as a designer?

- What designs, concepts, and projects were successful in your last job?

You also have the right to ask questions as this is a fact-finding procedure for both parties. You might consider:

- What is the firm like?
- What type of skills are you looking for?
- What are the expectations of the position?
- What are the opportunities for advancement?
- What is expected on the first six to twelve months of the job?
- Why is this position available?

The question of salary will not arise and it's a tricky area to navigate. Again, it is best to research the salary range

FIGURE 4.12
The interior design industry is very close-knit and many jobs are found through word of mouth, so be sure to utilize headhunters and network whenever possible.

THE INTERNSHIP

An internship is an excellent chance for students, recent graduates, and those looking to change careers to preview a particular area in the interior design field and obtain hands-on experience.

For students, internships can supplement academic classes and, in most cases, they can earn college credit. For graduates and job changers, it's a great way to test the proverbial waters in a particular field and sample a job before making a lasting commitment.

While most of the positions are unpaid, the competition for internships is fierce (paid internships are more the norm for graduates). Besides academic credit, the benefits include professional networking, a foot in the door for future employment, and valuable experience for your resume and portfolio. Internship programs are generally available part-time, during a school's "winterim" period, in exchange for a semester of school, or offered as a full-time position during the summer months.

There are several ways to find an internship. The first step is to check with the school's academic counselor or career services office. Second, search the Internet for the websites of possible companies you would like to work for, as many will list their internships under "About the Company" or "Careers" section. Lastly, pick up the telephone and offer your services—it never hurts to ask.

The following are a list of websites for internship information:

www.careerbuilder.com
www.collegegrad.com
www.entertainmentjobs.com
www.internships.com
www.internweb.com
www.monstertrak.monster.com

ahead of time if possible. If you are a recent graduate and seeking an entry-level position, there is rarely wiggle room in the competitive market of today. However, it's important to find the right fit as per Scott Ageloff, vice president for academic affairs and dean of the New York School of Interior Design. "We advise our students to do research on firms and look at their work, and not to be too hasty and accept the very first offer that they get, as if no one else will be interested in them," he says. "We tell them that it is important to go somewhere where they can learn and grow professionally."

If you have work experience, remember that employers rarely make their best offer the first one and successful salary negotiation tactics can only raise your profile. And lastly, be sure to follow up with the employer and thank them for the meeting, inquire about the possible next steps in the interview process and the status of the position. Be assertive as this is no time for shyness!

While talent, a knock-your-socks-off portfolio, and impressive educational credentials are certainly essential, employers are looking for designers with passion, drive, communication skills, and the ability to work well with others. Teamwork is an invariable part of the interior design process.

REFERENCES

Blanke, Gail. (1998). *In My Wildest Dreams: Living the Life You Long For.* New York: Simon and Schuster.

Buzan, Tony. (2002). *How to Mind Map: The Thinking Tool That Will Change Your Life*. New York: Thorsons.

Doyle, Alison. *Finding an Internship.* Retrieved December 1, 2007, from http://jobsearch.about.com/od/internshipssummerjobs/a/find internship.htm.

Finely Tailored Portfolios. Retrieved December 15, 2007, from www.dezignare.com/newsletter/portfolios.html.

Forest, Sara D. (2006*). Vault Guide to Interior Design Careers*. New York: Vault, Inc.

Hicks, David. *Living With Design.* (1979). New York: William Morrow and Company.

Knackstedt, Mary V. (1995). *Interior Design & Beyond: Art-Science-Industry*. New York: Wiley.

Linton, Harold and Rost, Steven. (2004). *Portfolio Design, Third Edition*. New York: W.W. Norton & Company.

Lowe, Janet. (1998). *Oprah Winfrey Speaks: Insight from the World's Most Influential Voice*. New York: Wiley.

No Experience and Looking For Work. Retrieved January 2, 2008 from www.dezignare.com/newsletter/work.html.

Piotrowski, Christine M. (2003). *Becoming an Interior Designer (A Guide to Careers in Design)*. New York: Wiley.

Siegel, Rita Sue. *Rita Sue Siegel Resources.* Retrieved January 6, 2008 from www.ritasue.com/resources/tools.html.

Tips for Graduates Entering the Interior Design Profession. Retrieved January 8, 2007 from www.asid.org/NR/rdonlyres/0A38FDC8-FE41-48AE-8FCA-182669B99936/0/ASID_SurveyWeb.pdf.

PART 2

The Traditional Interior Designer

5

"We all know that interior decoration is seen by many as a frivolous career full of ruffles and flourishes and preposterous fashion statements. Yet to transform the bleak and the barren into welcoming places where one can live seems to me an important and worthwhile goal in life. Sometimes this transformation can stun the eye, sometimes simply gladden it, but these are not frivolous pursuits."
— MARK HAMPTON, MARK HAMPTON ON DECORATING

The Residential Interior Designer

OVERVIEW OF THE PROFESSION

The morning begins with a 7:00 AM contractor meeting to review trim and moulding colors. While on the job site, a quick inspection of lighting fixtures reveals breakage and subsequent phone calls to the manufacturer are placed. The morning continues with a client meeting to discuss intricate bedroom window treatments and a quick visit to the stone distributor to approve granite for a countertop.

Back at the office, multi-tasking takes on a new meaning as lunch, phone calls, email, and the processing of purchase orders are tackled almost simultaneously. Both good and bad news awaits—the wallpaper hanger has an opening in her schedule and a new client contract arrives with a deposit check while a fabric dye lot is off-color and a client cancels a dining room table because he found one in a catalogue.

The afternoon's activities include pouring over blue-prints and sketching ideas for a custom club chair. The local newspaper calls for a quote on "how to decorate an inviting entrance hall" while a delivery truck waits on hold with news of a damaged chest. A staff meeting with fellow designers follows with the review of the design scheme for a country club, followed by budget reviews for a kitchen remodel.

The evening is spent tackling a stack of trade and shelter magazines, pulling ideas for a possible line of upholstered chairs to debut in the next year. A shopping bag of memo samples and design catalogues will have to wait until the following morning for review.

Such is the day in the life of the residential interior designer.

The residential interior designer is perhaps the best known and most popular of all the design specialties. From co-ops and condos to cottages and the occasional chateau-size structure, two-thirds of the design population practice in this area and are predominately female.

A large part of residential designers work as sole practitioners with home offices or storefronts or in small firms with less than five designers and a bookkeeper. They also work for firms that specialize solely in residential or commercial practices with a residential division, the interior design division of an architectural firm, or for builders and furniture stores.

The Bureau of Labor Statistics predicts the need for interior design services will grow faster than average for all occupations. Thanks to increased homeowner wealth, the growing number of baby boomers that traditionally use interior designers, and the need for the remodel of aging kitchens and bathrooms, residential interior designers will be in popular demand. While this demand is commensurate with the economy and housing, it represents a rapid growth industry.

Residential interior design is a discipline that requires education, skills, training, knowledge, and talent. It can involve the design of new construction and/or the renovation of existing spaces, as well as historic preservation and renovation. Designers must keep up with changing trends in technology and industry products, and be knowledgeable in a diverse number of areas more than ever before.

In this day of specialization, many residential designers have found niche design to be quite lucrative. There are a number of specialties within the field—kitchen and bath design, home office, home spas, home theater, condo/co-op/apartment, elderly, sustainable/green design, as well as consulting in the areas of color, fine art, antiques, and historic preservation for both consumers and corporations. Many residential designers lend their expertise to builders and real estate developers while others are applying their talents to design psychology, design journalism and overlapping contract design projects (health spas and wellness centers, boutique hotels, etc.) Recreational transportation in the way of houseboats, RVs, yachts and private planes, is another niche sector.

THE PROCESS

The practice literally involves everything from the design of one element or room to an entire house, drawing upon many disciplines to create and enhance both the function and aesthetics of an interior. They need to be well versed in floor and space planning, furniture, textile design, kitchen and bath design, plumbing, lighting, and the latest trends of the day.

The project begins with the initial client meeting, the presentation of a portfolio, and approval. Potential clients find the services of a designer in a variety of ways, from word of mouth to personal recommendation. Advertising, publicity, designer showhouses, and visibility in the industry all raise the designer's public awareness. This is a business that relies heavily on reputation, so make and keep an impeccably professional one.

The scope of services (with consideration given to the client's lifestyle and budget) is determined and the designer will decide and explain the fee structure as a result. Next, the client will receive a contract spelling out the services to be rendered along with a project schedule for installation and request for a deposit. Fees are charged in a variety of ways—set price, price per square foot, hourly

FIGURE 5.3 Presentation of a designer's work plays an important part in the hiring process.

consultations, hourly and cost plus, retail, or a combination of any of these.

The actual design process follows, beginning with the analysis of the client's new or existing structure/ furnishings, style and taste level, and the parameters of the job. Floor plans, elevations, and renderings are drawn. A preliminary budget is devised, and space planning, selection, and coordination of furniture, color, accessories, finishes, and materials all come in to play.

A design presentation is made to the client, accepted, and budgets are finalized. A variety of trades people and artisans are hired (after approval of competitive bids), scheduled, and supervised, and architects are brought in when necessary. The process continues with the shopping, ordering, and invoicing of furnishings and materials, and the execution and installation of design plans.

There is no one typical day for a designer in this field and flexibility, stamina, and the ability to juggle any number of tasks, figures, details and situations is essential.

THE PREPARATION

As previously noted, the residential designer has to wear many hats, from designer, shopper, budget maker, mediator, analyst, problem solver, organizer, and proverbial "wonder man/woman."

Requirements and Skills Needed
The following represent many of the qualities, requirements, and skills needed for the profession:

FIGURE 5.4
This design board includes floor plans, fabric swatches, and furniture recommendations.

Communication Skills

The designer has to deal with the complexities and emotions of the homeowner, as well as scheduling and working with contractors, painters, drapery installers, and a host of other trades people. Effectively working as a liaison between the client and architect and the ability to work as a team player will ensure job success.

Psychologist

Because much of the work takes place in the privacy of the home, emotions can run high and the designer must be able to effectively read, react, and understand the needs of the client and family.

Customer Service Skills

The ability to immediately solve a problem and assist the client in a variety of ways is of profound importance as so much of this business is based on service. The designer is called upon to follow up on orders, deliveries, and installations, and be ready for all types of situations.

Knowledge

The designer must be completely familiar with furniture styles and design, architecture, and design history. A working knowledge of building construction, codes, plumbing, lighting, and blueprints is crucial.

Sales

The ability to sell is a major factor as much of a designer's living is derived from the commissions from furnishings. Sales are also an integral part of the initial consultation and design presentation.

Mediation Skills

Quite often the designer will have to please several family members with varying opinions and tastes and problems can ensue as a result. Interior designer Clodagh resolves this dilemma up front by interviewing the husband and wife and others separately to get an idea of their likes and dislikes. The designer has to become a journalist of sorts, and gather useful information from the client for the job to truly be successful.

Vision

The ability to conceptualize the dreams and desires of homeowners will place

FIGURE 5.5
Designer meeting with client.

FIGURE 5.6
The ability to
read and draw
blueprints is a major
requirement for the
residential interior
designer.

FIGURE 5.7
Interior designer
Clodagh's designs
for a contemporary
dining room.

you ahead of the "eight ball" so to speak when making initial design plans. Creative expression both visually and verbally is crucial.

Time and Organization Skills

There are numerous tasks and elements to be juggled so organization and multi-tasking is necessary. One sofa can require as many as six different purchase orders so excellent bookkeeping is key. Managing time is also important—the successful designer must be adaptable and flexible as the workday has to be adjusted to suit the time of the client, workmen, and trades people. Projects finished in a timely manner will guarantee client satisfaction.

Business Brain

Mathematics will be required for everything from developing budgets to calculating square footage. A business mind is necessary as budgets will need to be developed, purchase orders calculated, and invoices processed as accounts receivable and payable are the lifeline of any business.

Other Skills

The need for problem solving will almost always present itself on a project and the designer will need to come up with space solutions for a variety of design dilemmas. Computer skills such as the use of AutoCAD, Adobe Photoshop, and Word programs are important.

Because this is a people business and networking is crucial in obtaining clients, designers often keep a hectic social schedule. The ability to handle stress goes without saying—you need to be able to survive in the organized chaos

of the job. Keep your life in balance and stay on top of every project. And lastly, possess a high ethical standard and enjoy what you are doing.

Education and Training

Most residential designers have either a two-year degree certificate or a four-year bachelor's degree in interior design from a bachelor of fine arts (BFA), bachelor of science (BS), associate of applied science degree (AAS), and/or a master's degree from an accredited university or design school. While many of the nation's top designers do not have a degree, it is strongly advised.

In terms of education outside of the classroom, be sure to attend museums, art galleries, exhibitions, and the cinema to learn about design history. Designer show-houses, design markets and industry events and architectural tours are also great ways to keep up with the trends—an imperative in residential design. Read and study the many books and magazines available on the field, watch design television, and network with professionals. Meet and talk with a variety of trades people from specialty painters, furniture makers, drapery workrooms, contractors, and architects, to discuss business. And lastly, taking and passing the NCIDQ exam and obtaining a state license is required to become a design professional.

Design Curriculum

Students who want to specialize in interior design are well advised to obtain a well-rounded education. Curriculum includes courses in the basics—drafting, perspective and rendering, color and design theory, art, furniture styles and design, historical interiors, visual concepts as well as residential design, kitchen and bath design, lighting, gerontology, environmental psychology, and design and art history.

With an eye towards the future, the student should take courses in marketing, accounting, sales, and business as well as public relations, journalism, and advertising. Classes in psychology are beneficial as you are dealing with human interaction and behavior within interior living spaces. Technology courses will also give the student an advantage in the workplace.

PROFESSIONAL ASSOCIATIONS

Students and designers can benefit greatly by joining a professional design association such as the American Society of Interior Designers (ASID), the International Interior Design Association (IIDA), and/or the many specialized organizations such as the National Kitchen and Bath Association (NKBA) and the Set Decorators Society of America (SDSA).

ASID has 12,000 student members in universities and design schools across America and offers student memberships. Established interior designers can join as professional members (the highest level of membership) or allied members (see Professional Organizations in Chapter Three for details). The benefits of joining an organization include networking, continuing education, research materials, seminars, workshops, discounts, and above all, credibility.

THE PATH

Assistant to Junior Interior Designer to Senior Interior Designer to Sole Proprietor or Firm Partner/Principal
Those starting on the path to a career in residential design should work for

FIGURE 5.8
Students and designers are urged to visit museums, exhibitions, and art galleries for inspiration.

FIGURE 5.9
Elements of the design presentation can include floor plans, renderings, and fabric samples.

several years with an established design firm that specializes in residential, if possible, and particularly before becoming a sole practitioner. Since most residential firms tend to be small, advancement is somewhat faster and hands-on experience more readily available (and the turnover can be high). While many firms vary in their employee positions and duties, the path to residential design is education, training, and ultimately, clients.

Positions on the career path can include:

Design Assistant

This entry-level position works primarily with junior and senior interior designers. Duties include updating the sample library, assisting with the design process, learning the various aspects of the business, and assisting with the coordination of the design scheme. Assistants should expect to spend anywhere from one to three years on the job training before advancing to junior designer.

This is an excellent way to learn the business and many have excelled to the top by starting out as the apprentice/assistant to the head. The venerable interior designer Betty Sherrill of McMillen began her career in 1951 working for then founder Eleanor Brown McMillen. She never left and today is chairman.

Designer showrooms are also excellent training grounds for a career in residential design. Many start in the sample room, coordinating schemes with fabrics and trims and working with designers and architects, assisting them with their projects. This is an excellent place to network and learn the showroom side of the business as well.

Junior Designer

This position includes assisting senior designer(s) on projects, supervising the daily aspects, and keeping track of orders and the activities of the various stages of project management. They attend client meetings, interface with vendors, contractors, and trades people. They also create purchase orders and invoices and oversee shipping, deliveries, and installations.

Senior Designer

One of the highest positions in the company, the senior designer is responsible for the entire design project and manage junior designers, design assistants, and other employees of the company. They are the primary contact person with the clients.

Principal

Also known as the partner, owner and/or president of firm, they are present at the initial meetings with the client and oversee all of the firm's designers. They also develop and sign off on the overall design direction of project and often shop with clients for antiques and furnishings.

THE PAY

As noted by the Bureau of Labor Statistics, the median salary for interior designers in 2006 was $42,260. (The middle 50 percent earned between $31,830 and 57,230.) The website www.salary.com lists salaries for design assistants ranging from $25,000 to 45,000, junior designers $32,000 to 45,000 and senior designers pull down anywhere from $45,00 to 60,000. Owners can

FIGURE 5.10
Vicente Wolf's
showroom in
Manhattan.

make six to seven figures a year depending on the economy and number of projects.

Salaries tend to be commensurate with the company, geographical location (metropolitan cities run higher), economy, and scope of the project. Designers in specialty areas and architectural firms tend to earn more than those in retail establishments such as furniture stores, etc.

For the self-employed designer, the sky can be the limit depending upon their client roster and subsequent project budgets and fee structure (and tend to work longer hours on the average). Consultants charge hourly, by the project or work on retainer with a company/client.

Perks with a design firm include (in most cases) healthcare benefits, expense accounts, and travel. Self-employed designers are naturally responsible for all expenditures. Some firms will cover professional fees and continuing education. All designers enjoy a healthy discount on purchases.

THE PROFILES

Alexa Hampton, President, Mark Hampton LLC

"It's a visual dictionary approach to design."

—ALEXA HAMPTON

The phrase "*studied at the feet of the master*" certainly applies to the career of interior designer Alexa Hampton.

The daughter of the late interior designer Mark Hampton (1940–1998),

Alexa no doubt inherited her talent through genes, osmosis, and personal experience—as well as the helm of the family business.

Her father's achievements were both remarkable and legendary. Making a name for himself as a designer of "restrained traditionalism," Hampton's client roster was a virtual who's who of political, social, and business luminaries from all over the world. Former President and Mrs. George W. Bush, Jacqueline Kennedy Onassis, Estée Lauder, and Ambassador to France Pamela Harriman were a few of the many who appreciated his iconic tailored yet comfortable style. He was one of the first designers to have a licensed collection of furniture for a leading home furnishings manufacturer (Hickory Chair) and was a profound book writer, gifted watercolorist, and popular lecturer.

Both father and daughter arrived to the field of interior design through a shared passion. After abandoning law school, Hampton pursued an art history degree at Michigan's School of Fine Arts and later received a master's degree at the Institute of Fine Arts at New York University. Upon receiving a bachelor of arts from Brown University, Alexa soon followed in her father's footsteps at the Institute and studied art and architectural history in New York and Florence, Italy.

While education was important, Alexa says "I was trained by my father my entire life. He taught me to look around and absorb everything I see. At the end of the day it's about referencing things, where to look, what inspires you, what looks wrong and right, what is missing? It's a visual dictionary approach to design."

Alexa worked side by side with her father, beginning her illustrious career at the age of 13, where she spent the summer picking up fabrics and trims from vendors in Manhattan. She took over the creative reins of the company upon his death in 1998, facing considerable skepticism. And while blessed with an incredible heritage, she faced a balancing act keeping her father's list of loyal clients, repositioning the firm to attract a younger generation, and most importantly, proving herself.

Today the talented designer successfully continues the legacy of Mark Hampton Inc., while making a name in

FIGURE 5.11
Alexa Hampton, interior, fabric, and furniture designer.

FIGURE 5.12
Alexa Hampton
interior featuring
furniture from her
collection with
Hickory Chair.

her own right. Overseeing as many as fifteen to twenty jobs a year, her approach to residential design centers on the belief that "we are a service industry and can never forget that. I help them (clients) get the best possible version of their style so it reflects them. And it is important to remember what being 'in service is'."

While the number of jobs she works on varies from year to year, they are all in varying stages. "They can be huge projects," she explains, "and I will sit down with the architect, do floor plans and electrical, the house will get framed and literally a year can go by with no calls until the house is ready. It's very unscientific and we have to really organize our time."

She also feels that design is a "tight-rope act" and finds planning to be the

biggest headache. "It's like weaving a basket. One thing can affect everything else," she states. Alexa cites the scheduling of a floor refinisher can literally make or break a project as one trade falls behind on their duties and it affects the installations of the rest of the project, "like a domino theory." As a result, time and management is crucial.

As head of the firm, she is lead designer on all projects and assisted by two senior and two junior designers. The company also has a draftsperson, bookkeeper, and office manager and utilizes as many as four interns, which is an entry-level position to the firm.

Alexa advises that to be successful, designers must learn how to run and market a business. She notes, "Its very important to have a serious business side, figure out what you need to make it and where you want to go. And be savvy about public relations. Self promote and make a name for yourself." Promotion begets more promotion, as her firm's projects have been featured in major shelter publications and newspapers across the country and Alexa has been named to *Architectural Digest*'s "AD 100" list and *House Beautiful*'s "America's 100 Best Designers."

For those starting out, she recommends a young designer will learn the most by "finding the hardest person out there to work for. Someone like a Martha Stewart who is incredibly organized and a tour de force would be a dream job!"

And like her accomplished father, Alexa teamed with Hickory Chair on a line of furniture. Her talent and energy were attractive to the North Carolina–based furniture company as she represents the demographic of the young metropolitan apartment dweller. Jay Reardon, President of Hickory Chair, wanted her to design a collection with a "youthful twist and not duplicate her father's line." Impressed with her knowledge and dedication, he notes "Alexa is literally on her hands and knees in the factory overseeing the production."

Alexa looked at the various categories of bedroom, dining and living room furniture and came up with antique adaptations for the 40-piece collection. "I was very fortunate with Hickory," she details, "and used a grass roots approach—the best thing to do is draw up your designs and approach a company (if you are interested in licensing). Sell yourself and only partner with the best firms. She also has a collection of fabric and trimmings with Kravet, lighting for Visual Comfort and rugs with Stark Carpet. (For more on licensing, see Chapter Ten: The Lifestyle Designer).

Alexa's interest in historic houses led her to the renovation of Trowbridge House, a townhouse in Washington, D.C., that is being renovated for visiting former presidents. Her father renovated a similar project, the official guest residence of the White House known as Blair House.

FIGURE 5.13
Armoire from Hickory Chair's Alexa Hampton collection.

The multi-talented designer is also a television personality and the first designer to appear on the PBS show *This Old House* and the top rated series on antiques, *Find!* Whether local or national, she recommends appearing on television to raise your visibility. Taking another page from her father's resume, she is also a popular lecturer, speaking at antique shows all over the country.

With or without her famous moniker, Alexa has established herself as a well-rounded and accomplished designer. And her father would be proud.

Nina Campbell, Nina Campbell Inc.

"My design work and private life all roll into one."

—NINA CAMPBELL

There is usually a moment in life when the proverbial die of the future is cast. For interior designer Nina Campbell, that moment occurred during her childhood. "We moved so much as a child," she explains, "and I was always redoing the bedroom. I was allowed to choose my own schemes and I used to go to wallpaper shops with my mother to pick out the colors and materials." At the tender age of twelve, an interior designer was born.

One of Britain's most renowned interior designers, Campbell began her career as a salesgirl at the General Trading Center, an upscale gift shop in London's Knightsbridge area. Her job was to "assist brides on what they should have in their home. That was the beginning for me . . . a desire to make life beautiful," she says.

She worked for the celebrated designer John Fowler of Colefax and

Fowler, who recognized her talents and hired her as an assistant. His tutelage proved to be a remarkable learning experience as he taught her invaluable design lessons. "The most important thing I learned was everything did not have to be new," Campbell details. "He

FIGURE 5.14
Sconce designed by Alexa Hampton for Visual Comfort.

FIGURE 5.15
Interior designer
Nina Campbell.

London, offering luxury items and she began her career in design retail.

Campbell moved on and opened her own store on London's fashionable Walton Street, combining both her retail and design businesses. Her career continued to soar with clients such as rockers Rod Stewart and Ringo Starr, the London residence of the Queen of Denmark and a number of historic castles, beach houses, hotels, yachts, and private residences from Beirut to Paris.

Campbell has been designing for over thirty-eight years and credits her success to several factors—her mentor John Fowler coupled with a few famous clients and editorial coverage, and lectures that gained her notoriety. In addition, the fact she is enormously talented, has a quick wit and inimitable sense of style, also helps.

In addition to her successful commissions, designing and manufacturing her own lines put Nina Campbell Inc. on the international map. It all began when she needed "copious amounts of a fabric for a bedroom in Scotland." Unable to locate the material, she decided to manufacture her own fabric in a small town on the Scotland border. Design inspiration came from a variety of places such as "old wallpaper falling off the walls of a castle" which turned into the best-selling "Brooklyn" pattern. Her career as a textile and wallpaper designer was launched and her products and home furnishings are licensed through Osborne and Little, The Rug Company and The Paint Library.

She feels the secret to her success is "I still think of myself as a small business. If I want to do something, I can

was very old school and lived through the war—back then you couldn't just go to Brunschwig and Fil and order eighty-six miles of silk. He was all about texture and making things look as if it had been there—a room is not really supposed to be the thing that is astounding, the life there is."

Campbell's clients soon realized her worth and she obtained the financial backing to open her own design studio. One of Campbell's first commissions was to decorate the historic Cullen House in Banffshire, Scotland. Other clients followed and she soon became known for her signature style of "timeless elegance and luxurious comfort." Her mix of rich colors and fabrics captured the attention of a London club owner who hired her to redecorate the famed Annabel's Club. The pair worked so well together and opened a shop in

FIGURE 5.16
Campbell's elegant
designs for a London
dining room.

FIGURE 5.17
Red match strikers
are one of the
many products in
Campbell's home
accessory line.

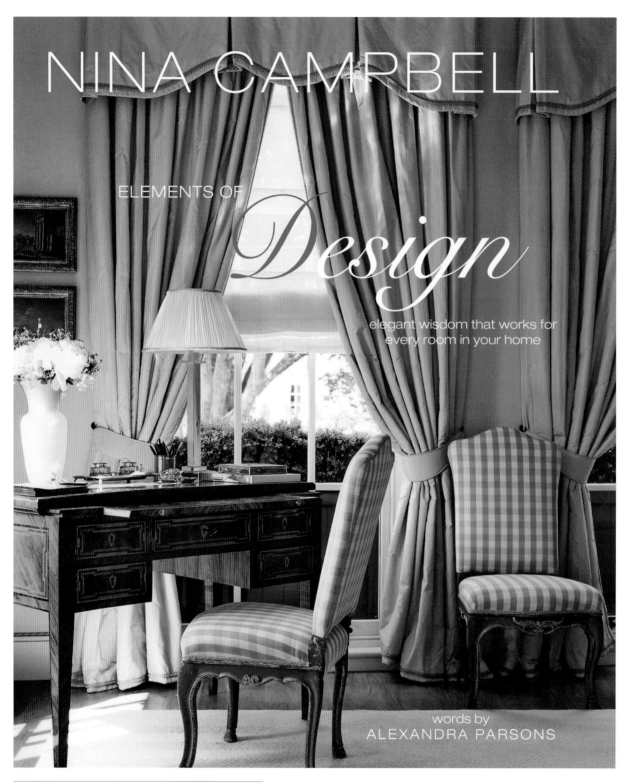

NINA CAMPBELL

ELEMENTS OF

Design

elegant wisdom that works for
every room in your home

words by
ALEXANDRA PARSONS

FIGURE 5.18
Nina Campbell's book *Elements of Design: Elegant Wisdom*
That Works for Every Room in Your Home.

do it, as there is no board of directors to answer to." Her son and right arm, Max Konig, is in charge of retail, locating manufacturers, and distribution, as well as licensing, and notes, "Licensing is actually common sense and keeping your eyes open. Love the name, love the product, and you won't get ruined." In addition, a staff of twenty (ranging in age from twenty-four to forty), including five decorators, two designers, and a publicity person, keeps things running smoothly. They work on as many as ten jobs at a time all over the world and Campbell makes it a point to attend every meeting.

Campbell's firm charges a design fee and a percentage on the goods purchased. She notes, "We used to charge retail and not a fee. Now people want to know the costs so we charge a percentage on top of wholesale and add the markup." She feels there is a marked difference in English versus American clients as "English jobs are more than likely going to be a 're-do' as opposed to clients with second houses who start with nothing and want a 'blanket look.'"

Her design philosophy is a simple one—"fashions change but good quality lasts," and feels "homes should always reflect the preferences and idiosyncrasies of the people who live in them." Her business credo is also straightforward, "Listen to your clients and observe how they live their life," she notes. "Their tastes and needs are my most important priority as a designer."

Campbell also adds the title of writer to her already impressive body of work. She has written four beautifully illustrated design books that guide the reader in recreating her signature look.

Giving back to the design world is an important priority as she travels all over the world lecturing at design schools. She advises students their most important quality is to be "super efficient." She explains, "Don't believe and be too trusting the painter will show up. Keep on the case and check everything. Keep your files in the right place. Design is 90 percent efficiency and l0 percent wafting in and out!"

And speaking of efficiency, Campbell must be one organized woman. She juggles an impossible schedule on her Blackberry and has been known to travel to Spain, Vietnam, Telluride, New York, and Paris in the space of a month. She shows no signs of slowing down and hopes in the future to "still be around a trolley of samples, extend my accessory lines and perhaps get the shop on Walton Street in a situation to franchise."

The adage of "design work and private life all roll into one" certainly pays off in this successful designing life.

FIGURE 5.19
Max Konig.

FIGURE 5.20
Vicente Wolf's signature style is often characterized by a white palette with clean classic lines.

FIGURE 5.21
Wolf's flatware line at VW Home.

FIGURE 5.22
One of Wolf's upholstery designs for Pucci.

Vicente Wolf, Principal, Vicente Wolf Associates, Inc.

"You have to love design because the compensations are often much more in artistic execution than money."

— VICENTE WOLF

The man known as the "white knight of contemporary design" took an alternative approach to his career.

Vicente Wolf, product, furniture and interior designer, author, and teacher happened upon the field of interior design admittedly by chance. "Fired from practically every job—fashion, merchandising, and acting—I have no formal training or schooling," he says. "When you don't have the limitations of a diploma, you will try anything because you don't have parameters."

Apparently, this approach worked and today Wolf is one of the country's leading residential and contract interior designers.

Wolf got his auspicious start in an entry-level position at Donghia, a prestigious fabric and furniture designer showroom. Enter Bob Patino, his future business partner who was working as a salesperson in the showroom. "By observing the path he had taken, for the first time I saw a direction and a sense of purpose," he notes. They eventually teamed up and formed Patino/Wolf and became known for their stylish minimalist designs and use of industrial materials for residential interiors. "One year I was sweeping floors in a showroom and the next year my first job appeared in *House Beautiful*," Wolf says. In 1988, he struck out on his own and never looked back.

His Manhattan firm Vicente Wolf Associates, Inc. employs twelve designers and assistants who work on projects as varied as a plantation in Natchez,

Mississippi, and model apartments for major real estate developers, to private residences, restaurants, retail, and hotels all over the world.

Wolf's design approach is all about "creating an environment that includes balance, elements, and juxtaposition." He explains, "I design every job and meet with every client. I assign one designer as a support person. I design the initial space and my staff does the construction, details, etc. I choose all the fabrics and furniture as well.

The self-taught designer advises that "You have to love design because the compensations are often much more in artistic execution than money. In return, I can live an incredible life.

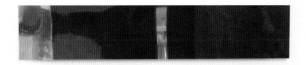

FIGURE 5.23
Vicente Wolf interior, from the Luxe Hotel on Rodeo Drive in California.

You have to pay your dues; these days students often have a sense of expectation. Many feel they have graduated and learned the tools but they haven't learned the process."

He also recommends to designers, "Be as professional as possible. Be a salesperson, businessperson and creative. If I cannot sell it, what good is the design? If you cannot run a business professionally, you will never make any money. Anyone can call themselves a designer and the true professionals are able to separate themselves from the 'wannabes.'"

Wolf is also a multi-faceted product designer and his creations range from furniture for Henredon and Neider-maier, lighting for Sirmos, china for Steuben and flatware collections for Sasaki. His signature line VW Home consists of treasures he gathers while traveling the globe. Over the past few years, the author of two books has added photography to his resume, displaying his passion at gallery shows and magazines.

REFERENCES

American Society of Interior Designers. (2007). *The Interior Design Profession: Facts and Figures.* Washington, D.C.: American Society of Interior Designers.

Brown, Patricia. (January 14, 1999). The Torchere Is Passed. *New York Times*. Retrieved January 12, 2008 from http://query.nytimes.com/gst/fullpage.html?res=9C07E7DF1331F937A25752C0A96F958260.

Bureau of Labor Statistics, U.S. Department of Labor, *Occupational Outlook Handbook, 2006–2007 Edition*, Interior Designers, Retrieved January 10, 2008, from http:www.bls.gov/oco/ocos.293.htm.

Connors, Jill. (July/August 2005). Classic Style, On Camera and Off. *Brown Alumni Magazine*.

Dampierre, Florence. (1989). *The Decorator*. New York: Rizzoli.

Forest, Sara D. (2006). *Vault Guide to Interior Design Careers*. New York: Vault, Inc.

Hampton, Mark. (1989). *Mark Hampton on Decorating*. New York: Random House.

Turner, William. (1989). *How to Work With An Interior Designer*. New York: Watson-Guptill.

Wolf, Vicente (2002). *Learning to See: Bringing the World Around You Into Your Home*. New York: Artisan.

6

*"I do think my team leaves a personal stamp on each space
we have designed, but it is more in the feel and essence of the
project, rather than in creating a certain 'look.' I have always
believed that it is important to create a timeless design that is
also comfortable and usable. The first thing I consider is the
client and what they want to achieve with the project. That is
what we mean by designing for the market."*

— Trisha Wilson, President and CEO,
Wilson Associates

The Contract Designer

OVERVIEW OF THE PROFESSION

The distinction is simple—residential design is concerned
with private dwellings, while contract design deals with public
spaces.

As the second most popular career choice among designers, contract (also known as commercial) design offers
the largest number of specialties within the profession and
encompasses everything from the design of a hotel lobby to
the conference room of a law firm. Hospitality, government,
retail, health care and transportation are just a few of the
areas within the practice that is further divided into "subspecialties." Hospitality designs may specialize in restaurant or
resort design while health care, designers may focus on nursing homes or wellness centers.

And like the practice of residential design, many of the
skill sets are similar and the basic principles of theory and
application apply in the planning and execution of the design
process. However, the work can also be quite different in
scope as the design of a home may require a few chairs where
a hotel conference center can require hundreds. The raw silk
for a club chair would not be suitable for a sofa in a hospital
waiting area, while a carpet yearly walked on by over 50,000

FIGURE 6.1
Wilson Associates have designed hotels in some of the most exotic places in the world. Shown here are the dynamic designs for the Park Hyatt in Dubai.

FIGURE 6.2
Kelly Wearstler's sophisticated yet informal designs for the Tides Hotel in South Beach, Florida.

people needs to be durable. The size, scope, duration, large fees, and budgets of the projects involved make this more of a business-oriented profession.

One of the primary differences lies in the face that contract designers must have a working knowledge of codes as much of the design must incorporate the safety and welfare of the public. The flammability of a fabric becomes not only a safety issue but a legal one as well. Consideration of handicap ramps and ample interior exits are just a few of the many requirements when designing for the public.

Designers specializing in office designs represent the largest area of the profession followed by hospitality and health care. Due to the nature of the business, contract designers are generally employed by large contract firms, corporate in-house design departments, and architectural firms. Small design practices have to compete with the giants of the industry for high profile jobs.

Contract Magazine's 2006 Hiring Survey indicates that large commercial design firms are hiring in overwhelming numbers, particularly those involved in commercial and institutional spaces. Project managers are the most in demand as well as AutoCAD operators and senior designers. In addition, employers cited "project, business and time management skills to be the most sought after traits among applicants" along with expertise in design and technology. "The well-rounded designer—possessing skills that can most likely only be honed with a few years of experience—is considered by many to be a professional catch," the magazine states.

The rise in travel and tourism indicates a demand for hotels, resorts, casinos, and restaurants in the hospitality industry and transportation design should benefit as a result. There is also a growing luxury segment demanding personal service, comfort, and high-end experience. Interior design services in the health care field are expected to rise due to the aging baby boomer segment of the population. Facilities in the way of senior assisted living, nursing homes, and hospice are anticipated in the wake of this aging demographic.

An increase in consumerism coupled with wealth is a key factor in the growth of retail design. Businesses are recognizing not only the aesthetic and functional need for good design but also the importance of marketing and sales that an attractive store image can bring. In addition, designers are jumping into the arena of branding as demonstrated by interior designer Clodagh's packaging design for the Awake skincare line.

There is considerable crossover with residential design as many firms have added contract design to their list of specialties. Residential designers are being called upon to design luxury spaces such as boutique hotels, spas, medical, dental and legal offices and other areas that need the personalization, warmth, and beauty often lacking in the design of public spaces.

Employing these concepts in her work, interior designer Kelly Wearstler's practice is 70 percent commercial. "I like the fact that I can crate more fantasy-driven designs with hotels—people tend to appreciate the escape when they visit a new place," says the designer of the Avalon, Maison 140, and Viceroy Hotels, and Bergdorf Goodman and Trina Turk boutiques.

FIGURE 6.3
Clodagh's serene
interiors for
Burlington House.

FIGURE 6.3
Clodagh's serene
interiors for
Burlington House.

FIGURE 6.4
Wearstler's dramatic
use of bold colors
makes a strong
statement in the
Viceroy Hotel in Palm
Springs.

TOP TEN CORPORATE/OFFICE DESIGN FIRMS

1. Gensler
2. Hellmuth, Obata + Kassabaum
3. IA Interior Architects
4. Nelson
5. Skidmore, Owings & Merrill
6. TPG Architecture
7. Leo A. Daly
8. Perkins + Wil
9. Kling
10. Mancini Duffy

Source: *Interior Design* magazine

TOP TEN HOSPITALITY DESIGN FIRMS

1. Wilson Associates
2. Hirsch Bedner Associates
3. DiLeonardo International
4. Concepts 4
5. H. Chambers Company
6. Wimberly Allison Ton & Goo
7. Gensler
8. Brayton + Hughes Design
9. The Gettys Group
10. Daroff Design + DDI Architects

Source: *Interior Design* magazine

TOP TEN COMPANIES IN RETAIL DESIGN

1. Pavlik Design Team
2. Callison
3. Design Forum
4. Gensler
5. FRCH Design Worldwide
6. Nicholas J. Tricarico, Architect
7. JGA
8. TPG Architecture
9. Cubellis Associates
10. Peter Marino & Associates, Architects

Source: *Interior Design* magazine

TOP TEN HEALTH-CARE/ASSISTED-LIVING DESIGN FIRMS

1. HDR
2. Cannon Design
3. Perkins + Wil
4. NBBJ
5. PageSoutherlandPage
6. Perkins Eastman
7. Hellmuth, Obata + Kassabaum
8. Zimmer Gunsul Frasca Partnership
9. HKS
10. Karlsberger Companies

Source: *Interior Design* magazine

THE PROCESS

The design process for residential and contract is quite similar. A design firm is contacted and interviewed based on their reputation, work, or by the recommendation of an architect, builder, or contractor. The designer's portfolio is presented, and during the initial consultation, fees are explained and the designer is subsequently hired. The scope of the job is determined and a design vision for the overall project is discussed with the client.

Architects may be brought in to create plans with input from both the client and the designers. The contract designer may work directly with the client/principal, project manager assigned to the job and/or their in-house design team. The contract design team will develop design plans, schedules, and budgets for the project. A presentation will take place in the form of sketches, drawings, elevations, renderings, models and fabric, furnishings, and material boards. Contracts are negotiated and signed, deposits received and the work begins.

Once the design concept is determined, the designer and team will specify materials, furnishings, lighting, flooring, wall covering, and other design elements. To ensure that the design meets building codes, drawings for approval will be submitted to a construction inspector and if structural work is required, an engineer and other trades are assembled and hired after obtaining competitive bids.

The next phase includes the ordering of furnishings, working with purchasing agents, vendors, and contractors. The design team visits the project site

FIGURE 6.5
Corporate offices
by Gensler.

often, overseeing the work and interacting with clients. Installation, follow-up, and invoicing are the final steps of the project.

THE PREPARATION

Many of the basic skills, attributes, and requirements of residential interior designers apply to the field of contract design. (See Chapter Five: The Residential Interior Designer for more information.)

Requirements and Skills Needed

The following are additional traits needed:

Communications Skills

Due to the large scope and number of vendors, architects, engineers, and assortment of trade and service people working on the project, designers must be effective communicators as well as good listeners. The ability to write contracts and business correspondence is also an asset. Working as a team player is useful as the field involves interaction with a variety of professional heads, architects, designers, and workers on all levels of the project.

Time and Project Management

Due to the extensive nature of the commissions and number of variables involved, the effective management of time and execution of project details is crucial. This can be a highly stressful business, so problem-solving skills and balancing projects under pressure are important traits.

Technical Knowledge

Contract designers must know and understand the structural requirements of buildings, codes, and safety and health issues such as the durability of materials, handicap accessibility, and making sure lighting is UL approved.

The ability to read, draw, and work with blueprints is paramount. Designers should possess expertise in AutoCAD (some employers also accept Micro station) and drafting and rendering skills. Any courses, experience and knowledge in architecture and engineering is always a plus. The ability to create presentation boards and 3-D modeling skills is also required.

Knowledge

Know your client's needs and business objectives. One of the goals of contract design is often successfully portraying an identifiable public image of the client. A high-powered attorney might want a "power office" look to portray a successful image to his clients while the needs and specifications for an obstetrician's office would have a completely different set of parameters.

Other Skills

Accounting knowledge and the capability to make and balance a budget is important as many projects can involve millions and millions of dollars.

Education and Training

A four-year bachelor's degree in interior design, bachelor of fine art (BFA), bachelor of science (BS), or associate of applied science degree (AAS) in interior design or architecture from an accredited college or design school is highly recommended for a career in this field.

Contract design is one area where actual professional experience in the field can be even more beneficial than a post-graduate degree although a master's degree can certainly supplement the designer's education. Ann Black, associate director of faculty and curriculum at the University of Cincinnati's acclaimed interior design program notes, "A master's degree is very impressive and certainly allows for a further honing of the skills used in contract design. While it might be impressive, I don't know that it is critical for success in the commercial field. Professional practice teaches so much that even the best graduate degree cannot teach."

Design Curriculum

Students should obtain a well-rounded curriculum of design courses including the basics and electives—drafting, rendering and perspective, design theory and principles, furniture styles and history, art and art history, color and design theory, historical interiors, fabrics and materials, and textile design. Classes in residential design, kitchen and bath design, lighting, and universal and

FIGURE 6.6
A single purchase order in contract design can involve hundreds of chairs.

FIGURE 6.7
Then: Camellia
House restaurant at
the Drake Hotel in
Chicago designed
by the legendary
Dorothy Draper.

FIGURE 6.8
Now: W Hotel
dining room shows
restaurant design
has changed over the
years.

environmental psychology should also be added to the student's curriculum.

Courses that will directly impact a career in this field are contract design, construction technology, construction documents, AutoCAD, modern architecture and design, building practices codes and standards, and professional portfolio development. Students would be wise to take specific courses tailored to their chosen specialty such as restaurant and hotel design.

Business, marketing, accounting, and a class in legal contracts are highly advisable as much of this business revolves around budgets. Sociology and psychology courses are helpful along with advertising, public relations, landscape architecture, ergonomics, and gerontology.

PROFESSIONAL ASSOCIATIONS

Both students and designers will benefit from joining a professional organization (See Chapter Three: The Design Education for further details) such as the American Society of Interior Designers (ASID), the International Interior Design Association (IIDA), and the National Kitchen and Bath Association (NKBA).

Becoming a professional member is important in contract design as it denotes credibility and stature within the design community as well as an excellent source of networking and resources for career growth. Contract designers also benefit by joining one of the more tailored groups relating to their specialty such as the Institute of

Store Planners (ISPO) for those in retail design or the American Academy of Healthcare Planners (AAHID) for designers involved in all aspects of health care. (A detailed listing of organizations is featured in the resources.)

THE PATH

One path: Entry level Assistant or Technician to Junior/Intermediate Interior Designer to Interior Designer to Senior Interior Designer to Design Director/Associate to Vice President/Senior Vice President to President

Many positions, titles, and duties will vary from firm to firm and the path for the technician who specializes in the execution of construction will differ from interior designers, the following represents the hierarchy of a contract firm:

Entry-Level/Assistant

Duties include assisting designers and project managers on day-to-day activities, learning how to specify furnishings, aiding in the coordination of materials and various aspects of the design process. Most of the large contract firms have internship programs in which the student/designer learns everything from design to marketing and human resources. The sample library is another excellent resource to get your foot in the door as the coordination, upkeep, and fulfillment of fabric and wallpaper samples is vital to the business of a showroom or design firm.

Technician

This position involves the primary technical aspects of a project, utilizing

AutoCAD to produce construction documents, elevations, sections, and details. They are also responsible for the execution of rendered plans and construction documents and understand building codes, structures and forms. A bachelor's degree is a must. This is an entry-level position in some firms while others require up to four years of experience.

Job Captain

This position requires a minimum of five years experience; strong technical skills utilizing AutoCAD; and knowledge in building codes, structures, and standards. A degree in architecture is recommended.

The primary responsibility is to provide team coordination for finished project plans and construction documents from the preliminary set of drawings to final construction. They are also in charge of the specification of materials and keeping track of purchase orders. Other duties include working with consultants, contractors, and fabricators.

Interior Designer

The duties of this position are different at every firm, ranging from entry-level to junior/intermediate designers to senior designers/design directors. The basic responsibilities include conception and execution of design concepts; coordination of color and materials, presentation, budgets, and specification of furnishings. A bachelor's degree in interior design, art, or architecture and AutoCAD is necessary.

Senior Interior Designer

This position oversees interior designers, provides design leadership, and is involved on all phases of the total project process including team management, schedules, and budgets. A bachelor's degree in interior design and AutoCAD is required.

Project Manager

Responsibilities include the management of project design teams, scheduling, budgeting, staffing, and the negotiation of fees and contracts. The manager is also the point person with clients. A bachelor of arts or science degree in architecture or interior design and knowledge of building codes and structures is needed along with three to ten plus years of experience, depending upon the firm.

Design Director

This position is in charge of developing design schemes, coordinating, and overseeing design firms. Strong leadership skills are required as is the ability to oversee a number of teams on multiple projects. The director acts as the primary design interface with clients. A bachelor's degree in interior design coupled with ten plus years of experience is preferred.

Vice President/Senior Vice President/President

These top positions are the design principals on all projects and are very involved in the business management of the firm, marketing, public relations, and a rainmaker for new projects. They may also be named associate, and maintain client

relationships and become very involved with activities at the corporate level.

THE PAY

Interior design salaries vary in range depending upon the specialty, type, size, and geographical location of the employer and the candidate's level of experience. Larger specialized design and architectural firms tend to offer more in salaries and benefits.

Salary levels are slightly higher than those in residential design. Interior design headhunters note the following ranges: beginners, $30,000 to $45,000; AutoCAD operators, $50,000 to

$47,000; junior/intermediate designers, $40,000 to $55,000; interior designers, $60,000 to $85,000; project mangers, $75,000 to $110,000; senior designers, $99,000 to $150,000; and vice presidents/principals/partners, $105,000 to $150,000 and up.

According to the ASID website, "Designers working in large, commercial firms in major metropolitan areas and those serving in management and consulting positions earn more than those in smaller firms and those who primarily do design work." The perks include working on prestigious high profile jobs and quite often, travel, expense accounts, and health care benefits. In some cases, profit sharing and year-end bonuses make up a large portion of a designer's income (based on both the designer's work and the financial performance of the firm).

THE PROFILES

Trisha Wilson
"Design for the market."
— TRISHA WILSON

It all began when the young designer Trisha Wilson made a "gutsy" phone call to a Texas hotel developer requesting the design commission for the Anatole Hotel. Against all odds, she landed the job.

FIGURE 6.10
Trisha Wilson, President and CEO, Wilson Associates.

Today she is President and CEO of Wilson Associates and has designed an astonishing number of over one million guestrooms across the world. Since 1978, her firm has designed or is currently working on over 2,750 projects to date in 46 countries. With offices in the United States, South Africa, Shanghai, and Singapore, the young woman who got her start selling mattresses has come a long way.

The firm employs over 280 professionals including architects, designers, design assistants, and administrative staff. The acclaimed designer has created four-star luxury resorts, restaurants, clubs and casinos all over the world from the Hyatt Regency in Orlando to the Palace of the Lost City in Bophuthatswana. Inducted in *Interior Design*'s prestigious Hall of Fame in 1993, the magazine noted Wilson's interiors "embody the cultural spirit of their client's particular needs." She possesses a remarkable knowledge of the hotel industry and is a twenty-time winner of the prestigious American Hotel and Motel Association's Gold Key Award for Excellence in Hotel Design.

A graduate of the University of Texas (bachelor of science in interior architectural design), Wilson began her practice in residential and restaurant design. She credits her classically elegant grandmother as a source of inspiration as she used to travel the world on business and it sparked wanderlust in her young granddaughter. No doubt this became the impetus for her desire to design for the world traveler.

Her contract design philosophy is simple—"design for the market." She explains, "Wilson Associates prides

FIGURE 6.11
Wilson's luxurious designs for the Inn at Palmetto Bluff resort in South Carolina.

FIGURE 6.12
Palace of the Lost City hotel's Crystal Court in South Africa.

FIGURE 6.13
The spectacular lobby of the Venetian Hotel in Las Vegas.

itself in attributing no specific 'style' or 'look' to the firm's overall work, but rather to create unique places, customized for each client. I have always believed that it is important to create a timeless design that is also comfortable and usable. The first thing I consider is the client and what they want to achieve with the project. That is what we mean by designing for the market."

For a career in contract design, Wilson advises "It is very important for students studying entire design to have architectural training. I look for graduates who have a strong architectural education. I also always advise architecture and design students to take a few business classes— remember that every business must make money and be profitable. And it's important to know how to manage and keep a budget," she says.

Design students start in her firm as interns, an area representing 75 percent of new hires. "It gives the intern an opportunity to see the type of work we do and determine wherever we are the right 'fit' for them and vice versa," she details. "It is important for students to take advantage of an internship opportunity and get as much from the experience as possible. I also encourage them to attend as many installations as possible. They will never work as hard as they will while doing an installation, but they will really enjoy the excitement and gratification of seeing a wonderful project come to life."

Wilson credits flexibility to be an important attribute in the fast paced world of hospitality design. "I am often up in the wee hours of the morning on the phone with my managing director in Singapore, with offices all over

the world, there is a Wilson Associates office open virtually around the clock!" She notes that design is often a juggling act as "designers in another part of the world can assist with a drawing or rendering and it will be on my desk the first thing the next morning."

Her personal and professional motto—"it can be done" has been a mainstay throughout her career. "Overall I believe attitude is everything. Beyond talent and creativity, my best designers have 'can do' attitudes." This philosophy has obviously served her well.

Kelly Wearstler (kwid)

"I like the fact that I can create more fantasy-driven designs with hotels. People tend to appreciate the escape when they visit a new place."
—KELLY WEARSTLER

First there were the Viceroy Hotels, filled with whimsy, strong color and mid-century modern elements. Next was the High Roller suite at the Hard Rock hotel in Las Vegas. Rose damask wallpaper and pink tinted mirrors designed to resemble an English rock star's apartment. An investment park in Century City of Los Angeles followed, old world designs mix with gold leaf for a modern glamour not commonly used in the design of high finance. These are not your traditional stodgy clichéd commercial interiors.

Los Angeles–based interior designer Kelly Wearstler has literally turned the commercial interior design market on its rear. Her trademark designs— modern glamour mixed with singular geometric elements and a dominant use of strong hues are not expected in the

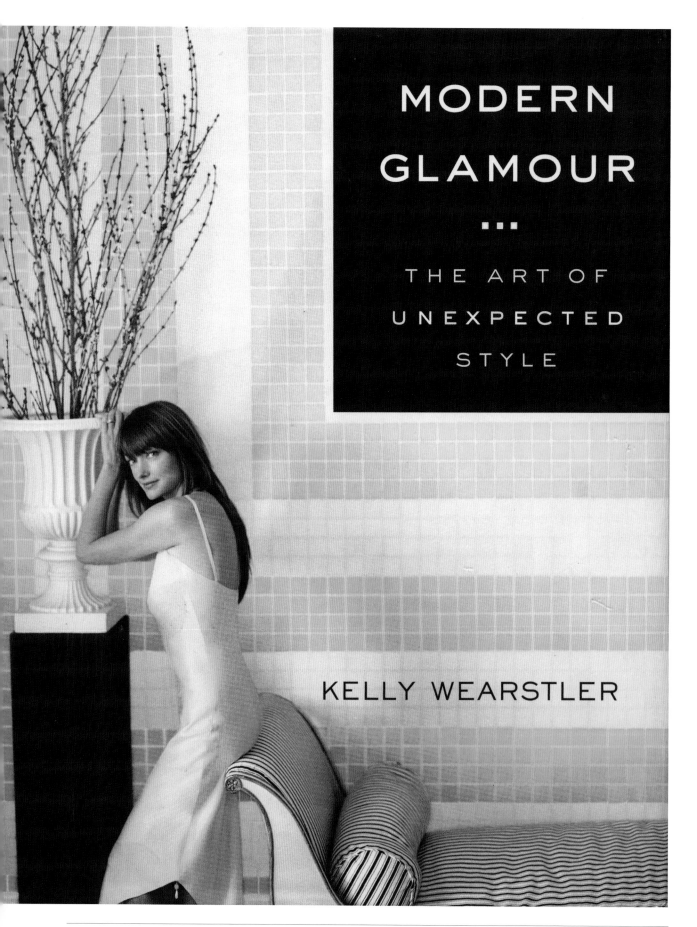

MODERN GLAMOUR

...

THE ART OF UNEXPECTED STYLE

KELLY WEARSTLER

FIGURE 6.14
Modern Glamour: The Art of Unexpected Style (Collins Design, 2004) by Kelly Wearstler.

FIGURE 6.15
Tides Lobby design by Kelly Wearstler.

various restaurants, hotels, and retail environments that display her work. And she literally redefined and redesigned the boutique hotel concept. (*Elle* magazine coined her Joan Crawford–like black and white interiors for one of the Viceroy hotel properties to be reminiscent of a Hollywood film set.)

At present, Wearstler and her staff at kwid (the acronym Kelly Wearstler Interior Design) are hard at work on no less than five luxury hotels, two of which she will be working with the noted furniture designer Pedro Friedeberg. She has also added the work of internationally known fiber artist Sheila Hicks to her commercial interiors as well. "I start with historical references because it can look cheap if you don't, and then I add the unexpected elements," she says of her interiors. "There's always something unexpected when you come around the corner. It's never vanilla." Seventy percent of her firm's work is commercial and they usually handle ten to twelve projects at a time.

The South Carolina–bred native got her start as an intern after receiving a bachelor of fine arts from the Massachusetts College of Art. "Internships with Milton Glaser Inc. in New York and Cambridge Seven and Associates afforded me access to the tools of our trade," she notes. She eventually opened her own firm in 1995, met and eventually married her biggest client and the rest is history.

Riding the wave of the future of multi-talented and multi-tasking designers, the hard working Wearstler expanded her empire to product and furniture as well as two books, *Modern Glamour: Art of Unexpected Style* (Collins Design, 2004) and *Domicilum Decoratus* (Collins Design, 2005). She also designed a line of fabrics and trimmings for Groundworks/Lee Jofa, floor coverings for the Rug Company, and a signature collection for the Kelly Wearstler Boutique in Bergdorf Goodman, where she designed the store's restaurants as well. She most recently made headlines as a judge in Bravo's *Top Design*, the interior design competition program. And if that is not enough, a chain of stores bearing her name is under consideration.

Wearstler may not have invented the boutique hotel, but she has certainly reinvented the way it is designed.

FIGURE 6.16 Wearstler's French-inspired interiors for the bar of Maison 140 hotel in Los Angeles.

CONTRACT DESIGN SPECIALTIES

- Educational: Schools, colleges, universities, and libraries use interior designers for everything from classrooms and dormitories to gymnasiums and laboratories.
- Entertainment: Theme parks, clubs, theaters, casinos, and industrial projects as well as stadium and arena design are a few of the specialties in this area.
- Government/Institutional: Government offices and agencies such as military bases, federal building offices, and child care centers represent opportunities for designers.
- Health care: One of the fastest growing industries in the nation, this category includes medical and dental offices, nursing homes, hospitals, wellness centers, clinics, and health and fitness clubs. Within this practice are subspecialty areas such as emergency room design, hospice clinics, etc.
- Hospitality: Restaurants, hotels, resorts, casinos, nightclubs, bars, conference centers, spas, senior living centers, convention centers, country clubs, and even bed and breakfast and sports bars are some of the hospitality categories designed by interior designers who want to create functional and exciting interiors for the masses. The acceleration of travel and tourism coupled with consumer wealth has made this a hot category.
- Professional office: This specialty includes the design of corporate and professional service firms such as law and financial offices as well as public and private areas from lobbies and reception areas to conference rooms, etc. Office design draws upon the principles of residential design to create spaces that are both functional and make a statement.
- Retail: Shopping center malls, national chain stores, outlets, and department stores to art galleries, showrooms, and specialty boutiques are among a few of the popular retail specialties. Creating a dynamic and identifiable image and store branding represents major design challenges in this area.
- Transportation: Airplanes and airports, cruise ships, transportation terminals, railroad cars, and yachts comprise this group and are dependant upon the economy and tourism.

(See Chapter 11: The Specialty Designer for a complete listing of niche design categories.)

REFERENCES

American Society of Interior Designers. (2007). *The Interior Design Profession: Facts and Figures*. Washington, D.C.: American Society of Interior Designers.

Apodaca, Rose. (Fall, 2007). Kelly Wearstler: What's Next. *Harper's Bazaar*.

Building Momentum: The 2006 Hiring Survey. (January 2, 2007). *Contract*. Retrieved April 13, 2007, from website http://www.contractmagazine.com/contract/web_features/article_display.jsp?vnu_content_id=1003526344.

Bureau of Labor Statistics, U.S. Department of Labor, *Occupational Outlook Handbook, 2006–2007 Edition*, Interior Designers. Retrieved January 10, 2008, from website www.bls.gov/oco/ocos.293.htm.

Davidsen, Judith. (January 1, 2005). Increases of Giant Proportion. *Interior Design*. Retrieved April 10, 2007, from website www.interiordesign.net/id_article/CA498691/id?stt=001.

DeVries, Hilary. (December 8, 2002). Creating a Scene from the Lobby Up. *New York Times.* Retrieved March 10, 2008 from website www.newyorktimes.com.

Forest, Sara D. (2006*). Vault Guide to Interior Design Careers.* New York: Vault, Inc.

Friesen, Craig. (February 15, 2007). Interior Design School Can Prepare You for Commercial Jobs. *Interior Design School Review.* Retrieved on January 12, 2008, from website www.contractmagazine.com/contract/web_features/article_display.jsp?vnu_content_id=1003526344.

Hall of Fame. (August 27, 2005). *Interior Design.* Retrieved January 10, 2008 from website www.interiordesign.net/HoFDesigners/95.html.

Knackstedt, Mary V. (2005). *The Interior Design Business Handbook.* New York: John Wiley & Sons.

PART 3

The Diversified Designer

7

"The only really good place to buy lumber is at a store where the lumber has already been cut and attached together in the form of furniture, finished, and put inside boxes."
—DAVE BARRY, HUMORIST AND AUTHOR

The Designer as Retailer and Merchandiser

OVERVIEW OF THE PROFESSION

At the very foundation of the interior design profession lays the component of sales. From planning and presentation to sourcing and consultation, the art of selling (both directly and indirectly) comes into play. Moreover, it explains why retailing is such a natural offshoot for a career in interior design.

Retailing and merchandising is defined as the sale of products and services, acting as the intermediary between vendor and consumer. For the interior designer, it can mean everything from opening a home furnishings shop or turning a design office into a storefront to becoming a national retailer with a chain of stores. A designer can work as an in-house consultant for a furniture store or become a furniture buyer for a retailer, buying office, or catalogue. They can team up with a retailer and sell their wares in a cozy special boutique environment (known as a "store within a store" concept) or specialize in retail store design and display. In addition, retailing does not have to stop with the proverbial brick and mortar location as designers are venturing into direct mail via print catalogues and online retailing in cyberspace.

One of the nation's top growth industries, retailing has long fueled our economy and will continue to grow and expand as home furnishing sales are predicated to hit $87 billion in the year 2008. As we enter the next decade, look for more changes as retailers adjust to meet the demanding needs of a retiring yet active and affluent baby boomer market, many of which will purchase second homes that result in furnishings for these properties. Whether the home-selling market is up or down, home improvements and interior design will always be a mainstay.

The proliferation of shopping malls, websites, catalogues that are more specialized, and the new "lifestyle shopping areas" abound. Simply having a storefront will not be enough as technology and a computer-savvy public require access 24/7 and online orders will be the norm. Website presence is as mandatory these days as a business card and represents one of the three of the most vital elements of retailing along with stores and catalogues.

THE PROCESS

Career options and opportunities abound in almost every type and size of retail venue. For those with an entrepreneurial spirit, owning a store might be the answer. Buying offices, showrooms, catalogue houses, and numerous other firms utilize designers with a knack for retailing and merchandising.

The Shop Owner

For many, a shop of one's own symbolizes the American dream as many interior designers hang out their shingle for interior design services and home furnishings. If entrepreneurship is in your genetic makeup, this is both an excellent career choice and a logical extension for the design practice.

The designer as shop owner must serve in a variety of roles from the buying, handling, and receiving of merchandise to sales, store maintenance, and customer service. Responsible for both profits and losses, financing is another important consideration. Start-up costs are expensive and include rent, merchandise, security, utilities, and salaries and good financial planning can make or break a business. Upscale linen store retailer Linda Berry notes "Having a war chest is critical to long-term success and staying power," and something start-up businesses may not be able to do.

The benefits are many. Owning your own store means being your own boss (although the customer is the ultimate person you must answer to). Designers can increase their visibility and client list as well as develop and sell their own product line. The store becomes a working laboratory, allowing the designer to showcase their talent as well as experiment with ideas. The shop can develop into an extension of the office, housing a sample library that can be

FIGURE 7.2
Branca is a full-service interior design firm in Chicago.

directly offered to the public. Trunk shows and special events offer partnership with vendors with increased sales and visibility as a benefit. And for many, it feeds an ongoing passion for buying and shopping as well as arranging and display.

There are downsides as well. The hours are long and holidays non-existent due to peak sales time. Designers often find it hard to concentrate on interior design duties in the back of the store and sales in the front. It is common for the shop owner to play housekeeper, security guard, and stock person and finding and keeping good personnel can be a constant problem. Bad record keeping and miscalculating inventory and the public's tastes and needs can prove to be risky. The survival rate is gener-ally low and retailing success is in direct correlation with the economy.

One of the more interesting retail concepts in home furnishings was the Charlotte Moss Townhouse. A five story building on Manhattan's Upper East Side, the retail store displays merchandise from its namesake interior designer Charlotte Moss as if it were in her home. From a conservatory with garden items to merchandising linens and china in the dining room, the concept takes the designer showhouse one step further, offering every design element (both large and small) for sale.

The Store(s) Retailer

The success stories are full of retailing lore.

FIGURE 7.3
Shown here is an interior vignette from a Branca store.

Home furnishings giant Pottery Barn began as a simple store in Lower Manhattan in 1949. Crate & Barrel displayed its wares on you guessed it, crate shelves and empty barrels in a single Chicago shop in l962. Mitchell Gold and Bob Williams (MG+BW) built their empire upon a single theme, "Relaxed Design," and today sales have reached in excess of 100 million (see profile). And all of these retailers began with a simple premise, a single store and became national empires.

They also share a common theme—lifestyle branding, a marketing concept that speaks to the lifestyle and psychology of a particular customer base. (See Chapter 10: The Lifestyle Designer for further information on this subject.) Retailers today are not only serving the desires of consumers but their emotional needs as well. Many are primarily concentrating on one category line (such as California Closets) or one stop shopping for stylish home furnishings and customers who want to furnish their entire home in one place with a designer look.

Home furnishing retailers are creating synergy with retail partners and commercial ventures. Mitchell Gold (MG+BW) sell their upholstery through other giants such as Crate & Barrel, Pottery Barn and Restoration Hardware as well as designing the guest rooms and lobbies of the W Hotels and Rande Gerber's Whiskey Bars across the country.

If your sights are not as lofty as those who have multiple stores, design opportunities are available as in-house interior designers; furniture buyers; product, accessory, and furniture designers; and visual merchandising and display designers.

Catalogues and E-Commerce

Print catalogues have filled consumer mailboxes since the early 1900s with staples Sears and Roebuck and Montgomery Ward, and by the end of the century, the average American household received twenty-one print catalogues a week. Today they are an integral part of retailing, as the majority of catalogue houses are going hand in hand with online (also known as "e-commerce" and "e-tailing"). An abbreviation of "electronic commerce" and a play on the word retailing, these terms refer to

**FIGURE 7.4
Chester Sofa by
Mitchell Gold +
Bob Williams.**

the distribution, marketing, and sales of products or services over the Internet.

According to the Direct Marketing Association (DMA), approximately 10 billion catalogues are mailed annually with the category of home furnishings representing 31 percent. Online sales are lucrative as well, topping 2.5 billion in 2007. Statistics show that the fastest-growing merchants are smaller niche retailers who specialize in one particular area such as home accessories. More than 25,000 design-oriented consumers purchased from the West Elm Catalogue (average order $200.00) in the past six months.

The United States Postal Service reported that consumers who receive catalogues are more twice as likely to purchase online, accounting for 15 percent more transactions, and will spend on average 16 percent more than customers who did not receive catalogs, regardless of household income, education levels, or location. The DMA also notes that the average catalogue customer is female (71 percent) in her early 50s, married (63 percent), and employed (58 percent), with roughly a $53,000 income. Research also shows that consumers are more likely to shop in the store once they receive a catalogue as well.

FIGURE 7.5
Mitchell Gold + Bob Williams also design for retailers such as Restoration Hardware. Shown here is their Clifton Sectional.

As a result, many successful designers are finding that a storefront is simply not enough and an online presence is as common as a business card and a key contributor to sales.

E-tailing has its many advantages. Most Internet retailers have a lower overhead structure than typical retail stores and do not have to deal with commissioned salespeople or staffing requirements. The limitations of display space are not a factor so they can offer a wider selection. Consequently, many enjoy a major pricing advantage over retail-furniture stores. In this day of stay at home shopping and instant gratification, consumers use home furnishings sites for purchasing as well as research and comparison-shopping. Those with a product line can market and sell directly to the consumer without the financial outlay of a physical store. Designers are finding success with everything from small niche areas (think pillows and lampshades) to online design consultations.

While retailing via mail and online is a science onto itself, it is strongly recommended that designers seek help with all areas of direct marketing from list management, fulfillment, and distribution to creative. Designers can also find work as furniture and merchandise buyers, marketing managers or on the creative end with catalogue and website layout, copywriting, design, and display.

Furniture/Merchandise Buyer

Designers with a knack for merchandising, a love of purchasing, and a brain for business may find a career as a furniture and product buyer rewarding. Responsibilities include developing business strategies and seasonal plans for department and furniture specialty and chain stores, buying offices, catalogues, and online retailers. They must keep abreast of new trends and identify the "next big look" in home furnishings. They must be very knowledgeable about what and how much they purchase and work closely with vendors, sales, and promotion.

RETAIL STORE DESIGN

From a luxuriously upscale boutique to the mass-market monolith, retail design is responsible for the mood, image, and function that sets an establishment apart from its competitors.

Retail store design is a vital contributor to the overall profitability of a store. Successful design establishes branding, targets the customer base and invites them into the store and communicates the retailer's overall vision. Interior designers specializing in this area can also be involved in packaging (store shopping bags have become an art in themselves) and visual merchandising and display design.

Retail interior designer plan and executes drawings for store layouts and design schemes and can be involved in the remodel for various locations. They develop approved plans for the construction team and work with storeowners to understand their business plans, needs, consumer base, branding, and marketing strategy.

FIGURE 7.6
Home furnishings
retailer Nina
Griscom's storefront
in Manhattan.

Visual Merchandising and Display

Designers in this highly specialized area are responsible for everything from the design conception to execution of store windows, in-house visual display, and unique boutiques and selling areas within a store space. They must also take into account the corporate brand and seasonal design for holidays and coordinate design activities with buyers and sales staff. Combining creativity and maximizing space, they are responsible for creating an image, increasing store traffic and guiding a customer to the point of sale.

Manhattan interior designer Tracy Bross specializes in luxury store and showroom design and works on presentations twice a year. She often has to call on her residential design talent for a linen manufacturer and explains,

"I create a showroom that feels like the lifestyle that the bedding would live in and what it was inspired by to give it a subtle theme. Its more interior decorating than display in feeling, which I like." She also notes that classes in photography proved to be a valuable asset for this career.

THE PREPARATION

First and foremost, it is understood that a strong retail sales background is extremely beneficial for a career in retailing (along with expertise in the design field). If the goal is to own and/or manage a store, they must have solid financial backing and be prepared (in some cases) to go without a salary for the first couple of years.

FIGURE 7.7
Interior layout of
Griscom's store.

Requirements and Skills Needed

Designers should also have excellent interpersonal skills to assist customers, handle complaints and manage employees as well as excellent organizational skills needed to oversee the daily operation of a store or a department. Customer service is crucial as the age-old adage of the "customer is always right" will apply.

It may be a cliché, but a shop owner must be a "people person" as they are constantly on stage. Flexibility is key as the shop owner wears many hats both behind the scenes and in the public eye. Being able to chart trends and target the lifestyle and needs of the customer base is also crucial.

For those that want to increase their sales and visibility through online and catalogue retailing, extremely high technological skills are a necessity.

Becoming familiar with technology related to Internet sales, distribution, and inventory tracking will also give your business an advantage. Since e-commerce is linked to technology, coursework in database management, web design, systems analysis, and Internet technologies will supplement traditional business fundamentals.

Retail and display designers and visual merchandisers need to be artistic, have a sense of flair and space and knowledge of lighting, ergonomics, and commercial building codes and standards as well as the basic tenets and theory of interior design.

For all positions, it is advisable to develop excellent communication and interpersonal and problem solving skills. Gain as much knowledge about the products and services being sold and be a highly motivated self-starter.

Education and Training

A four-year bachelor's degree in interior design, bachelor of fine arts (BFA), or bachelor of science (BS), or associate of applied science degree (AAS) in interior design, architecture, or art from an accredited college or design school is highly recommended for a career in this field. A bachelor of arts or bachelor of science degree can be obtained in more targeted areas such a retail merchandising, furniture design, retail store design, and visual display and merchandising.

When available, internships and assistant positions are strongly advised. Related retail sales experience is also a plus.

Design Curriculum

In addition to a degree in interior design, students would be wise to take as many retail business courses as possible such as store merchandising and management, planning and control, inventory management, and retail consumer science. Basic business classes could include accounting, marketing, finance, economics, and advertising. Specialized business courses structured for start-ups are strongly recommended. Tailored computer courses for online retailing and marketing and catalogue business and development are useful as well.

Understanding the mind of the consumer would be helpful with psychology courses. Design curriculum can include retail store design, visual merchandising and display, product and furniture design and development. For those interested in visual merchandising, take courses in color, graphic design, lighting and art, as well as furniture building.

THE PAY

Salaries in the field of retailing run the gamut, depending on sales versus management, type and size of retailer, if you own your own business and of course, education, experience, and location.

For the self-employed shop owner, the range can be literally anywhere from zero to becoming hugely successful as many interior design shops will supplement their sales with design services, develop their own wholesale and/or retail line, and perhaps preside over a national domain. A unique inventory and good cash flow are paramount. According to Berry, "A working rule of thumb is to be prepared not to take a salary for three years and after that. If the business is growing then use every cent to keep growing and after five years (you can) collect dividends."

For a position in sales, large retailers report that in-store salaries, based upon store volume, range from $48,000 to $150,000 according to the National Retail Federation. Many entry level sales positions will be minimum wage or commission based. Salaries for sales associates range from $20,000 to $30,000, assistant store managers $30,000 to $50,000, and store managers between $40,000 and $70,000 depending upon the size of retailer and geographical location. Small boutique owners and specialty sales owner report that salaries for design associates run $39,000 to $50,000 with the median salary at $42,000.

Salaries for buyers generally run higher, starting at $40,000 and running up to $150,000 again, depending upon retail store, buying office, or catalogue company.

FIGURE 7.8
Chapman Radcliffe store in Los Angeles.

For retail store designers, no pay information is available at this time for retail store design but it is commensurate with that of contract designers (see Chapter 6: The Contract Designer). For general positions, with contract firms, salary levels are slightly higher than those in residential design. Interior design headhunters note the following range: beginners, $30,000 to $45,000; CAD operators, $40,000 to $47,000; junior/intermediate designers, $40,000 to $55,000; interior designers, $60,000 to $85,000; project managers are the next pay level up at $75,000 to $110,000; senior designers, $99,000 to $150,000; and principal/partners, $105,000 to $150,000 and up.

Visual merchandising specialists start out at $21,000 to $32,000 for entry-level positions and range up to $60,000 depending upon the retailer and location. Many designers move on to management positions where the salaries are significantly higher.

THE PATH

There are no set roads on the path to a career in design retailing and the journey is as varied as the destination.

The Shop/Store Owner
Starting your own interior design shop and/or home furnishings store requires

FIGURE 7.9
Interior designer Kelly Wearstler's boutique at Bergdorf Goodman.

FIGURE 7.10
Environment
Furniture's
Manhattan
retail store uses
sustainable
materials in its loft-
like space.

several criteria—knowledge of what you are doing; a willingness to work harder than you ever have; and capital, capital, capital. There are no tried-and-true paths to this destination as many have arrived from various roads. Designers may work in retail as an assistant, salesperson, in-house designer, or buyer before venturing on their own. Other designers have a solid practice with a substantial client base and want to hang a shingle to be more available to the public. They may also have created their own line of furnishings and accessories and need a place to sell. Designers have also arrived via working for national retailers and buying offices in sales, merchandising, and marketing.

Catalogues and E-commerce

E-commerce covers a wide range of business activities as professionals plan, manage, supervise, and market electronic business operations, products, and services provided online via the Internet. Jobs are very similar to those in the brick and mortar store and corporate world with the added knowledge of the methodology and technology of the Internet. For those who want to become buyers for a catalogue or e-commerce, starting as an assistant is an excellent way to begin. Buyers plan and purchase a well-balanced assortment of products and work with inventory, vendors, and sales.

Furniture Buyer

Sales>Assistant Buyer>Divisional Merchandise Manager> General Merchandise Manager>Upper Level Positions
Most jobs in retail at the higher level begin as management or sales trainees. They generally work within a specific category or department for one to two years to gain experience and move up to positions such as assistant buyer and on to furniture buyer or merchandise manager, to other upper-level positions that vary in title from company to company.

Unlike other industries, retail offers valuable experience without special qualifications for the entry-level job seeker. Internships and sales associate jobs are available for young designers and those with college degrees targeted to a specific area have much easier access. Most retailers promote from within and while this is a competitive industry, it is indeed a very open one.

Retail Store Design
Intern/Assistant>Store Planners and Specialist/Manager of Retail Design>Senior Store Planner/Director of Retail Design>Retail Store Designer
Interior designers specializing in this area will find work with contract firms that specialize in any form of retail design from shopping malls and boutiques to entertainment arenas with specialty shops. They work with architectural firms that are involved in the contract/retailing area and major retailers in a variety of industries (home furnishings, fashion, and home improvement remain the most popular).

Professional titles will vary from type of retailer to contract design firm but the overall basic job function remains the same. Store design planners are responsible for new store layouts, develop detailed drawings, work with architects and construction teams, and implement overall design plan. A minimum one to two years of experience in retail planning is needed and internships and assistant positions are the best ways to get started.

Visual Merchandising
Entry Level Assistant>Visual Display Designer>Director–Senior Vice President–Vice President of Visual Merchandising
Designers interested in this area can begin as an assistant to a major retailer and work their way up through the system. Many designers have found lucrative careers as visual display designers for fashion giants such as Bergdorf Goodman and The Gap, designing windows, in-store displays, and individual boutiques. They find work with trade showrooms, industry tradeshows, specialty shows, and any other areas where items are displayed and sold. Many will specialize solely on holiday and seasonal display and decoration.

PROFESSIONAL ASSOCIATIONS

As discussed in previous chapters, interior designers and students will enjoy benefits from joining professional organizations such as the American Society of Interior Designers (ASID) and the International Interior Design Association (IIDA).

In addition, there are several organizations targeted to the retail profession such as the Institute of Store Planners (ISPO), National Retail Federation (NRF), Furniture Marketing Group (FMG) for furniture retailers, and the Association for Retail Environments (ARE) which offers membership for visual and display designers. Designers involved in catalogue retailing should check out the Direct Marketing Association (DMA). A detailed listing of organizations is featured in the resources list.

THE PROFILES

Linda Berry—The Shop Owner (Bella Linea)
"Retail is not for the faint of heart. It takes a total commitment—time,

energy, money, a vision, and the willingness to stick it out in good times and bad. It's just like marriage."

—LINDA BERRY

As with the birth of many business ideas, Linda Berry was exposed to something she loved and could not find—European linens. Having experienced the concept of "European sleep style" while over-seas (down comforters and duvets, high thread count, etc.) and frustrated with the local department store's polyester selection, she decided to fulfill her dream and open a store. Over twenty years ago—and two days after the 1987 stock market crash—Bella Linea was born.

Berry came to shop ownership via the world of retail and pharmaceutical sales. Armed with good timing, an

BELLA LINEA
fine linens • down • bath

FIGURE 7.11
Beautifully photographed postcards are used for retail promotion as seen here by Bella Linea.

untapped niche market, and courage, the entrepreneurial southerner decided to intuitively "go with the flow." Realizing her target customer was traveling to Europe in record numbers, she wanted to bring this feeling—as well as the product—to her store in Nashville, Tennessee. "In those days, 'going to market' consisted of buying from perhaps ten European manufacturers altogether and buying could be accomplished in a day, as it was a new industry and choices were limited. Today, it requires a full week to buy for the upcoming season," she explains.

She grew the business by offering state-of-the-art designs and establishing basics in bedding in all price ranges, colors, and quality. "When I opened my retail store, I was one of the first in the United States to have three beds on a showroom floor outfitted with linens from top to bottom like the old-fashioned stores that displayed linens in a glass counter," she says. "Three beds grew to ten over the years and I expanded to bath, furniture, and four to five designers on staff."

In-house designers are useful in not only selling the store's merchandise but bring in a "value-added" factor to the many customers who would not necessarily hire a designer. While most designers in stores work on straight commission, she finds her staff performs well under a salary structure (with a step up incentive program plus benefits), particularly in uncertain economic times as she notes, "They do not blow sales because of feeling too pressured. I want them focusing on the client 100 percent." All of her design staff have a degree and Berry feels it provides great credibility to the store.

Berry advises that in "order to create a business that will last for generations, you must either tap into a niche or create one. Generally those who make it to the finish line usually stay there because they change with the times and do what it takes to stay on top," she states. While she found a "hole" in the bedding market in her area, she feels "It's not enough to start a business because there's a preconceived 'need'—it needs to be a business that sets you on fire because that fire will keep you going long after the customers go home."

Mitchell Gold + Bob Williams— The Store(s) Retailer

"People want to know who makes the furniture they're spending their lives on and want to buy a brand associated with the lifestyle they want to live."
—MITCHELL GOLD

The year was 1989 and the economy was unstable. And to think the pair almost became the proud owners of a vineyard.

Partners in life, Mitchell Gold and Bob Williams were looking to partner in business as well. Instead of fermenting grapes, they chose to design and manufacture furniture. Gold was at The Lane Company in their in-store gallery division and Williams was an art director in New York City and their collective marketing and creative talents were natural for the furniture industry. The gamble paid off in droves and today they own a $100 million dollar business with signature stores in eighteen cities.

The talented duo began their line with dining room chairs and bedroom furniture that consisted of headboards and platform beds. While the beds did well, the chairs were a big hit and soon the line was launched.

Their mission statement was to make the world a more comfortable place. According to Williams, they also wanted to "make furniture they would have in their own homes and do it differently from anyone else." Based on this premise of "Relaxed Design," they paid attention to how people lived and dressed, sensing a move towards comfortable yet fashionable. Using pre-washed fabrics such as denim, silk, and velvet

FIGURE 7.12
Gurus of comfort Mitchell Gold, Bob Williams, and the late Lulu.

FIGURE 7.13
MG+BW based their
company on the
concept of "Relaxed
Design." Shown here
is the Carter Chair.

FIGURE 7.14
Picture frames are
an exclusive to the
MG+BW line.

They have made revolutionary additions to the business of the furniture industry, setting new standards in the workplace by adding the first on-site daycare center for their employees, and a health-conscious café, and gym. The company even provides free medical physicals and offers a much-coveted concierge service. Their corporate culture and support of non-profit groups is extraordinary.

Customer service is also another consideration as their motto of "Sincerely treating all customers as we ourselves would want to be treated became our principle for customer service," says Williams. "Early on I decided there would be incredible synergy with furnishing homes, creating products, and (the look of our) showrooms."

"We put ourselves in the consumer's shoes. Buying furniture can be an anxiety-ridden purchase so we have figured out every detail to make it as pleasurable as possible," says Gold. They developed the TAPS program (The Answer People), which consists of a team traveling the country educating the sales people.

for slipcovers and making choices easy and affordable, the line eventually grew to slip covered and tailored upholstery, leather, sectionals and accessories, rugs and lighting (and even dog beds!).

Unlike many manufacturers who go overseas, the line is made in a state-of-the-art factory in Taylorsville, North Carolina where they employ 700 people.

They are credited with being one of the very first to have a website. "We quickly learned that this was becoming a best way for consumers to 'shop around' without even going to bricks and mortar store," says Gold. By focusing on making it a research-friendly site, the company has enjoyed steady sales. The website also has a unique on-line mini-magazine "Comfortmag.net" which features decorating ideas and personality profiles.

The furniture line is public driven and every pattern you see is in inventory as Gold notes, "Our biggest selling

point is instant gratification." Mitchell seconds this, explaining, "Many furniture companies will make you wait until fabric is made before they make the furniture. So we make sure its in inventory and we know when you order we can tell you when it will be done."

The furniture design cycle takes up to six months for upholstery and 18 months for case goods. Their largest division is residential and contract accounts are primarily in the hospitality industry. The accessory line is comprised of pictures frames, vases, lighting, and rugs and are all designed internally and exclusively.

In addition, the designing duo are ardent human rights activists and have added the title of author to their resumes with the publication of the book *Let's Get Comfortable* (Meredith, 2007).

One wonders how they do it all? It beats picking grapes.

Laura Daily—The Catalogue (Ballard Designs)

"Our design philosophy is creative layering of style."

—Laura Daily, Vice President of Merchandising

It all began when Helen Ballard Weeks submitted photos of her Atlanta condominium to *Metropolitan Magazine*'s home of the year contest and won the award for the southern region. As a result, more than 500 people contacted the magazine, clamoring for information on her designs. Ballard promptly quit her job, sold her condo and began Ballard Designs, becoming a one-woman entrepreneur. In August of l983, a two page, black and white brochure

FIGURE 7.15
Area rugs are one of the many product offerings at MG+BW. Shown here is the Sherlock design.

was developed, featuring a copy of a table from her home.

Ballard sold her company a decade and a half later to Cornerstone Brands (who also publish Frontgate, Garnet Hill, Smith and Noble, and Grandin Road catalogues). The tradition lives on and Ballard Designs is one of the most popular home furnishings catalogues in the country, featuring full-color products ranging from upholstered headboards to garden accessories with a European inspired flair.

The catalogue has evolved over the past twenty-five years and is based on natural trend making, says Laura Daily, vice president of merchandising. "It changed as aspects of Helen's sophisti-

FIGURE 7.16
Ballard Designs
expanded their
catalogue operations
to retail.

cation level changed. She had a natural inclination to explore trends and the catalogue followed that." This translated into European influenced looks offered at moderate prices.

Lured by Ballard from a catalogue company in Chicago, Daily got her start in the business as an assistant buyer at Carson Pirie Scott. One of her goals is to show the versatility of their multi-category products. They do five core creations a year, keeping in mind seasonality aspects (the Fall Home Office issue is the biggest). She explains the products' versatility by noting, "We move product through rooms. A thirty-three-inch console with a fourteen-inch depth would fit in the hallway and would be great in the dining room."

The design team also takes into consideration the various trends and color palette through the year. "We look at Pantone studies and use it as a reference check. We have very distinct colors such as cheetah and Ballard green (that are synonymous with the brand)," she states.

The unique product mix includes upholstery, home office, garden, and dining with wall décor ranking as their top-selling segment. Eighty percent of the catalogue items are exclusive and their upholstery collection is made in the United States. Seventy-five percent of items are exclusive and sourced in Europe, Asia, and South America as well as factories in the United States. They also enjoy a "healthy balance between catalogue and Internet (50

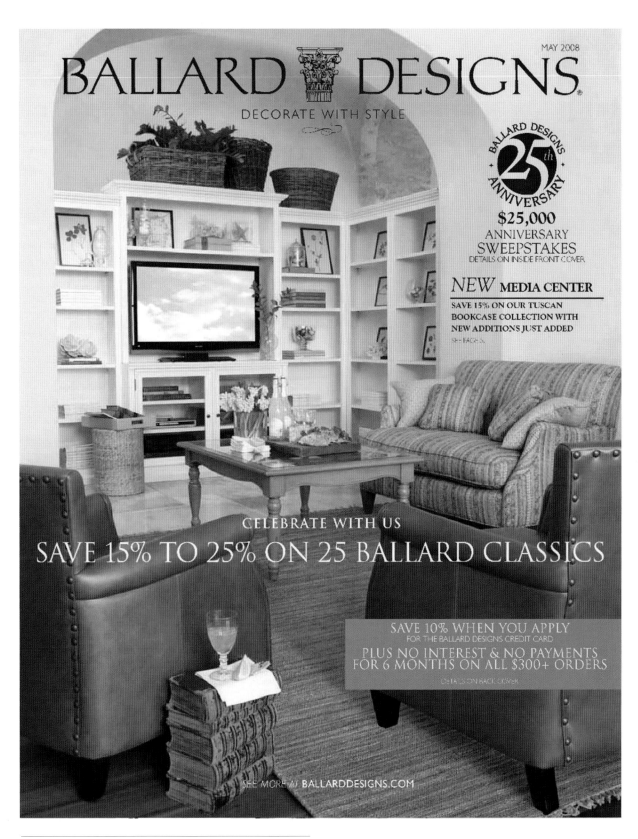

FIGURE 7.17
The Ballard Designs catalogue.

FIGURE 7.18
Custom furnishings make up a large part of the product mix at Ballard Designs.

FIGURE 7.19
Innovative displays jump right off the catalogue pages to Ballard Designs' retail outlets.

FIGURE 7.20
Sue Fisher King's eye-catching storefront in San Francisco.

percent). With the catalogue, there is limited space and on the Internet we can spread out wings," she says. Many retailers start with an actual store first and the Internet and catalogue will follow, but Ballard did the reverse. They recently opened their two retail stores in Tampa and Jacksonville, one in a mall and the other in an outdoor lifestyle center with both the planning and design very different. The store is an extension of the catalogue with stock ranging from urns and candles to armoires and antique reproductions. Many of the items are exclusive to the Internet as well as retail stores. Some items show better in print and some need to be seen in person. Daily notes that merchandising and product development takes up to eighteen months. They decide one theme for their issue twelve months in advance; from merchandise to layout to assembling, the process takes eight to twelve months. As vice president of merchandising, she oversees a lean staff of six buyers and their assistants and a sourcing group of ten employees as well as the process of assembling the book and color stories and trends.

She notes it's not unusual for her team to come up with design sketches on napkins which get turned over to the sourcing team who travel the world to produce. They also have three AutoCAD specialists who implement the design ideas as well. To become a buyer, Daily advises students to have "a retail background and be good on the analytical side. They should take art, art history, and public speaking, and a liberal arts degree with a business minor

are acceptable. An undergrad with a liberal arts degree is an excellent way to go with this career path as it teaches you to think."

Daily also counsels students to "never shut their eyes—they need to be open to every little piece of inspiration. Great students should study design with an adolescent eye—it could be an ironwork fence that turns into a headboard, a pattern on a fabric becomes the pattern on dinner china, etc. Always be open to the possibilities an object has in terms of design."

James Pope, manager of new business development oversees all new business, partnership marketing, and in-house public relations. He credits their success to the fact that "We are all about great options. We give people the choice as to how they get that product—website, retail stores, or the Internet. We give the customer solutions and beauty in a busy world."

Sherri Donghia—CEO, SD International

Many careers in the field of interior design have begun in a parallel universe. For Sherri Donghia that universe was the world of fashion.

The multi faceted designer has worn many hats—product designer, marketer, textile editor, merchandiser, author, consultant, lecturer, and mentor. Her illustrious career has been built upon the concept of exploration— her love of travel, seeking new artisans, and creative methods of design and production have given birth to many a product.

Donghia's career began in the early seventies as an assistant to the late Katherine Murphy, prominent fashion director of Bloomingdale's where she traveled the world designing products for their private label brand. Stints as rival Gimbel's fashion director and product development manager at Federated Stores soon followed along with design and consultant work for European fashion designers and the retail shops of Laurence Rockefeller's RockResort hotel group (which included properties from Little Dix Bay in the Virgin Islands to the Boulders Resort in Carefree, Arizona). "Mr. Rockefeller—who had his own museum quality collections of arts and crafts from all over the world—seamlessly integrated each setting into its unique, individual environment. I learned as much about understated elegance as I learned about authentic design from my ten years working for Laurence Rockefellar in indigenous cultures," Donghia notes.

Her exposure to fashion and fabrics, travels around the four corners of the world and retailing and product development all proved to be an important foundation when she took over the reins of cousin Angelo's home furnishings company Donghia Furniture/Textiles. As the executive vice president of design and marketing, she continued the company's legacy, overseeing the design direction and providing a singular voice for their multi-category luxury lines. Her many roles included opening new showrooms (today they are sold to architects and designers in more than fifty countries) and working with design staff while developing new design ideas for the company's extensive collections of sophisticated and timeless furniture, fabric, wallcovering, trim, and lighting.

Donghia took her couture sensibilities and transformed the company into an international custom home furnishings brand. "Our company is all about couture artisan production. Our textiles are hand-embellished and our Venetian accessories are made in Murano," says Donghia. "The community is shrinking every year, but we continue to support the industry. We do the designs. But they make the magic happen. These pieces will become collectors' items."

She is known in the industry as the consummate textile editor and it certainly shows in the product lines. "We work with all the best mills around the world. As a hands-on textile designer, I worked with two talented associates who made up our textile studio. We worked with the best weavers internationally to create the original and exclusive Donghia signature designs."

Donghia also notes the correlation between fashion and design. While at the firm, she often tapped into these worlds, hiring fashion designers such as Romeo Gigli to collaborate on fabric collections. "This is an exciting time within design, art, and fashion are so related and the boundaries are blurred. Designers need to be aware and informed as there is more pressure to be fluent in the latest in art and architecture and technology." For those interested in product design, she explains, "There are so many consumers at the top economic tier now and they collect unique limited editions. The savvy designer with these clients needs to constantly research galleries and shops and sell the unique pieces."

A BFA graduate of Penn State with an honorary doctorate of fine arts from New York School of Interior Design and RISD, Donghia believes in giving back. While at Donghia, she mentored a group of students in business, marketing, and product design with the goal of finding and developing "the next generation of designers." She notes, "Many textile and furniture (students) come out of international design schools. Donghia's intern program hires from the top design schools around the world." She also advises student to "travel, travel, travel," particularly the Middle East, Far East, North Africa, and India. "Go to the local markets and look for the arts, crafts, and clothing of the local cultures. Attend major and smaller museums in less visited places," she notes.

Her accolades are many. A former board member of the Fashion Group International, Donghia is on the board of the Rhode Island School of Design and is chair of the Color Association of the United States (CAUS) interior colors committee, a color-forecasting group. She was also the first American to receive the esteemed Master of Linen award by the European Union's Master of Linen Group. During her tenure, the firm received the first Elle Deco Design Award for Textiles and Chicago Athenaeum's Good Design award for a record four years in a row.

She also adds author and guest lecturer to her already staggering list of accomplishments. Her illustrated book *Donghia: The Artistry of Luxury and Style* (Bulfinch Press, 2006) is a celebration of the Donghia design philosophy, clean sensual lines elegantly mixed with compelling colors. It has been heralded as one of the first books on design fusion.

REFERENCES

Allegrezza, Ray. (February 11, 2008). "Keep Your Eyes On The Target." *Furniture Today*. Retrieved January 10, 2008 from website www.furnituretoday.com.

Bureau of Labor Statistics, U.S. Department of Labor, *Occupational Outlook Handbook, 2006–2007 Edition*, Interior Designers, Retrieved January 10, 2008, from www.bls.gov/oco/ocos.293.htm.

Brohan, Mark. (June, 2007). The Top 500 Guide. *The Internet Retailer*. Retrieved February 12, 2008 from website www.internetretailer.com.

Dolber. Rosyln. (1996). Opportunities in Retailing Careers. Chicago: NTC Publishing Group.

Emerson, Jim. (July 26, 2005). Special Report: Catalog Marketing.

Retrieved Febraury 9, 2008 from website www.directmag.com.

Forest, Sara D. (2006). *Vault Guide to Interior Design Careers.* New York: Vault, Inc.

Kealoha, Ami. (April 11, 2007). Mitchell Gold and Bob Williams Interview and Giveaway. Cool Hunting. Retrieved December 20, 2007 from website www.cool hunting.com.

Perry, David. (December 10, 2007). Internet Guru: Ikea No. 1 in Online Visits. *Furniture Today.* Retrieved March 2, 2008 from website www. furnitureday.com.

www.monster.com.

www.salary.com.

The Designer and the Showroom

OVERVIEW OF THE PROFESSION

The view can be both intimidating and intoxicating for the first time visitor as well as the seasoned veteran. Rows and rows of beautifully appointed spaces showcase wings of luscious fabrics and custom furniture. Fragrant lilies, bowls of candy, and baskets filled with stylish pencils and pads grace the reception desk. A bustle of activity occurs as designers coordinate color schemes, present ideas to clients and place orders. While the setting is no doubt a glamorous one, serious business takes place. The work is hard, the days are long, the choices are endless and the stamina and energy of Superman (or Wonder Woman) is required.

Such is the world of the design showroom.

The primary resource for the interior design field, mammoth multi-leveled design centers house a diversity of showrooms that carry furniture, fabrics, floor coverings, lighting, linens, accessories, kitchen and bath, and much more, all available for purchase at wholesale or "designer discount."

Over sixty design centers are located in twenty states in major metropolitan cities. The most frequented are the Decoration and Design Center (D&D) in New York, Pacific Design Center (coined the "Blue Whale") in Los Angeles,

FIGURE 8.1
Brunschwig and Fils
showroom in New
York's Design and
Decoration Building.

FIGURE 8.2
To the Trade
Only: New York's
Decoration & Design
Building is known
as D&D.

centers include the International Home Furnishing Center in High Point, North Carolina, home to biannual furniture markets.

Designated as "To the Trade Only," these centers require that industry professionals provide appropriate credentials (usually a resale tax identification certificate and/or business license—some showrooms also ask for a business check) upon request to gain admittance. The industry term "trade" refers to interior decorators and designers, architects, buyers, space planners, and design consultants. At one time, entrance to these hallowed halls was about as hard as arranging a private meeting with the Pope, but due to changes in the industry and the economy, some centers have relaxed their entrance requirements so consumers can purchase these much-coveted items. At one point, several of the centers considered opening to the public but the idea was nixed.

Like many industries, the state of the design showroom has been in a flux in recent years. Thomas Lavin, the savvy owner of the high-end Thomas Lavin showroom in Los Angeles, comments, "Every industry is changing as design, music, film, and TV are in constant evolution." He notes that many segments of the market and consumers will feel an economic crunch, but not high-end. "Wealthy clients will always use interior designers period," he concludes.

When the economy is down, the trickle down theory is often seen in the design centers. Many will downsize due to high rents and products can be affected. Donna May Woods, design director of high-end fabric showroom Brunschwig & Fils notes, "High rents

and the Chicago Merchandise Mart. To put it in perspective, the famed Merchandise Mart consists of approximately 130 showrooms representing over 2,000 product lines (boasting the largest collection of home furnishings under one roof worldwide). Other important

FIGURE 8.3
Thomas Lavin showroom in the Pacific Design Center in Los Angeles.

FIGURE 8.4
J. Robert Scott
showroom in
West Hollywood,
California.

push out the workrooms which means fewer people to hang $200.00 a roll pre-trimmed wallpaper" and thus, fewer production or increasingly discontinued stock. Mike Sands of Tui Pranich showroom at the DCOTA in Florida has noticed the lack of salary bonuses and foreclosures due to a bad economy has a direct impact on sales.

The designer showroom is the yin to the designer's yang. While traffic on the Wilton carpeted floors may be down, the design centers will be a mainstay and these partners in business will always need each other. Much like the retailer is the intermediary between the vendor and the public, the design showroom functions in the same way. It's a symbiotic relationship and the lifeblood of the industry.

In terms of a career, interior designers can utilize their skills in showrooms of all types from large metropolitan city centers to independent single operations or home furnishing companies in industry meccas such as High Point, North Carolina. Positions can include sales, marketing, merchandising, customer service, archivist, furniture, and product design as well as showroom manager or owner. They also represent one of

the best training grounds for the young designer, starting in the sample room and advancing to creative or sales.

Designers in mid-level cities are opening their own design showrooms, offering many of the amenities and products of their cousins at a smaller scale. Donna Hysmith, owner of Designers Gallery in Nashville, Tennessee, services designers all over the Southeast, offering a wide number of lines in multi categories. A former manufacturers' sales rep, she attends market twice a year, and cultivates relationships with designers and architects (particularly the independent designer) in her 7,000 square foot showroom. "I wanted to empower designers and help them make huge commissions," she explains. "It's all about selling merchandise and handling problems and follow-through." Hysmith bases everything on retail price and gives designers a healthy discount from 40 to 50 percent. Retaining only 10 percent for the firm, volume is the name of the game. She feels that retail stores across the country are turning to mass marketing (and offering a smaller trade discount in the process) and designers need an alternative.

THE PROCESS

Life in a showroom is all about the activities revolving around sales, marketing, display, and customer service to the client, mainly the interior designer and decorator, buyer, and architect. The typical design showroom houses samples of furniture on the floor, racks (known as wings) of fabrics, trimmings and wallpapers on the wall, displays of lighting and accessories, and cases of catalogues (depending on the product and type of business). In most instances, prices are marked in code and the variety of offerings is staggering. Image and style are everything as design takes on an elevated nature with displays and rooms rivaling the pages of a shelter magazine.

Showrooms will carry their own exclusive lines and/or a variety of vendors and commission is the order of the day—the showroom makes a profit from the sale and often the designer marks up the sale to the client. Behind the scenes, executives manage the business, conceptualize and plan new lines, determine the showroom displays, and dictate marketing and advertising strategies while customer service agents tend to a variety of needs. On the floor, personnel are involved in sales, assisting customers with product inquiries (known as tear sheets and memo samples), and place orders for both residential and contract areas.

THE PREPARATION

Many of the basic skills required for the interior designer and retailer will be put to use in this specialty category.

Requirements and Skills Needed

The following traits are useful for these positions:

Customer Service

Since a single order can involve many steps ("strike-off" or "CFA" a.k.a. cutting for approval, estimate, purchase

FIGURE 8.5
Brunschwig and Fils bedroom vignette in their Manhattan showroom.

FIGURE 8.6
Room vignette showcases merchandise as shown here in Brunschwig and Fils showroom.

order and delivery), customer service is a daily activity. The ability to solve problems along with assistance to the client is vitally important. Computer skills are an absolute must in ordering and tracking materials. "Customer service and quality are very important to success. I believe strongly that back up in customer service is as important as sales," says Sally Sirkin Lewis, president of J. Robert Scott showroom.

Interior Design

Showroom salespersons will often tap into their interior design skills to assist clients and make recommendations with design schemes. Textile and furniture knowledge, space planning and scale, and the ability to read blueprints are also invaluable.

Showroom Sales

The ability to sell, sell, sell is one of the primary skills for a career in wholesale. Being a self-starter, excellent communicator, negotiator, and networker is important along with organization, time management, and follow through. A talent for making presentations is also required. Knowledge and usage of the product line is imperative. As with many careers of this nature, appearance and style is important as the designer is representing the image of the showroom.

Showroom Management

The ability to oversee personnel, arrange displays, work with vendors, maintain sales, and be extremely organized is required. Business and marketing skills are also needed along with a talent for merchandise display.

Education and Training

While no specific education is required, a degree in interior design is preferable. A well-rounded liberal arts, marketing, or business degree is also useful. Students are advised to take advantage of internship programs to get their foot in the door. Many showroom owners recommend the best training is to start at the ground floor and work up the proverbial ladder. Retail sales and management experience are also great additions to the resume.

Design Curriculum

In addition to basic interior design courses, classes in art and furniture history, visual display and furniture, textile, retail, and product design are suggested.

Business classes such as marketing, sales, accounting, business management, and computer technology is also advised. Since this field deals directly with the public, classes in psychology and communications are a bonus. For those interested in becoming an archivist, look for schools that offer museum studies and classes geared for the curator.

PROFESSIONAL ASSOCIATIONS

As with other specialties, students and designers will benefit by joining a professional organization such as the American Society of Interior Designers (ASID) and the International Interior Design Association (IIDA). The International Furnishings and Design Association (IFDA) consists of full-time managers or executives in the furnishings or design industry as well as supervisors, executives, or associates who work in a design related field (student memberships are also available).

Many design centers will have their own groups such as the High Point Showroom Association. For a detailed listing of associations, see resources at the end of the book.

THE PATH

*Sample Room>Customer Service>
Showroom Sales>Sales Representative>
Showroom Manager>Owner
Assistant>Showroom Sales>Road
Representative>Vice President of Sales
Design Director, Marketing, Merchandising, Display, Archivist, and Furniture*

and Textile Designer arrive with previous experience in most cases.

Showroom positions are found by word of mouth, direct application, design employment agency, professional organization resource center, or college placement office. Many interior designers will move from design firm to showroom sales and management and vice versa. Positions on this career path can include:

Stockroom/Sample Room
This is an excellent entrée to the design showroom.

Duties include coordinating and hanging fabric wings, filling requests for memo samples and tear sheets. Other responsibilities include assisting the sales force, shipping, delivery and showroom upkeep and assisting with displays.

Archivist
This position is similar to that of a museum curator and supervises the collection of antique wallpaper and fabrics, artwork and books in the company's historical archives. Primarily firms that carry English lines (where the printer is also a weaver) will have this position and the jobs are few. Judy Stratton, archivist at Brunschwig and Fils got her start at the Metropolitan Museum and oversees the company's collection dating back to the forties as well as discontinued items. (Note: This is a similar position to librarian which oversees the memo sampling program in residential and contract firms).

Customer Service
This area primarily deals with the livelihood of the business, the purchase

order. Representatives may place orders and check stock (showroom sales will also handle this) and expedite all aspects from the CFA to invoice, deposit, vendor order, final invoice, and delivery. Due to the nature of the business, it's fraught with the occasional problems—damaged deliveries, lost shipments, bad dye lots, and the dreaded "out of stock" dilemma.

Showroom Sales

Salespersons will deal directly with designers and architects, assisting with the product needs of a design project (including design direction, checking stock and dye lot availability, supplying tear sheets and/or written quotes, and placing orders).

Road Representatives

Also known as outside sales reps, they build relationships with interior designers and architects, and often have a territory of several states (mostly in areas that do not have design centers). Sales reps will visit accounts at retail offices, corporations, architectural and design firms, or smaller design centers that carry their accounts and manage their memo-sampling program. They usually specialize in several product lines or categories.

Showroom Manager

This position manages all aspects of the day-to-day operations that directly and indirectly affect financial performance of the showroom. They will maintain showroom sales, develop relationships and interface with clients and vendors, assist in marketing and promotional efforts, and oversee the sales staff and other showroom personnel.

Duties will also include setting up product display, showroom maintenance, planning new furniture layouts, and new collection introductions (usually occurs twice a year). This position generally requires two to five years of prior sales experience in a retail environment. Interior design and merchandising experience is also an advantage.

Vice President of Sales/ Territory Manager

This position will direct all activities of the showroom and outside sales force. They are responsible for developing a sales team, conducting on-going product training, and most importantly, delivering sales results in the residential and contract segments of the business. They may also have input on new product development.

Merchandising Director

Primarily dealing with product development and merchandising, duties can include developing a brand strategy and product for international markets, including design, color selection, and construction. They may set wholesale prices and margin parameters, source mills, and work with the sales team to ensure they understand the product.

Marketing Director

This position is involved in increasing client awareness nationwide of all product lines through advertising, client

presentations, special events, promotional activities, and mailings. This area works with public relations as well.

Product and Furniture Designer/ Textile Design

Designers are responsible for developing new product, furniture, and fabric design, and they are occasionally found in showrooms that carry their own exclusive lines as well as wholesale furniture manufacturers. For further information, see Chapter Nine: The Product and Furniture Designer.

Design Director

The director can oversee everything from the look of the showroom, determine the design direction of the product and furniture lines, as well as the advertising and marketing campaign. They can also be involved in selecting and managing vendor product lines. This is a very specialized position and not all showrooms have one on staff. Donna May Woods, design director of Brunschwig & Fils, says, "I step in when

FIGURE 8.9
Celerie Kemble Collection for F. Schumacher and Company.

there are dramas and custom work to be done and help the interior designer through the process." When Gracie Mansion (New York City's mayoral residence) requested a fabric with the color purple, Woods made sure it was the correct historical shade.

Owner

Responsible for all aspects of the business, owners set the overall image and direction of the design and image of the showroom. They are ultimately responsible for maintaining the firm's capital and bottom line as well as locating, securing, and keeping product lines in a very competitive marketplace.

THE PAY

As with all specialties, salaries will depend upon the level of experience, type of showroom, and geographical location.

Entry-level positions pay anywhere from minimum wage to $22,000 to $30,000 depending upon the firm and location. Customer service agents and archivists make a salary of $30,000 to $40,000.

Showroom sales range from $35,000 to $60,000 base with commission, depending upon the level of experience. Territory reps can make $60,000 and upward to $120,000 depending upon the type and number of accounts. Showroom managers can start at $50,000 base and go up to $100,000 plus.

Salaries for design directors can range from $60,000 to $120,000 while furniture and product designers make $60,000 to $75,000. No information was available for marketing and merchandising. Perks in this business include commissions and expense accounts when applicable, product discounts, and benefits.

THE PROFILES

Sally Sirkin Lewis, President and Founder of J. Robert Scott
"My family is my company. I live and breathe what I do."
—SALLY SIRKIN LEWIS

If you were to look up "Renaissance woman" in the dictionary, no doubt it would say "see Sally Sirkin Lewis."

As an interior designer, Lewis is credited with the style "California Design," and her sleek and timeless neutral palettes have appeared in everything from a corporate jet to a Malibu beach house. A celebrated hall of fame furniture and textile designer, she is particularly known her unparalleled exotic veneers and mirror-like finishes. Her passion for textiles led to the creation of a line of couture award-winning evening gowns.

And if that weren't enough, Lewis is president of J. Robert Scott, the company she founded in 1972, which provides high-end home furnishings to the design trade. The original showroom opened in Los Angeles and today there are five J.P.R. showrooms all over the world along with representation in six United States showrooms and fourteen international markets. Based on the desire to provide furnishings that reflect her design philosophy of a "simple yet gracious formality," the showrooms were a logical progression.

The indefatigable designer got her start in the early sixties when the design showroom was literally in its infancy. "I didn't really want to open a showroom as a merchandising center but wanted to do one that looked like someone's home. At this time the only stand alone showrooms were F. Schumacher and Scalamandre in New York," she explains. "It motivated me to open a showroom as I wanted to bring chic lines to Los Angeles."

The J.R.S. showrooms gave Lewis the perfect showcase as well as an experimental laboratory for her ideas. An inveterate traveler, inspiration came from a variety of places—woven straw became the catalyst for a textile while batik sarongs found their way on upholstery. The J.R.S. collection consists of furniture, lighting, textiles, and accessory items, with some 900 fabrics alone.

Her company is literally her family, so to speak, and enjoys a very low personnel turnover. Many of her staff have been there for more than twenty years (a textile designer clocks in at twenty-two years). Her sales people are the lifeblood of the business, having built long-standing relationships with interior designers and architects all over the world. A passion for the product must

FIGURE 8.10
Hall of fame member Sally Sirkin Lewis, president of J. Robert Scott.

FIGURE 8.11
Josephine Sofa is from the J. Robert Scott upholstery line.

ask every prospective applicant to do a portfolio of magazine pictures of things they love and hate."

Note: For more on Sally Sirkin Lewis and her career, see Chapter Nine: The Product and Furniture Designer.

Dotty Travis, Owner, Travis & Company

"I found to be successful, I had to be different."
— DOTTY TRAVIS

Like Sally Sirkin Lewis, Dotty Travis remembers the days when you had to visit Manhattan to shop in a showroom. "Atlanta was stuck in a rut at the time, everyone wanted Queen Anne and Chippendale chairs, pedestal tables, and secretaries," she explains, and the Georgia native wanted more selection and sophistication.

She opened a brownstone shop with antiques dealer Jane Marsden and practiced interior design before taking the plunge, opening Donahue & Travis at the Atlanta Decorative Arts Center in 1976. "I found to be successful, I had to be different. I opened the showroom with dhurrie rugs, contemporary art, Alan Campbell fabrics, and my own line of acrylic furniture," she states. Eventually partner Eden Donohue left Atlanta and sold her share of the business, and Travis & Company was created in 1978, going from a location with less than 2,000 square feet to eventually a two-story 16,000 square foot space.

Since this time, Travis & Company has built a reputation as one of the premier high-end showrooms, representing over forty lines of fabric, wallpaper, trimming and upholstery companies.

be reflected in the people she hires, noting, "I don't want people to take the job unless they want it badly—there are hundreds of showrooms they can work for. They must love the product as it will only hurt them in the end unless they are able to sell it."

Entry-level positions at J.R.S. can start in the production department (products are made in a 100,000 square foot factory in neighboring Inglewood, California) or as a librarian in the sample room. "If an applicant's portfolio is good, they might start in the design department," Lewis notes. "I look for a sense of design and scale, originality, sketches of fabrics and furniture. I

FIGURE 8.13
Lewis has been
credited with
the invention of
California Style as
evidenced in this
master bedroom in
Stinson Beach.

FIGURE 8.14
Dotty Travis, founder
of Travis & Company.

Antiques, reproduction, lighting, and accessories also supplement the product mix. Spanning the globe, a diverse selection of Manuel Canovas fabrics and Zuber wallpapers from France to Jane Shelton fabrics from Mississippi is available to designers and architects. Travis also has a retail antiques shop at a nearby location in the Buckhead area of Atlanta filled with French antiques, art, and accessories.

Daughter Ann Travis Davis is Vice President of the company that consists of a director of product display, showroom manager, sales staff of eight, memo sample room of four, and a staff of six in customer service.

For the design graduate, Travis recommends starting in the sample room filling memo requests, learning the

FIGURE 8.15
Tastefully arranged objets d'art are the characteristics of a Travis interior.

product lines, and eventually moving up to showroom sales. "Everyone sells everything—from sofas to antiques—and everyone participates in the profits," she says. "The business is structured around a team concept and if one sofa sells, everyone benefits."

Starting your own showroom is not for the weak as Travis details, "It's very difficult unless you come up with a unique line and work yourself to death. You must have great people and an active road program. We service six southeastern states which is geographi-

FIGURE 8.16
Classic mix of contemporary and traditional marks a Travis interior.

FIGURE 8.17
Well-appointed
interior mixes Travis'
love of antiques
and contemporary
artwork.

cally the largest per square mile in the country." Reps (known as road program representatives) go on the road twice a year to meet with interior designers and architects showcasing the latest addi-

tions to the product lines. Business is conducted at a hotel conference room or in-store presentations in a flurry of back-to-back cities and sales meetings over a month-long period.

FIGURE 8.18
Custom built-in
banquette takes
center stage in
Travis's kitchen.

In addition to inventory and hard work, working capital is mandatory. Design center rents can be staggering and showrooms work best for designers when they are all under the same roof.

The costs of memo samples loaned to the trade, overhead, salaries, catalogues, promotional materials, and display must betaken into account. Competition to attract and keep lines is fierce and most

showrooms work on commission with the manufacturers who keep an eye on the presentation and sales. "We are middlemen, we have to produce," she concludes.

Cathy Mitchell, Director of Merchandising, Hickory Chair
"Sometimes the best-laid plans involve a detour or two."
—Cathy Mitchell

Such is the case of Cathy Mitchell, who began her career as a residential interior designer with a luxury retailer in Westport, Connecticut. The University of Illinois design graduate quickly found she didn't have the patience for residen-

tial work and moved back to her roots, finding a job at the Century Furniture showroom in Chicago's Merchandise Mart.

"I worked as a jill-of-all-trades, redoing layouts, furniture plans, and in customer service," she says of her five-and-a-half-year stint. She moved to furniture giant Baker, Knapp and Tubbs, serving on a team of five designers in charge of the showroom design across the country (each one had a different look). Showroom management followed in the Boston location and she ultimately moved back to Chicago, working for fifteen years in product development.

Today she is director of merchandising for Hickory Chair, a 100-year-old furniture legend located in Hickory, North Carolina. Responsible for the firm's overall product development, she explains, "The company is very small, so I wear lots of hats. I see what products and finishes we need to add and drop, hire outside furniture designers, and work with interior designers." Working twelve to eighteen months in advance, she will work with a licensor such as Alexa Hampton on product design. "Alexa will put together a notebook of ideas and thoughts and we will narrow this down to what pieces are doing well," she says.

Mitchell notes, "My career path is a little unconventional for an interior design graduate but I love what I do and would be very happy continuing to do product development and merchandis-

ing for the rest of my career. It's a great marriage of the subjective and objective skills sets (right brain/left brain)." She also cites internships as an excellent way to gain entry. "This is one of the industries where you can rise through the ranks," she says.

REFERENCES

Forest, Sara D. (2006). *Vault Guide to Interior Design Careers.* New York: Vault, Inc.
Slesin, Suzanne. (July 15, 1993). "Trade Only" Walls Weaken. *New York Times.* Retrieved March 1, 2008 from website www.newyorktimes.com.
www.interiortalent.com.
www.salary.com.
www.ritasuesiegel.com.

FIGURE 8.19
The versatile pull-up Oxford chair with monogram from Hickory Chair.

FIGURE 8.20
The iconic Knole Sofa from Hickory Chair.

FIGURE 8.21
Continental Demi-Lune cabinet from interior designer Mariette Homes Gomez collection by Hickory Chair.

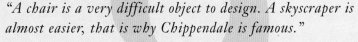

"A chair is a very difficult object to design. A skyscraper is almost easier, that is why Chippendale is famous."

—Ludwig Mies Van Der Rohe

The Product and Furniture Designer

OVERVIEW OF THE PROFESSION

The names and styles range from the exotic and the whimsical to the timeless and the utilitarian: the elbow chair, the confetti bowl, the bargello pillow, the Bollicina lamp, Kabuki bullion fringe, tree of life fabric, and the classic Chippendale chair. Literally thousands upon thousands of items in every category share their origins in the mind of a designer.

Designing home furnishings—be it furniture, products or textiles—represents another popular career choice for the interior designer. For those who dream of the perfect table or a line of tableware, this is a creative itch that no doubt needs to be scratched. Using a variety of artistic, aesthetic, and technical skills, furniture and product design employs many of the basic theories of interior design. Designers are finding the design of home furnishings for wholesale, retail, and custom one-of-a-kind pieces for commercial and residential markets to be both lucrative and creatively satisfying.

While furniture design has technically been around for centuries (the first discovery of a chair, table, couch, and a canopy were found in a fourth Dynasty Egyptian tomb in

FIGURE 9.1
Scratch Your Itch
for Stich: From the
Bargello Pillow
collection by
Jonathan Adler.

FIGURE 9.2
The elbow chair was
designed by William
Haines in the 1930s
so women would
have a place to sit in
their ball gowns.

2600 BC), the industry is continually changing. Many manufacturing jobs are going overseas and positions as a staff designer are more difficult to find.

Opportunities have shifted from the pure furniture manufacturers (many located in the southeast) to ones that are solely marketing furniture. Moreover, a downturn in the economy will affect the high-end custom market of products as well.

Whether you are an entrepreneur with a signature collection or designing for a manufacturer, furniture and product design takes skill, vision, drive, hard work, and most importantly, knowing your customer. And while a passion for the profession is required, designers develop products with the intention to sell. They must keep up with trends, the competition, production costs and materials and the vagaries of the marketplace.

THE PROCESS

It all begins with an idea.

For international interior and product designer Clodagh, "the design process can be as simple as seeing something out of the corner of my eye and it becomes a design. A carved wooden bowl from a flea market turned into a bathtub while a massage table was made longer and turned into a spa chair."

Often a product is born out of a specific need (thirties designer William Haines created the elbow chair for women to sit in while wearing ball gowns). Products are developed to target a specific market as with architect Michael Graves line of "products for everyday people with everyday budgets" for Target. Jonathan Adler found

his calling for ceramics at a young age, signaling the starting point for a multi-dimensional design career. Palm Beach designers Mimi McMakin and Brooke

FIGURE 9.3
International interior and product designer Clodagh.

FIGURE 9.4
Spa Lounger from Clodagh's Sanctuary Collection for Oakworks is a relaxation bed.

Huttig brought their home-grown knowledge to Laneventure with the Palm Beach Collection.

Once a design is conceptualized, the process begins. John Black, a former vice president of design at Baker, Knapp and Tubbs, explains, "The process can take a year from the first discussion with a client or company to the specific needs of the collection to the next stage of the design presentation through working drawings" (which is when the real design takes place). Detailed drawings, rough sketches or formal renderings are prepared along with samples and prototypes. "The process also involves working with sales and marketing. It is just as important to design the entire project, beyond the furniture, to include input for the showroom presentation, catalog and advertising design. These are the key elements as to how to appeal to the end customer, which is where I start my design process," he details.

Many hands can touch a single piece of furniture. Jay Reardon, president of Hickory Chair (maker of classic high-end wood and upholstered furnishings), notes, "Approximately 540 people actually touch a piece from start to finish." Working with designers such as Alexa Hampton, Mariette Himes Gomez, Suzanne Kassler, and Thomas O'Brien, the process involves all phases of design from drafting, purchasing, upholstering, sewing, merchandising, cutting, and finishing to marketing, sales, and display.

THE PREPARATION

Requirements and Skills Needed

Those who wish to specialize in this area should possess a high degree of both artistic and technological skill as the appearance of a chair will be just as important as the levels of ergonomics, comfort, and practicality. They should also be self-starters, have a strong aesthetic eye for color, space, proportion and style. Veteran furniture designer John Black recommends, "Learn to draw by hand as it is a great communication tool and it will develop your design sense."

Education and Training

Formal training for those entering this area of the profession can include a bachelor of science degree in interior design as well as a specialized bachelor of fine arts degree and master of fine arts in furniture design. Industrial and product design and textile design degrees are also available. At present, there are not a large number of schools offering furniture design. Several of the most notable ones are the Kendall College of Art & Design at Ferris State University, Northern Michigan University, Savannah College of Art

FIGURE 9.6
Hickory Chair room vignette.

and Design (SCAD), and Rhode Island School of Design (RISD).

Decorative painting, millwork, and furniture restoration are other great skills to acquire along with woodworking, metalworking, welding, fabricating, and upholstering (depending on the products of interest).

Design Curriculum

Courses in furniture design will cover aesthetics, techniques, structure, and materials. Technical drawing and Auto-CAD, fabrication and finishes, rendering and presentation, construction, and spatial composition should also be added to the course load. It is also advisable to take courses in furniture and product marketing and merchandising.

Textile design majors will take color theory, drawing, art, fabric and fiber composition, textile science, weaving, surface design, screen printing, and 2-D and 3-D fine art. Fabric construction and product merchandising classes are also recommended.

Since these areas are deeply rooted in history, it is strongly advised to take art history and furniture history classes.

PROFESSIONAL ASSOCIATIONS

The American Society of Furniture Designers (ASFD) is the primary organization for professionals in this specialty. For membership requirements, see their website www.asfd.com.

THE PAY

Salaries in this field will vary depending upon the company, scope or responsibil-ity, and geographical location. Entry-level assistants can start at $36,000, which is consistent with other areas of the interior design industry. Furniture and product designers can make anywhere from $40,000 to $150,000 for the more seasoned individual. And the perks naturally include discounts!

THE PATH

Furniture and product designers enjoy a variety of opportunities. They can work in-house by contract and residential furniture firms, manufacturers and showrooms or architectural firms, act as consultants or work solely and develop their own (custom or mass produced) product and furniture lines. They can design for mass-market retailers such as Restoration Hardware and Mitchell Gold or high-end luxury custom furnishings or industry giants such as Baker, Knapp and Tubbs or Hickory Chair.

Textile designers will find employment through fabric houses and some furniture companies. A good portfolio is necessary and internships remain one of the best ways to break into the industry. The fashion industry is also enjoying a crossover—Donna Karan and Calvin Klein have bedding lines and the Italian luxury firm Fendi opened Fendi Casa. Successful product and furniture designers partner with companies and license their product lines as well. (See Chapter 10: The Lifestyle Designer for more on licensing.)

Furniture designers also move into furniture buying, ergonomics, conservation, industrial design, marketing representatives, and teachers.

Black advises job seekers be open to working in a multi-disciplined office or company. "Understand that fresh out of school, you must pay some dues, maybe work in an environment that is less than ideal. I have yet to meet a good designer fresh out of school," he says.

THE PROFILES

Michael Graves, Architect and Designer, Michael Graves Design Group

"Design has nothing to do with economic class. If I were designing for Cartier or Tiffany, I would expend the same energy."

—MICHAEL GRAVES

Chances are you have seen a Michael Graves creation and did not even know it.

A singing kettle teapot, an innovative paper towel holder, or the design of the Dolphin and Swan hotels at Disney World are just a few of the designs by the architect extraordinaire.

American architect Michael Graves has been an iconic figure in the design world for over forty years. His many accomplishments, awards, and achievements are almost too numerous to mention. His practice has designed over 350 buildings worldwide and includes an architecture, interiors, graphic design, and three product design studios in Princeton, New Jersey. He has designed furnishings, light fixtures, and

FIGURE 9.7
Michael Graves, architect and designer.

FIGURE 9.8
Whimsical Alessi teapot collection by Michael Graves.

FIGURE 9.9
Leather chair design by Michael Graves.

dinnerware for the likes of Steuben, Alessi, Phillips Electronics, and Black & Decker. His product reach ranges from a bath fixture collection for Dornbracht to door handles for the Italian hardware manufacturer Valli and Valli—a reach that extends to over 1,000 items ranging from chess sets to cleaning tools.

While the contemporary product and furniture lines of an architect are often available only for the very elite, the witty designer made a simple realization—good design doesn't have to be expensive. Over lunch one day with Ron Johnson, then-vice president of general merchandise for uber-retailer Target, Graves was told "We've been knocking you off for years. Why don't we come to the source?" Afterwards, the pair toured a Target store and Graves put yellow stickers on the products he thought he could improve. They ran out of stickers and a partnership was born.

Extremely affordable prices without sacrificing quality has become a mission statement of sorts for Graves, who explains, "Whenever we design a product, we insist on seeing manufacturer prototypes that we review for both design conformance and quality control. If we see defects, we reject the prototypes and send them back. I feel fortunate that Target is as committed to good quality as I am," explains Graves.

As a product designer, he has revolutionized the mass-market industry, offering the world new ways to view something as simple as a garlic press. Instead of losing his cache as a luxury designer, he has become a household name. Graves has done for domestic households what he does with architecture—taking conventional forms and adding a touch of unexpected whimsy with function. "As an architect, I find myself interested in the artifacts of daily life and how they can be related to architecture," he explains. "Because I see architecture and design as part of the same aesthetic continuum, I don't distinguish between making a building, a piece of furniture, or a tea kettle, aside from the differences of size and function. What is important in creating all of these things is to have a sense of domesticity, which enriches designs at any scale."

Sidelined by illness (an untreated sinus infection turned into paralysis and today he is wheelchair bound), Graves plans to tackle household products for the disabled. Designing from a world he now unfortunately knows, his plans include bath safety and mobility equipment and aids to daily living such as: "Items like bath benches, handheld showers, tub rails, and portable bath

FIGURE 9.10
Breakfast room
interior with Michael
Graves product line.

benches for traveling that fold up with handles that can assist someone in getting balance. We notice that while one person in the family uses [the device], everyone has to live with it, and there is no need for it to look terrible. We are trying to make ours look not like medical devices but furniture that is meant to help you," he states. "My recent paralysis has inspired a new vision for my design team and me. We are just beginning to explore the world of health care products. There are huge opportunities in this arena for good designers to make a real difference."

John Black, Furniture Designer and President, J. Black Designs
"Study and learn artistic influences outside of your personal likes; it will open your eyes to other ways of approaching design and life in general."
—JOHN BLACK

John Black has had one of the more traditional routes to a career in furniture design.

After receiving a degree in the field from the Kendall School of Design, he worked for twenty years with freelance design offices in Montreal, Chicago, and Washington, D.C. "Both were good training experiences," he explains, "as I was exposed to different styles and types of furniture. For the first ten years I was drafting on full-size drawings of designs done by senior designers, learning materials and construction techniques."

Black's first company position was with the prestigious furniture company Baker Knapp and Tubbs as a designer on the Milling Road Collection and later vice president of design. Under his jurisdiction, he worked on the impressive collections of interior designer Barbara Barry, Stately Homes, Colonial Williamsburg, and Historic Charleston.

For the aspiring furniture designer, Black recommends developing a personal style that will distinguish your work. "I am very much a modernist but have great respect for and draw upon traditional design to influence my style," he says. "I do my best to make it seem fresh or what I call relevant for today and make my modern designs timeless and classic. First and foremost, scale and promotion is the driving force that makes my style recognizable. It's also about categories and existing collections to keep them current and make them saleable, this is what keeps clients coming back."

Jonathan Adler, President, Jonathan Adler Inc.

The year was 1978 and the place, summer camp where a young Jonathan Adler first tried his hand at pottery. A year later, his parents placed a kiln and a wheel in the family basement and a career was born.

Years later (and several careers later), Adler returned to his first love and showed a line of Chanel-inspired quilted pots to New York's trendsetting Barney's department store. "I made a decision to pursue my passion and I got an order. I made them and delivered them by hand without an invoice," the engaging Adler says, "I didn't know what an invoice was!" The rest, as they say, is history.

The debut line consisted of a dozen contemporary high-fired pottery pieces that grew into two dozen lines (approximately 200 models in all) a decade later. Storefronts with the Adler name followed from Soho to San Francisco.

In 2000, he and his wife opened their company, J. Black Designs.

Black has been in the industry for decades and has seen the changes come and go. "I think the role of the specialized furniture designer is in a state of flux, in large part because a good deal of product today is 'designed by interior designers.' The most significant change I have seen is the multitude of retail options the consumer now has for buying furniture. The traditional furniture retail store is being replaced, or at least challenged, by a growing myriad of buying choices such as Crate & Barrel, Williams Sonoma Home, and the like. And they are doing a brilliant job of displaying product with the added benefit of having a full range of home products," he details.

FIGURE 9.12
"I am very much a modernist, but have great respect for and draw upon traditional design to influence my style," says John Black, furniture designer.

FIGURE 9.13
Table by J. Black
Designs.

FIGURE 9.14
Jonathan Adler,
ceramist, designer,
author, and
television star.

Adler expanded his interests and product line to furniture, handbags, pillows, bedding and bath, rugs, and lighting. Interior design projects ensued, designing private residences as well as contract installations such as the whimsical designs for fashion retailer Trina Turk and the Parker Palm Springs hotel.

While admitting to never hatching a master plan, the colorful New Jersey native says, "I have been very lucky and I am having fun (and stress) along the way while enjoying a very circuitous and serendipitous career." For those who want to walk in his Gucci loafers, he advises, "Be willing to work mega-hard and be patient. My first three years as a production potter meant eighty hours a

LIBERACE
refuses to poop in the rain

JONATHAN
is in the gift community

SIMON
lied about his height on his passport

FIGURE 9.15
Adler interior is
marked by whimsy
and strong use of
color.

week at the wheel producing the same mug or pot over and over again." He also learned to delegate, explaining, "When I became overwhelmed with production, I found a workshop in Peru to produce my designs, allowing me to step back and figure out the real spirit of my work. Instead of becoming 'that guy who makes striped pots,' I was able to develop a sensibility that became the road map for all my future work. In short, be very analytical about who you are and what your work is about."

The admittedly never-bored designer finds inspiration for his product line "in so many different places . . . fashion, architecture, nature and even rap music!" he exclaims. "Watching old movies has inspired entire collections of furniture and traveling to Palm Beach fueled moi's obsession with waspy-chic style. Do things you love and they will find their way into your designs."

The ceramist and interior designer also added author (*My Prescription for Anti-Depressive Living*, Collins Design,

FIGURE 9.16
Adler's high-glazed
stoneware put him
on the map. Shown
here is his Utopia
line of pottery.

FIGURE 9.17
Red walls make a
bold statement in
this Adler designed
interior.

FIGURE 9.18
Adler's book *My Prescription for Anti-Depressive Living* (Collins Design, 2004).

2004) and judge on Bravo Television's competition reality show, *Top Design* on which Adler weekly bids the losing contestant adieu with his signature phrase, *"See ya later, decorator."*

For more on Adler and licensing products, see Chapter 10: The Lifestyle Designer.

REFERENCES

Adler, Jonathan (2005). *My Prescription for Anti-Depressive Living*. Collins Design: New York.

Encyclopedia: Furniture. (2006). *The History Channel* website. Retrieved March 14, 2008 from www.history.com/encyclopedia.do?articleId=209952.

Forest, Sara D. *Vault Guide to Interior Design Careers* (2006). New York: Vault, Inc.

Gogoi, Pallavi. (August 18, 2005). Michael Graves: Beyond Kettles. *Business Week.*

Graves, Michael. (June 2002). *Michael Graves On Design*. Retrieved March 10, 2008 from website www.pbs.org.

Gross, Kim Johnson and Stone, Jeff. (1993) *Chic Simple Home*. New York: Alfred A. Knopf.

Lipman, Mary J-Lo G. (February 11, 1999). *Bullseye! Michael Graves Does Target.* Retrieved March 11, 2008 from website www.cnn.com/STYLE/9902/11/target/.

Newman, Ellen. *San Francisco Market 2004 Presents Design Integrity In A Global Economy.* Retrieved March 13, 2008 from website www.sfdesign center.com/pressroom/press_press archive33_integrity_middle.html.

Perman, Stacy. (August 15, 2006). Michael Graves New Target: Medical Devices. *Business Week.*

Singer, Matt. The Making of a (New) Modern Master. *Modernism Magazine.* Retrieved September 10, 2007 from Jonathan Adler website www.jonathanadler.com/shop/mod_page1.php.

Tischler, Linda. (August, 2004). A Design for Living. *Fast Company* magazine. Retrieved March 11, 2008 from website www.fastcompany.com.

THE KNOCK-OFF

While it's said that imitation is the sincerest form of flattery, furniture and product designers often look more on this as a form of insult.

Sally Sirkin Lewis, President of J. Robert Scott, unveils new furniture, fabric, and wallcovering lines each year. Designed and produced in her 100,000 square foot factory outside of Los Angeles, the celebrated interior designer operates in a total hands-on manner, overseeing prototypes from fabrication to completion. June Triolo, Marketing Manager of J. Robert Scott, notes the company is known for their "unparalleled finishing techniques, utilizing dyed exotic veneers hand-polished lacquers, chinoiserie, and 22-karat gold finishes." It is not unusual to see artisans hand sew dressmaker details on a sofa and apply silver leaf to a mirror with squirrel hairbrushes.

Lewis is also known for her exquisite textiles and is credited with bringing couture to the home furnishings market. "For many fabrics I design, in the back of my mind I imagine a ball gown—(I ask myself) is it suitable for fashion? The most important thing is how it feels and drapes and of course is it suitable for upholstery," she comments.

With all of these distinguished accomplishments, it's probably no wonder that she has been "knocked off."

While staying in a hotel room in Atlanta, she was astounded to find her fabric designs had been copied by the hotel chain. She later found an unauthorized facsimile of her gold mirror in a catalogue and decided something needed to be done. Frustrated with the antics, Lewis organized industry leaders in 1994, forming the Foundation for Designer Integrity to educate designers and manufacturers about protecting their work.

Lewis eventually sued the hotel chain and the catalogue company and won an undisclosed amount in damages. "You need design patents and thousand of dollars to defend yourself. Otherwise there are no protections," she says. She notes that it costs between $2,000 and $5,000 per design patent (her company has been awarded more than 100 patents in the United States and the United Kingdom already). Legal fees can be exorbitant, running upwards of $50,000. "With lawyer's fees at $450 an hour, how can young designers afford to protect themselves and their designs?" she states.

Patents, copyrights, and trademarks all exist to protect designers and their work. While it may not always be successful, at least it's a deterrent. Perhaps one day "copies," along with fake designer bags sold on city streets will be a thing of the past.

Cloud Chest by designer Sally Sirkin Lewis for J. Robert Scott.

Lewis is known for her use of exotic finishes and clean contemporary lines. Shown here is the Tuscan dining table.

life-style n
The way of life that is typical of a person, group, or culture.

gu-ru n
Somebody who is prominent and influential in a specific field and sets a trend or starts a movement.

The Lifestyle Designer

OVERVIEW OF THE PROFESSION

The role of a lifestyle guru is to impart information on all things home and evoke images of the good life to a domestically challenged audience. From tips on design and decoration to gardening, entertaining and cooking, this new breed of designer/personality turned expert/guru reaches audiences through a variety of multimedia and retail outlets. Considered by many to be the pinnacle of the interior design career, the practice consists of a combination of several or more specialties.

Targeting a specific segment or marketing to the masses, lifestyle branding is a form of marketing that encompasses the core values and aspirations of a culture. Ralph Lauren and his Polo brand are a classic example, portraying a preppy, Ivy League life "to the manor born." Lifestyle marketing emerged in the seventies as mass production moved overseas and the economy and culture began to shift. Fashion was first to jump on the bandwagon, as witnessed by the immensely popular line of Calvin Klein jeans, targeting an affluent consumer (or those of middle income with a charge card) who longed for designer identification with an aura of chic.

The home furnishings industry followed as consumers looked for guidance on how to live, eat, design, and do

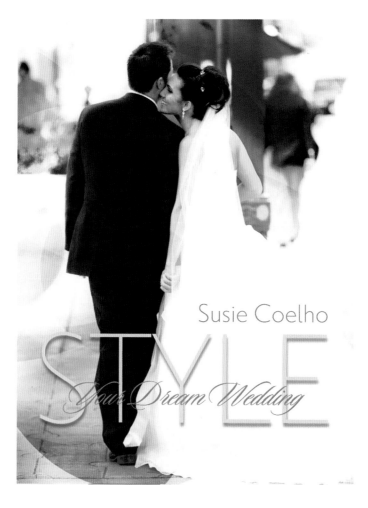

Susie Coelho
STYLE
Your Dream Wedding

FIGURE 10.1
Lifestyle guru Susie
Coelho teamed
with Grandin Road
catalogues as their
style expert.

everything from making a lampshade to selecting the perfect sofa. Interior designers soon discovered that developing their own personal branding strategy coupled with an image, a line of products, and/or services marketed through multimedia channels is a winning formula.

Perhaps the best-known expert in the field is the poster child for lifestyle design, Martha Stewart, whose career path became a blueprint for countless designers.

THE PROCESS

The formulaic strategy appears simple yet is one filled with many goals. While all of this sounds amazingly straightfor-

ward, it is a path not easily attainable for most designers.

The interior designer gains success and notoriety through projects, garnering national press through television, newspapers, and magazines. Vendors and/or licensing agencies take notice and the designer receives contracts to develop and license their luxury products and home furnishings. Subsequent books follow and the designer goes on book tours and lectures across the country. A product line expands to the mass-market level when Target calls. The designer signs with a national speakers bureau and gets an agent. The television networks follow suit and offer a prime-time show. Satellite radio joins the fray and signs up the designer for a weekly half-hour segment. Other companies vie for commercial endorsements. And the business practice of licensing plays a part like never before.

A record number of interior designers are sought by companies to develop a specific niche or style that a company does not have (i.e., a modern collection for manufacturer that is known more for traditional). Many companies look to notable designers for name recognition, supplying a fresh approach to an existing product category that has grown stagnant and may have lost sales. Designers are consulting with the industry, supplying marketing ideas and bringing an added *"star power"* through the deal of the licensed product.

For many an interior designer it is the ultimate dream. Their name and logo is placed on everything from bedding and towels to fabrics and wallpapers, and visions of dollar signs and empire building dance in their heads. While this no doubt sounds glamorous and lucrative, licensing is a serious, difficult, highly competitive, and elusive business.

"Celebrity worship will fuel licensing deals in the future. Pop culture is replacing real design luxury," says Steve Nobel of Nobelinks, former president of The John Widdicomb Company furniture, and now an industry consultant. He advises designers to "Pick their partners carefully (when considering a licensing deal). Look for a collateral nature with brands. If you want volume, then talk to Target, JCPenney, and get your product out there."

Nobel recommends that you "make sure your goals are consistent with their goals. Designers might want to go high price with their products and the

licensee is thinking lower. Be sure each party can deliver on what they promise." Many a designer has a deal go south after two years of product development. Quality control is another issue; some may have very little while other designers like Jonathan Adler have maintained 100 percent control over their designs.

Michael Graves agrees, "Licensing design is akin to sending your children to boarding school. So long as they are happy and doing well, they can stay in school. But if they misbehave, they are sent home! So long as my products perform well at retail, they remain on

FIGURE 10.2
A Martha Stewart–styled interior.

FIGURE 10.3
Sleek contemporary interior featured in *Martha Stewart Living* magazine.

the market." He also notes that his firm insists on retaining some of the control of the aesthetic character of their designs right thorough the manufacturing process.

Keith Granet, head of Granet & Associates, a consulting firm for the design industry, feels there should be plenty of room for qualified designers in the licensing arena. "I go into department stores and see at least twenty-five fashion designers and there should be plenty of room for interior designers. Companies today are seriously looking at the cache of 'celebrity' designers, and people like to know who is behind a product."

The agent to the stars suggests one of the first ways to start is by getting to know editors and thus, get published. "We tell designers to build relationships with editors, as they want to know you and see if there is a story (behind your products) and where placement could happen in the magazine," he explains.

It is also important to have some sort of idea where you would like to be vis a vis low end or high end. Granet notes that the mass market manufacturers tend to "cycle through designers faster" while the designers at the more middle- to high-end companies have longevity. Others have successfully straddled both sides of the fence—Target designer Thomas O'Brien is also at Hickory Chair.

If you are interested in teaming up with a company, do your homework. See what is in the marketplace, aim for something unique and different. You can approach a company directly or get a licensing agent, but go armed with top-notch sketches and well thought out plans. Industry stalwarts such as

Century, Baker, Knapp and Tubbs, and Hickory Chair receive over fifty requests a year from designers wanting their own lines. Jay Reardon, president of Hickory Chair, has aligned his company with only four interior designers—Mariette Himes Gomez for contemporary, Alexa Hampton and Suzanne Kasler for traditional, and Thomas O'Brien as a bridge between the two.

Companies and licensing agents look for designers with name recognition, uniqueness, style, glamour, and the ability to design a custom line of products.

Give the company a good story behind the product such as the Hemingway line of furniture with Thomasville. They will also look to the designer as a marketing partner and expect them to articulately promote the line. For their efforts, they will receive anywhere from 3 to 24 percent (only two to three get the top 24 percent fee). Add to this a minimum 10 to 20 percent fee for the licensing agent. (See sidebar at the end of the chapter for more on the practice of a licensing agency.)

Chris Casson Madden partnered with JCPenney and notes that the "company's core values matched my own in terms of what to deliver to the customer—great style and quality at affordable prices." Of the overall process, Madden says, "I have creative control to set all of the wheels in motion—define the trend, outline the design, tweak it pre-production and give it final approval. JCPenney does the sourcing and pricing."

Many designers will forgo the agent route as was the case of interior designer Celerie Kemble. The Manhattan and Palm Beach based designer made a name for herself with a younger

explains, "These companies will have an annual minimum and guarantee a fee per year, paying X amount for five years plus a percentage of wholesale sales."

THE PREPARATION

To succeed in this high-powered, highly visible specialty, designers will have to develop or draw upon many skills:

Requirements and Skills

Interior Design

To be a well-rounded lifestyle designer, it is important to know as much as possible about the theory and practice of interior design as well as trends and the industry.

Communications

Since this area is deeply rooted in multimedia, the ability to communicate is paramount. Designers in this specialty are front and center and must be able to manage the media behind and in

FIGURE 10.4
Celerie Kemble of Kemble Interiors.

FIGURE 10.5
Celerie Kemble's fabric line for Valetkz has both commercial and residential applications.

affluent market and among the pages of *Domino* and *House and Garden* magazines. Kemble's urbane yet fashion-inspired look earned her lines with F. Schumacher, Laneventure, and Beacon Looms for home bedding. Kemble

front of the camera. Public speaking at lectures and book signings, being interviewed on television, hosting a radio and/or television show and promoting products at events are just a few of the media activities.

The role of teaching is often a vital component of lifestyle design. Imparting and promoting products in the media require teaching and instruction to the consumer.

Entrepreneurial Spirit

The foresight of business; the forecasting of trends; and the ability to create and build an empire with enthusiasm, drive, passion, and spirit are just a few of the many requirements for this area. Also essential is choosing the right business partners, managing staff, and delegating tasks while still maintaining a hands-on approach. "You must have a high level of commitment as you are your own boss," says Coelho.

Organization

Due to the many varied areas of activities, designers must be highly organized and task oriented as the ability to juggle a variety of businesses and goals is vitally important. You might be working on designs for a home bedding line and writing the chapter of a book in the morning, conducting an interview over lunch, and meeting with a team of merchandise buyers in the afternoon. For more insight, see the various chapters pertaining to the particular specialty of interest.

Education and Training

While a bachelors degree in interior design is an excellent foundation for the lifestyle designer, it would be wise

FIGURE 10.6
Martha Stewart at book signing promotion.

to take as many courses and/or obtain a minor in business, marketing/merchandising or communications due to the varied areas of knowledge and expertise required.

Design Curriculum

Since many of the activities center around multimedia, courses in broadcasting, acting, public relations, public speaking, journalism, and the Internet are essential. Lifestyle design is quite entrepreneurial; therefore courses in finance, business, accounting, marketing, advertising, and management are vital. For those with the desire for a home furnishings line, take product, furniture, and textile design courses. If retail store(s) are in your future, courses in all aspects in retailing and merchandising should be added to the curriculum.

Psychology courses are also important as you must be able to understand, market to, and deal with the public.

THE PATH

Since lifestyle design is such a unique career destination, it is advisable to take a variety of avenues if possible as this is clearly a career for the renaissance man/woman. Martha Stewart was a model, caterer, and stockbroker and Susie Coelho a restaurateur, television host, model, actress, and shop owner before building their empires.

Establish Who You Are

Determine your strengths. Consultant Fred Berns recommends the "5-5-5 Drill: Create a list of the five assets/qualities that differentiate you (from other students/designers/businesses, etc.)."

FIGURE 10.7
Martha Stewart is the poster child for lifestyle design.

Susie Coelho contacted everyone she knew and asked one simple question, "Considering everything I have done, what do you think the essence of Susie is?" By querying candid and supportive friends, she was able to ascertain that her strongest quality was helping others, one of the major tenets of lifestyle design.

Martha Stewart honed her craft of gardening, sewing, and cooking during her teenage years in New Jersey. Modeling put her in front of the camera, catering gave her the necessary culinary and entertaining skills for a domestic diva, while Wall Street provided the business backbone for creating her legendary career.

Develop a Platform

Coelho found that her strongest career asset was her experience on television as an entertainment news reporter. Capitalizing on this skill set (along with her suggestions of friends), she approached pro-

ducers (*Home and Garden Television* was in its infancy, so add foresight and luck to the mix) with an idea for a "how-to" show on gardening, "Surprise Gardener."

It is also important to develop a media presence. Becoming a well-known industry expert and personality will go a long way in getting a book, television, and licensing deal. Get as much good press as possible.

Determine Your Niche Market

While lifestyle branding often goes hand in hand with marketing to the masses, it helps to know who your market is. Niche marketing is the process of addressing a need for a product or service to a particular consumer base or market segment.

Martha Stewart and Michael Graves excel in this while others target a more segmented (and often higher end) consumer. Interior designer Celerie Kemble. her mother Mimi McMakin.

FIGURE 10.8
Kemble Interiors partnered with Laneventure for a line of sophisticated furniture.

and design partner Brooke Huttig brought the Palm Beach lifestyle to the general public with their home furnishings lines for Laneventure while Barbara Barry brings her own brand of luxurious living through elegance, and laid-back California glamour.

Devise a Simple Mission Statement

Mitchell Gold and Bob Williams based their company along the idea of relaxed design and comfort while Michael Graves' credo is "everyone should have access to beautiful things." Jonathan Adler's mission statement is "We believe that your home should make you happy" which reflects in his colorful and whimsical line. Coelho's simple yet to the point mantra is "Keep Creating."

Passion and Plan

Martha Stewart no doubt lives and breathes her business, saying, "All the things I love is what my business is about. The delightful secret of the entrepreneurial life is that when you love your work, you rarely get tired." To succeed in this area, you must possess a strong desire to succeed, create, and teach.

Planning is also vital. While Stewart is highly ambitious, she dared to dream big. "It's within everyone's grasp to be a CEO. You really can do anything," she says. Devise a business plan as to how best to promote your product and/or service and through which medium is marketing 101. And while it's great to think big, some may be happy being a large fish in a small pond. Designers located in smaller cities can benefit from less competition and increased visibility. If you are not in a large media market

and want exposure, try doing design segments on a local news show.

Vision is also key. "Everyone should start with a vision of where to go and what to create. Really look at the big picture and what is achievable this year. You don't have to emulate someone else's career exactly as it will never happen that way. Take your strength in one area and parlay it in your own way," says Coelho.

While a very small percentage of the population will enjoy success of such magnitude, mirroring the various areas of Stewart's multifaceted career in her words is "A Good Thing."

PROFESSIONAL ASSOCIATIONS

It is advisable to join organizations that pertain to the various areas of interest beginning with an overall professional organization such as the American Society of Interior Designers (ASID). See the resources list for a more detailed listing of groups available.

THE PAY

Due to the nature of the highly diverse and specialized areas, no set salary figures are available but it is safe to say with book, product, and media contracts, the virtual sky is the limit.

THE PROFILES

Martha Stewart, Founder and President, Martha Stewart Omnimedia
"It's a Good Thing."
—Martha Stewart

The facts say it all:
- 755 Employees
- $33 million in revenue
- $3,565,969 yearly salary
- Household name
- World's most successful businesswoman

Martha Stewart, founder of Martha Stewart Omnimedia, oversees an empire that Julius Caesar would never have envisioned.

The true poster child of the lifestyle design movement, her multimedia ventures include a magazine (*Martha Stewart Living*), television (*The Martha Stewart Show*), radio (*Martha Stewart Living* on Sirius), retail (product lines with Kmart, Lowe's, and Macy's). In addition, there's Martha Stewart weddings, crafts, food, paint, furniture, and even a collaboration with KB Home for Martha Stewart inspired houses in New York, Connecticut, and Maine. In the business of all things home, it's world domination.

Stewart represents the American dream come true. Countless stories have been told of her success—and her well publicized missteps—but one thing is certain, this Renaissance woman has changed the landscape of the home industry forever. A graduate of architectural history from Barnard College, she credits learning the art of research and the power of a single idea (homemaking as an art) as the key to her success, using her domestic expertise and creativity in every area from product to television show.

The former model-turned stockbroker became a successful caterer in 1972. Stewart's best-selling book *Entertaining*

(Crown, 1982) is considered the Rosetta stone that launched her empire. More books, videotapes, dinner CDs, and appearances on Oprah followed and made her a celebrity. In 1987, Stewart received a five million dollar advertising and consulting contract with Kmart, followed by more books, and the launch of a quarterly magazine, *Martha Stewart Living*.

FIGURE 10.9
Martha Stewart.

FIGURE 10.10
Martha Stewart in the early years.

Her most successful venture came in 1993 with the weekly half-hour lifestyle/ magazine show, *Martha Stewart Living* (now known as *The Martha Stewart Show*). Two years later, the domestic diva founded her umbrella multimedia company, Martha Stewart Omnimedia (MSLO). Despite an insider trading charge and subsequent prison setback, her groundbreaking career is the proverbial "stuff of legends."

Always the teacher, Stewart wrote the book *The Martha Rules* (Rodale, 2005), imparting her valued business knowledge to those who want to follow in her well-heeled pumps. A few of her pearls of wisdom:

FIGURE 10.11
The Martha Stewart Show.

1. Find your passion. Stewart loves what she does and it shows. Rumored to work twenty-hour days and sleep four hours a night, her love of homemaking was successfully converted into a multimillion-dollar business and phenomenon.

2. Know your customers. Stewart is there to serve her customers and has developed a loyal and devoted cult-like following as a result. She maintains a personal connection through her interactive website, magazine, radio, and television show, reaching over 30 million people.

3. Develop an A team. She recognizes the importance of a supportive staff and partners that share the same vision, noting, "Without a sense of teamwork, I think it's really hard to build a great business." She recommends choosing the right advisors for your business, forgoing well-meaning friends (unless they are strong business

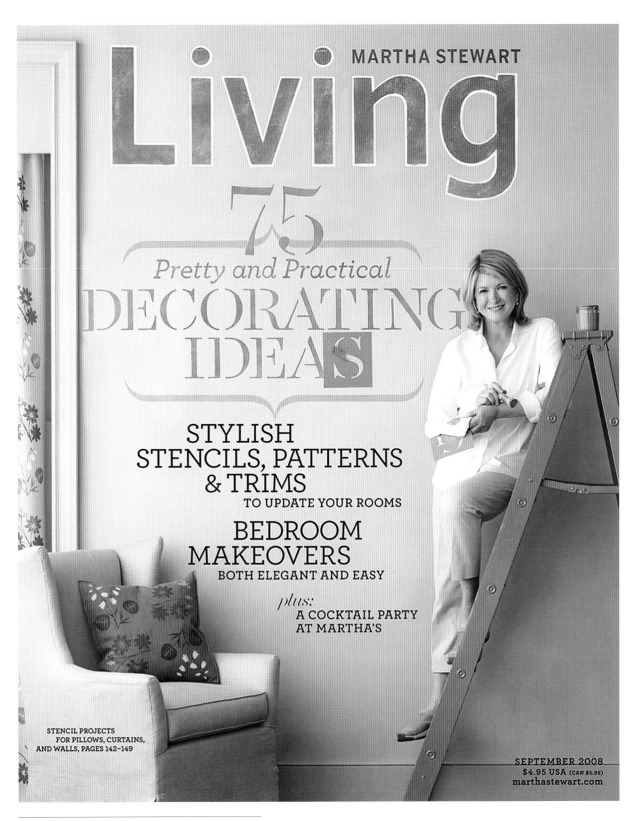

FIGURE 10.12
Martha Stewart Living magazine.

FIGURE 10.13
Martha Stewart
was one of the first
designers to have
a mass-market line
with Kmart.

people). Known for her hands-on approach, her personal stamp is instilled and seen on everything from gardening gloves at Kmart to a can of paint primer at Lowe's.

With a net worth of $1.2 billion, it's good to be Martha.

Susie Coelho, President, Susie Coelho Enterprises

"Take a look at your own goals and resources. Decide where you want to go, who you want to be and what is the best path."

—SUSIE COELHO

She has been called the "next Martha," a "home style guru," and a "style diva."

Susie Coelho is a leading lifestyle guru with a rare career that encompasses the four main areas of home,

garden, cooking, and entertaining. Considered a forerunner in the home makeover genre that began in the nineties, the former Ford model has over twenty years of on-camera experience as a television personality.

Coelho's career has all the essential ingredients. The former host of HBO's *Entertainment News* is no stranger to the camera; she appeared on more than 200 HGTV shows and specials (the top-rated *Surprise Gardener* and *Outer Spaces*) along with regular appearances on ABC's *The View* and NBC's *The Today Show*.

In 1997, she formed Susie Coelho Enterprises (SCE), a multimedia lifestyle company centering on "practical solutions for everyday living" through television, publishing, products, and endorsements. Targeting the "homeowner who wants to get great style, I give tips for the person who does not have a lot of time and needs help," she says.

Coelho's accomplishments are impressive and she has a background as diverse as her products and books. While married to the late singer and ex-mayor, Sonny Bono, she designed and ran Bono's restaurants, giving her experience in food and entertaining. She was also a successful retailer with her "A Star Is Worn" resale celebrity collectibles stores in Los Angeles.

Her desire to impart wisdom and inspire people to "cultivate their own creativity" led to the publication of four books—*Styling for Entertaining: 8 Simple Steps, 12 Miracle Makeovers* (Simon & Schuster, 2003), *Secrets of a Style Diva: A Get-Inspired Guide to Your Creative Side* (Thomas Nelson, 2006), *Susie Coelho's Everyday Styling: Easy Tips for Home, Garden, and Entertaining* (Simon & Schuster, 2002) and *Style Your Dream Wedding* (Thomas Nelson, 2008). Her writing skills were also honed with a column for *Palm Springs Life* magazine.

Coelho's eclectic background (East Indian heritage and raised in England) and multicultural heritage connects her to a wide audience. She serves

as a spokesperson for Grandin Road catalogue, Sears, Betty Crocker, EBay, Vanity Fair, and Meridian Vineyards.

In terms of product design, Coelho explains, "every company works in different ways. For the bedding and bath line, we will show the vendor sketches and a color palette and work with them to develop it further. For our luggage line, we deliver an actual pattern, tell them we want to use our logo, and ask how to fabricate on a two-tone jacquard. Basically, we deliver and they figure out how to make." The vendor will lay out the design, produce a mock up on

FIGURE 10.14
Susie Coelho based her multimedia lifestyle company on "practical solutions for everyday living."

HOST OF
HGTV's
Outer Spaces

STYLING *for* ENTERTAINING

8 SIMPLE STEPS

12 MIRACLE MAKEOVERS

SUSIE COELHO

FIGURE 10.15
Styling for Entertaining: 8 Simple Steps, 12 Miracle Makeovers (Simon & Schuster, 2003) is one of four books by the author.

a bigger scale, develop CAD drawings and have one to two versions made in China. Coelho and the buying team review, approve the color, tweak the design, and a product is launched.

The process is not always cut and dried. "You have to coordinate all the time. I am constantly looking at the marketplace, statistics, what is sold, and the prices," she explains. She has learned every facet of the process on the job and has a licensing agency to guide her through. Her support staff also includes a business manager, lawyer, licensing agent, and bookkeeper and uses freelancers for graphic design and product development.

"I had a dream with no restrictions. I did this on sheer determination and put the whole plan into motion," she says of her extraordinary career.

Chris Casson Madden,
Chris Madden, Inc.
"Affordability, durability and style—my mantra."
—Chris Casson Madden

For Chris Casson Madden, it's all about lifestyle.

In 1998, Oprah gave Madden a design challenge to "de-mystify decorating" on her television show. The author and designer responded with advice on helping women to find their own decorating style, whether it be Adventurous, Romantic, or Serene. She challenged women to explore their passions and collections in order to discover their own personal style and "create spaces that will nurture, restore and make an emotional connection to their life—that's what true lifestyle design is all about."

Founder of a 30-year multi-million dollar home furnishings business that encompasses design, publishing, licensing, and television, Madden launched her career in magazine publishing, learning the basics of great magazine photography at *Sports Illustrated*. Book publishing experience followed, working for Random House, G.P. Putnam and then as director of publicity for Farrar, Straus & Giroux, G.P. Putnam, and Simon & Schuster.

In 1988, Madden focused her journalistic and visual talents on her passion—interior design—with the publication of *Interior Visions: Great*

FIGURE 10.16
Chris Casson Madden is a noted lifestyle designer.

FIGURE 10.17
Madden's book *A Room of Her Own* (Clarkson Potter, 1997) is in its twelfth printing.

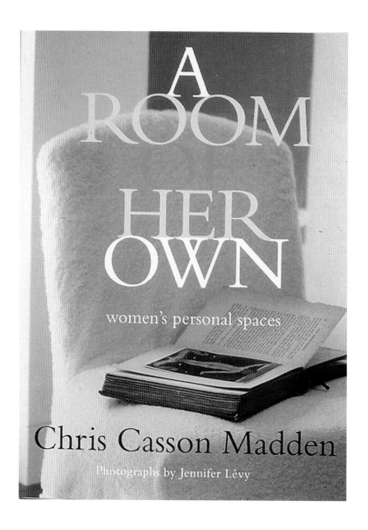

American Designers and the Showcase, (Stewart, Tabori and Chang, 1988), an immensely popular and beautifully illustrated book that featured rooms of designer showhouses across the United States. Fifteen books followed, including the bestselling *A Room of Her Own* (Clarkson Potter, 1997), and *Kitchens* (Clarkson Potter, 1993) among many others. "With my publishing background, books became a natural outlet for my creative energies. With my textile sciences and art history background, interior design was a logical direction for me," she notes.

Madden's message of "home as haven" became the foundation of her business. "I have been preaching it for two decades. Of course, after 9/11, home became everyone's haven, a place for comfort and sanctuary for all," she says. Her unique vision of home landed her roles as Oprah's first design correspondent, host of her own show on Home and Garden Television, and a syndicated newspaper column, *Interiors By Design.*

A landmark licensing deal with JCPenney followed, soon becoming the company's most successful home furnishings launch in its 102-year history. Madden created her collection based on her three decorating lifestyles—"Adventurous," "Romantic"

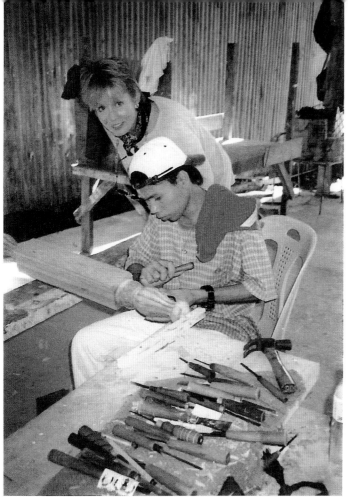

FIGURE 10.18
A hands-on approach: Madden
checks the finishes on her
first furniture collection being
handcrafted in Cebu, Philippines.

FIGURE 10.18
A hands-on approach: Madden
checks the finishes on her
first furniture collection being
handcrafted in Cebu, Philippines.

FIGURE 10.19
Embarkation Table is one of
Madden's most popular designs.

A LICENSING PRIMER

The first and most successful licensing deal can be traced to the World of Bob Timberlake who sold more than $1.4 billion (since the nineties) for Lexington Home Brands. Since this time, designers have put their names on everything from home fragrance room sprays to kitchen faucets.

The Beanstalk Group is a licensing consultancy agency representing a variety of licensors from celebrities and interior designers to museums. They recommend using an agency as "designers need to focus on what they really love—designing and product development." Like many agencies, they manage everything from strategic planning and market evaluation to licensee selection and royalty collection.

"Retailers are enjoying success with licensed products like never before. They are constantly looking for new and unique products that their competitors do not have and licensing products is one effective way of differentiating themselves," says President and CEO Michael Stone.

While the satisfaction of creating a line is important, making money is also a key factor for the designer. The royalty rate can become a major bargaining factor and is usually based on the percentage of net sales. Another consideration is minimum guaranteed royalties—the minimum amount that the licensee has to pay even if the products do not sell well. This is usually paid as an advance upon signing the license agreement.

Stone notes "Ultimately licensing is all about creating a lifestyle for a brand by extending the credibility and authenticity into diverse product categories. The result of a successful licensing program is the development a more holistic and all-encompassing brand experience for consumers—a lifestyle experience. As a result, lifestyle designers are ideal candidates for strategic licensing as their brands are already credible. They are a licensing dream!"

The Beanstalk Group is one of the leading licensing consultants in the industry.

---

and "Serene." She has since added the CM Hotel collection and a bestselling tabletop line to her already extensive furniture, bedding, rug, window, and accessory designs.

Madden notes, "The new trends in manufacturing have incredibly reduced time of design—from drawing table to market. The manufacturing process has accelerated so much with computer technology being able to deliver plans and sketches to factories around the world, samples being returned quickly, and product shipped on the shelves in a much shorter time frame!"

Madden also feels strongly that designers lending their names to products must resonate with the consumer to be successful. Establishing authority and credibility with lectures, television, books, and the rest of the package is an important component in building a successful brand. "I have the proven design authority that the customer knows they can trust and rely upon. I really feel that one of my greatest strengths is knowing what the customer wants, what she is ready for, and what excites her."

REFERENCES

Aaron, Susan. *Career Lessons from Celebrity Women: What You Can Learn from Madonna, Martha and Oprah.* Retrieved March 22, 2008 from website http://career-advice.monster. com/job-promotion/women/Career-Lessons-from-Celebrity-Women/ home.aspx.

Ingram, Cinde W. Licensing: The Product Has to Support the Name. (May 2007). *Home Accents Today.*

Michael, Evan. *Lesson #5: Build a Great Team.* Retrieved March 20, 2008 from website www.evanmichael. com.

Powell, Alvin. (March 22, 2001). *Stewart Shares Her Secrets:* Retrieved March 22, 2008 from the website www.news.harvard.edu/ gazette/2001/03.22/10-stewart.html.

Stewart, Martha. (2005). *The Martha Rules.* New York: Rodale Books.

The Luxury Market: Trying to Hit a Moving Target. (March 30, 2005). Retrieved March 25, 2008 from website http://knowledge.wharton.upenn. edu/article.cfm?articleid=1126.

Williams, Mary Elizabeth. (1999). *She's Martha and You're Not.* Retrieved March 22, 2008 from website www. salon.com.

11

Mr. McGuire: *"I want to say one word to you. Just one word."*
Benjamin: *"Yes, sir."*
Mr. McGuire: *"Are you listening?"*
Benjamin: *"Yes, I am."*
Mr. McGuire: *"Plastics."*
— *The Graduate* (Embassy Pictures, 1967)

The Specialty Designer

OVERVIEW OF THE PROFESSION

Benjamin stands alone at his celebratory graduation cocktail party, disconsolate and unsure of his future. His confusion escalates when a family friend approaches with one word of advice about his future . . . *"Plastics."*

The familiar event is actually a scene from the sixties film *The Graduate* (Embassy Pictures, 1967) and if Benjamin graduated with a design degree today, no doubt the advice would be "specialization."

In an increasingly competitive market, many interior design professionals are expanding the usual disciplines of residential and contract design, venturing into areas known as *"subspecialties."* For example, an interest in both residential and hospitality can develop into hotel design followed by boutique hotel interiors and a career is born. There are numerous opportunities available and it takes imagination to uncover the right fit. Identifying a potential demand, addressing a need for a product or service and targeting a market segment are also important elements of specialization.

Becoming a specialist has its own rewards and challenges. A greater knowledge and expertise are required

FIGURE 11.1
Resort hotel design is one of the most popular of the design subspecialties. Shown here is the dramatic lobby of the Hyatt Hotel in Aruba.

which often translates into increased schooling and certification. By focusing their unique talents on a particular niche, interior designers can enhance

the financial bottom line. And by becoming an expert in the field, professional recognition and increased business opportunities can result as well.

THE SPECIALTIES

Choosing a specialty is not easy, as an array of avenues are available depending upon your distinctive talent, level of expertise and above all, interest. Pay attention to economic and market trends and world events; increased wealth fueled the luxury design market which contributed to private airplane and yacht design, the increase in global warming spawned the green design movement, and the proverbial "graying of America" created new opportunities for elderly design.

The following represents a listing of the various specialties and subsequent subspecialties within the interior design field.

Contract Design

Contract design is one of the most lucrative, labor intensive, and popular of the interior design specialties. Also

FIGURE 11.2
A colorful and contemporary conference center in Dubai represents the new trend in corporate and hospitality design.

known as commercial design, the field focuses on the interior design of spaces used for corporations and businesses, hospitality, educational institutions, and governmental offices. The design process is quite extensive and involves planning, coordination, material specification, purchasing, and installation. Many of these areas are divided into subspecialties as well. (See Chapter 6: The Contract Designer for further information.)

Corporate Design

Corporate Campus Design

From the fifties modernist designs of General Mills in Minnesota to Microsoft's sprawling monolithic compound in Seattle, corporate campuses abound. Encompassing the total corporate environment from administration buildings to manufacturing facilities, the *corporate campus* design concept (think campus style business parks) must balance function and aesthetics, meeting the special needs of the company as well as its employees.

Corporate In-House Design

Designers oversee the various phases of the interior design process, specifying and implementing office and facility design for the company.

Corporate Office Design

From small businesses to large corporations, designers can provide an overall corporate image as well as improve employee productivity through the design of workstations and office interiors.

Facility Management

This area is responsible for the coordination of office expansions and moves and the design and maintenance of office interiors for hospitals, universities, and museums. For more information, check out the websites of the International Facility Management Association (www.ifma.org), World Workplace (www.worldworkplace.org), and Building Owners and Managers Association International (www.boma.org).

Funeral Home Design

This highly unique niche area includes the building, remodeling, and interior design of spaces for visitation, chapel, burial, family viewing, worship, and reception areas in an appropriate atmosphere.

Institutional Design

Institutional interior design involves the programming, planning, design, and management of spaces used by public and private organizations such as churches and religious organizations, federal and governmental offices and buildings, military bases, fire and police stations, embassies, libraries, museums, visitor centers, and recreational facilities. Child-care, libraries, museums, schools, colleges, and universities also fall into this area.

Health, Fitness Club, and Spa Design

This segment represents one of the hot growth service industries in the nation, as personal fitness remains an integral part of daily life in our society. The discipline applies the knowledge of color, state of the art technology, psychology, lighting, and function to everything from national fitness clubs to therapy and relaxation centers. The field also crosses over into residential, as bonus

FIGURE 11.3
Traditional
residential interiors
are adapted for
contract use in spa
at the Kiawah Island
resort in South
Carolina.

and guest rooms are being transformed into home gyms, spas, meditation, and yoga rooms.

Hospitality Design

The design of environments that meet the overall physical and leisure needs of the public such as restaurants, theaters, hotels, and country clubs comprise this extremely popular segment.

Hotel Design

Designers can specialize in one or more types of lodgings and accommodations from large chain hotels and motels to resorts and boutique style hotels as well as bed-and-breakfast homes. Spaces include not only guest rooms and suites but lobbies, large conference centers, auditoriums, spas and health club facilities, and restaurants as well. Many designers choose to further specialize in one area of the industry such as resort design. Incorporating the best of residential and commercial environments, this luxury niche varies from spa resorts to specialty theme and destination environments.

Country Club Design

Residential settings such as dining and guest rooms and the contract areas of sport facilities (golf, tennis, and swimming pools), lobbies, and banquet halls incorporate the design of a country club. A knowledge of architecture, indoor and outdoor landscaping is also a plus.

Restaurant Design

This area covers a wide variety of eating establishments ranging from fast food

FIGURE 11.4
Hotel design combines both residential and contract design disciplines. Shown here is a guest suite at South Carolina's Inn at Palmetto resort.

FIGURE 11.5
Pan Pacific ballroom.

franchises to upscale bistros, corporate and employee dining rooms to casino buffets. Designers can specialize in interior spaces and kitchen design as well as the product and furniture design of bars, seating, china, and linens. Kitchen design specialists are a hot commodity and consult independently or for equipment supply companies.

LEED: Leadership in Energy and Environmental Design

A LEED specialist consults with homeowners, home and commercial builders, schools, retailers, and architects on the standards for environmentally sustainable construction (also known as "green buildings"). Designers must be certified to practice in this area. For more information, see the U.S. Green Building Council's website www.usgbc.org.

Lighting Design

Professional lighting designers are well versed in the illumination of both interior and exterior environments, taking in account technical, functional, design, and energy-efficient criteria. Designers must be proficient in not only technique and application, but also keep up with the latest technologies. A working knowledge of physics, ergonomics, codes, and construction is also recommended. See the International Association of Lighting Designers www.iald.org for further advice.

Office Design

Businesses and corporations utilize specialty designers in this area, focusing on both public (conference rooms, lobbies, and bathrooms) and private areas (offices and workstations). The design of financial firms and law offices are two of the most popular areas in this sector.

Codes and construction, ergonomics, psychology, color, and lighting are a few of the requirements needed.

Ergonomic

Ergonomics is an engineering scientific discipline based on interactions among humans and elements of a system (such as tools, equipment, etc.) or more simply defined, how things are designed to make the body comfortable. The practice is most commonly used in office design to improve employee efficiency and enrich the quality of life for the elderly

Universal Design

Merging both the disciplines of barrier free and accessible design, universal design was developed for individuals with disabilities to increase the ease, use, and access of spaces as well as accommodate the safety and comfort of

FIGURE 11.8 Kitchen design remains one of the most popular of the design specialties.

all users. This area can include "aging in place" design for baby boomers that want to remain in their homes, creating spaces for wheelchairs, lowering counters and controls, user-friendly faucets, and other safety and utilitarian features.

Communications

Specialties in the field of communications with a focus on interior design are an interesting niche market for those with a flair for writing, consulting, marketing, promotion, and even performing. Some of the areas include:

Consultant

Designers with an expertise in a particular area offer their services as consultants to manufacturers, organizations, and businesses. This can include everything from advice on product evaluation, placement, and marketing to raising awareness for a local or national design organizations. Designers are hired on a retainer or project basis.

Headhunter

Interior design employment agencies concentrate on the recruitment of interior designers in this growing niche segment of the employment industry. Firms also serve as "matchmaker," connecting interested prospects (homeowners and businesses) with interior designers and architects.

Journalism

The proliferation of "shelter" and trade magazines, design books, and websites have created the need for creative and knowledgeable writers on a variety of design subjects. Interior designers may find themselves on the masthead of a magazine as a design editor or writing a weekly newspaper column.

On-Air Television Personality

The huge success of interior design and lifestyle television has spawned a new breed of stars as "on-air television personalities." Interior designers with the special ability to appear on camera and communicate effectively are discovering careers as hosts of television shows, teaching a talent or skill on "how-to" and lifestyle programs. Many successful designers branch out to production as well.

Public Relations

Showrooms, vendors, interior design firms, and other allied areas of the industry are now requiring the need of either an in-house or outside public relations firm for help in promoting their products.

This can include everything from magazine story placement and writing press releases to placing clients on television and radio appearances.

Public Speaker

Designers can enjoy lucrative fees lecturing and conducting seminars to students, consumers, and the design industry. Lecture outlets include corporate and interior design events, colleges, and cruise ships.

Spokesperson

Manufacturers, vendors, and retailers often hire interior designers (many with a high profile) to act as spokespersons, representing their product line through seminars, trade events, magazine, radio, and television promotion. Designers

secrets of a

Style Diva

A Get-Inspired Guide to Your Creative Side

STYLE JOURNAL

SUSIE COELHO

FIGURE 11.9
Home style guru Susie Coelho is an interior design personality with a line of products and furnishings, books, and a television show.

with excellent communication, speaking, and public relations skills can benefit in this area.

Education

Design Educator

Design education is a rapidly growing field across the country, making the demand for qualified instructors very high. Designers must not only be qualified as design professionals, but as teachers and instructors as many educational facilities will require some sort of teaching credentials. Opportunities include working full or part-time at a college, university, design or secondary school, or part-time in the studio doing critiques.

Design Psychology

Tapping into the psychological underpinnings of a client's psyche is a vitally important component to the interior design process. Design psychology is a newly emerging field inspired by the contemporary concept of the "home as a mirror of the owner." A variety of tools are used to gauge a client's taste, preferences and personality, and their emotional connection to the past which include color psychology, feng shui, and holistic design. An expertise in psychology and human behavior is naturally required.

Entertainment

This segment combines the use of interiors, lighting, sound, and other technologies for movies, television, videos, dramatic and musical theater, clubs, concerts, theme parks, and industrial projects. Some of the subspecialty areas include:

Amusement Design

Designers create both atmosphere and interior space for themed amusement parks, ranging from the design of amusement rides to movie set props for a haunted house attraction. Ergonomics, color, and space come into play and designers will find illustration, space planning, and computer skills also handy.

Aquarium Design

Aquariums are designed for homes, offices, retail, and restaurants and make this an interesting niche category. The practice involves not only the

FIGURE 11.10
Aquarium design is one of the more unique niche areas of interior design as seen at the Georgia Aquarium.

knowledge of aquatic life, but lighting, color, materials, and underwater environments as well.

Casino Design

From slot machine placement to creating an artificial daytime interior environment, casino design is one of the most comprehensive of the specialties. Psychology, color, codes, lighting, and commercial design experience are just a few of the many criteria for a successful practice in this exciting segment of the field.

Museum and Exhibit Design

The display and placement of museum artifacts and exhibits comprise this area. A background in art, art history, product display, and lighting is quite useful as the work can include everything from concept and research to curation, design, fabrication, and installation.

Special Events

Interior designers are often hired for large-scaled balls, weddings, and special party events for corporations, charitable organizations, and individuals to create highly imaginative, unique, and often over-the-top themed environments, tabletop and floral displays, and even invitations.

Stadium Design

This segment comprises the interior design of public and private spaces in stadiums, arenas, and other sporting venues such as kitchens and catering areas, hospitality suites, bathrooms, signage, press boxes, locker rooms, restaurants, and stores.

Health Care Design

Hospitals, clinics, hospice, surgical suites, and examination, emergency, and operating rooms are just a few of

FIGURE 11.11
Casino design is a rapidly expanding specialty, one that involves both psychological and technical theories of interior design as seen at the Wynn Las Vegas hotel resort.

the many health care environments that comprise this multi-faceted area of contract design. An extremely lucrative and continually burgeoning market, *Interior Design* magazine cites the top commercial design firms have seen a 50 percent increase in the design of medical interiors in the past year.

Designers must have a vast knowledge of all aspects of health care design as the technologies, standards, and requirements are extensive and continually changing. In addition to the basic principles of design, planning, safety codes, and material specification, designers will need excellent AutoCAD, presentation, and communication skills as well.

For those interested in the field, attend the annual symposium on Healthcare Design to learn more. In addition, see the website for the Center for Health Design (www.healthdesign.org)

for an overview of the profession as well as the American Academy of Healthcare Interior Designers (www.aahid.org).

Dental and Medical Office Design

This highly segmented area of the field requires both technical and medical knowledge, incorporating equipment functionality with patient comfort. Designers must understand all medical requirements of the field as color, space planning, storage, and file management are an integral part of the design process. The image of the practice is also an important design consideration.

Hospital Design

One of the most complex areas of health care is hospital design, an area so extensive that there are numerous subspecialties as a result (a maternity ward will have entirely different requirements than those for an emergency room). A

FIGURE 11.12
For the designer with an interest in history, culture, and display, museum and exhibit design is a natural. Shown here is the exhibition "If These Walls Could Talk" at the Biltmore Museum in Asheville, North Carolina.

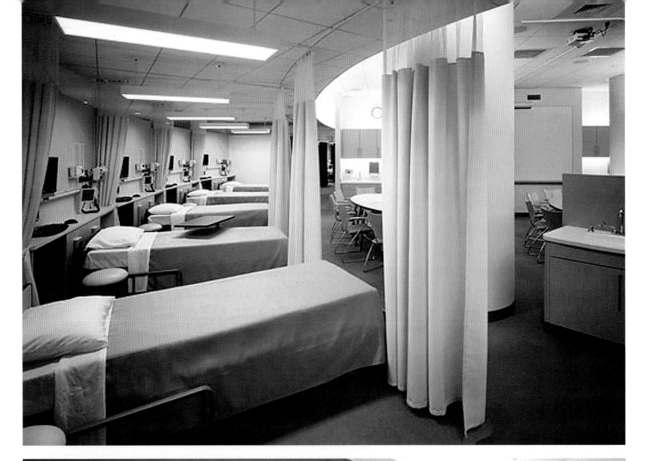

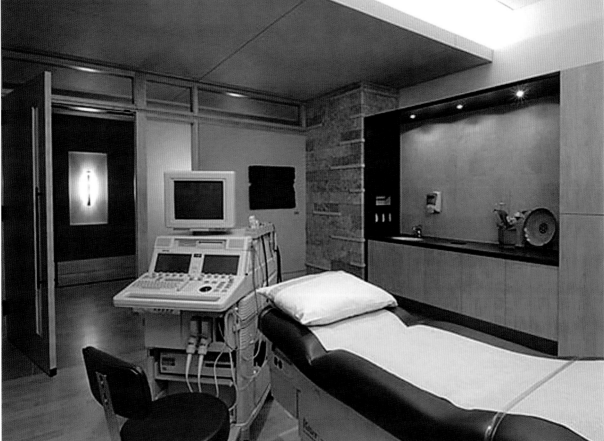

FIGURE 11.13
Hospital design is one of the most intensive and specialized areas of medical design. Shown here is the Seattle University College of Nursing.

FIGURE 11.14
Medical design represents one of the most popular contract areas. Shown here is the Swedish Medical Center.

hospital facility is composed of a wide variety of services ranging from patient functions and clinical laboratories to public cafeterias and administrative offices.

Medical Specialty Design

The emerging market of medical specialty design includes medical spas, wellness centers, cosmetic dentistry, plastic surgery centers, and other forms of treatment centers that integrate aesthetics with state of the art medical facilities.

Nursing Home Design

Incorporating both residential and contract disciplines, nursing home design must fit a variety of patient needs from long-term physical care to the emotional comforts of home. Special design challenges must be met and designers should have a working knowledge of ergonomics, psychology, elderly/geriatric, universal, and health care design.

Retirement Center/Assisted Living

With the number of Americans age sixty-five and older set to represent 20 percent of the population by the year 2030, design meeting the needs of the elderly will be paramount. This area includes the design of retirement centers, assisted living, nursing homes, and special requirements for those living at home. Designers will find classes in ergonomics, psychology, and universal and elderly design beneficial. (Note: This area is also known as elderly/geriatric design.)

Product Design

For the highly innovative and creative designer, product, furniture, and home furnishings design is a natural extension of the design practice. Designers can create and manufacture their own line or license their concepts for a company to produce and market. Ideas are often born out necessity as many a line was launched from a chair designed for a client. In addition, designers also specialize in product display, marketing, and sales. (See Chapter 9: The Product and Furniture Designer for more details.) The various lines can include:

- Art/Wall Decor
- Ceramic Tile
- China/Glass/Silver
- Fabric/Textiles/Trimmings
- Floor Coverings—hard surface, carpet/rug
- Furniture—casegoods and upholstery, casual/outdoor
- Garden Ornaments
- Hardware—drapery/cabinet
- Home Accessories
- Home Fragrance
- Lamps and Lighting
- Linens and Bedding
- Office Furniture and Accessories
- Wallpaper
- Window Treatments

Residential Specialty Design

One of the primary practices within the field, residential design focuses on the coordination, planning, specifying, renovation, and installation of the interior design of all types of private homes. Projects range from renovation and new construction to art consulting and historic preservation, spawning a variety of subspecialties within the field:

FIGURE 11.15
Vicente Wolf's line of home accessories for VW Home.

FIGURE 11.16
Interior designers
are branching out to
tabletop collections
as seen with Nina
Campbell's line of
"Perroquet" limoge
dessert plates.

FIGURE 11.17
Architect turned
lifestyle product
designer, Michael
Graves' faucet line
for Delta.

Apartment/Condominium/Co-Op Design

Designers work with builders, real estate developers, and architects on the public areas of these dwellings such as lobbies, offices, service rooms (laundry and mail), and exercise rooms.

Art Consultant

Highly knowledgeable designers are hired to advise, select, and search for suitable art for home and corporate environments. They must be familiar with art, art history, placement, and framing and either work independently or for art dealers or corporations.

Artist

Artists who specialize in murals and faux finishing techniques for walls and furniture are often required for residential and commercial interiors. A background in fine arts or tailored art classes in special finishes is preferable.

FIGURE 11.18
Mural designers are in popular demand for both residential and commercial projects. Seen here is Michael Graves designs for the interior of a Federal Reserve Bank in Houston, Texas.

FIGURE 11.19
California Closets was one of the first companies to specialize in storage planning and organization systems for the home and office.

Closet Design

One of the fastest rising specialties, there are design practices that specialize solely on storage and closet design for every room in the house (particularly the media room, bedroom, kitchen/pantry, home office, and garage). Jean Chené, General Manager of California Closets, notes other popular areas are hobby (gift wrapping, scrapbook, and

craftmaking), wine cellars, and children's offices/rooms. She also advises that space planning, design theory and application, and sales to be important assets for this growing field.

Color Consultant/Specialist

Color is not only one of the most important design elements that has a direct impact both visually and psychologically, it is also represents a hard decision for the consumer. Many designers specialize exclusively in the selection and coordination of colors for both home and commercial applications from paint choice to color scheme.

Feng Shui

Feng Shui is the contemporary design theory that focuses on the balance of the energy and flow of a space through the planning of internal furniture arrangements. With roots in ancient Chinese philosophy, it is said to have an effect on health, wealth, personal relationships, and good fortune.

Green Design/Sustainability

Also known as eco-design, this segment is concerned with protecting nature and improving the environment through design. Designers use materials that are eco-friendly and integrate green materials and systems into the building, remodeling, and manufacturing process.

Greenhouse Design

Greenhouses and conservatories are an increasingly popular addition to residential and contract interiors. The factors of climate and temperature control, materials, light, humidity, installation,

energy, and solar efficiency must be taken into consideration.

Historical Preservation

The goal of historic preservation is to preserve and restore history, keeping the original features, repair, and/or redesign with original style and skill of work in mind. Designers should have knowledge of architecture, preservation, historical design, and art history.

Home Interior Redesign

The basis of the redesign concept lies in working with the client's existing furnishings, accessories, and artwork through the art of rearranging the living space. Redesign has become a popular trend for homeowners on a budget.

FIGURE 11.20
The Zody Chair by Haworth is designed with both ergonomics and the environment in mind.

Home Office Design

With an increasing number of Americans choosing to work from home, home office design has become extremely popular as designers draw on both residential and contract office design disciplines. Designers are turning small guest rooms, kitchen pantries, and large bonus rooms into functioning office interiors, applying the same parameters for computers, task, and meeting areas sans the codes and standards.

Home Staging

Home staging represents one of the hot trends of the decade as many homeowners, real estate agents, and builders turn to home stagers to help sell their houses. Designers focus on universally appealing paint colors, furniture arrangement, and artwork to attract potential buyers. They must be able to work in a short period, have a storage center for stock or use merchandise on loan from vendors in lieu of free advertising or for a nominal rental fee.

In-House Designer

Staff designers are responsible for the coordination of interior design services in corporations, home offices of retail firms, catalogue companies, home improvement centers, health care, hospitality industries, architectural firms, and furniture stores.

Kitchen and Bath Design

One of the most popular of all the subspecialties, this area requires the renovation or new construction of high use spaces. Designers are often in high demand and certification and knowledge of space planning, codes, color, universal design, electrical, and plumbing systems and materials are crucial skill sets. Those interested in the field work independently, as a designer on site in a kitchen, bath or related materials showroom, or for builders and contractors. Many work in the sales of cabinets, faucets, and appliances as well. For more information, check out the National Kitchen and Bath Association website www.nkba.org.

Library Design

Designers consult on the design of home libraries from acquiring, storage, and display of books to specialized lighting and climate control.

Media Room Design

Home theater rooms involve the effective use of good interior design, acoustics, electrical engineering, technology and control systems, and video design. Designers must be knowledgeable in sound proofing, noise control, lighting, wiring, acoustics, theater design, and technology.

Model Home Design

Designers work with builders to decorate and furnish a sample interior, using design as a property enhancement technique. Furnishings are often borrowed from furniture vendors for free advertisement.

Nursery/Children Design

This area targets the design for nurseries, children and teen rooms, emphasizing comfort, learning, stimulation, development, and socialization using color and design.

FIGURES 11.21, 11.22
Bridging both the disciplines of interior design and architecture, interior architecture is a popular specialty. Shown here are the sleek contemporary lines of a media room and updated "pool room."

Outdoor Design

Outdoor spaces transformed into living areas for relaxation and entertaining have become a significant design trend in the past decade. From the design of the terrace and screened-in porch to the lanai and pool area, designers must have knowledge of outdoor furnishings, weather resistant materials, and accessories. They often team up with landscape designers and architects to further enhance the space.

Pet Design

With some 71 million homes in the United States having a dog(s) and/or cat(s), the need for designing homes that are fashionable and functional with our furry friends in mind has become a popular notion. Specialists are consulting not only on residential areas but hotels, day care centers, kennels, veterinary hospitals and offices as well.

Renovation

With real estate prices soaring, homeowners are looking to get the most out of their home through the renovation (also known as home makeover) of existing spaces. Designers with a working knowledge of construction, electrical and plumbing, kitchen and bath, and architecture are in popular demand.

Space Planning

Experts are needed to figure out how to best optimize the space on everything from a small bathroom to a 7,000 square foot house. Designers need to be adept at space and furniture arrangement; interior architecture; and kitchen, bath, and closet space requirements.

FIGURE 11.23 Careful space planning incorporates a home office and master bedroom.

Storage Design

With every square inch a vital commodity, storage can be very important. This area can encompass everything from closet and attic design for residential interiors to file and equipment storage for commercial offices.

Vacation Home Design

Often a luxury market, this niche includes the interior design of cabins, ski chalets, lake homes, beach houses, corporate condominiums, and villas. Many vacation homes are turnkey situations with designers specifying everything from soup to nuts.

Window Treatment Design

Whether residential or commercial, every interior has a window that requires some sort of treatment. Designers specialize solely on drapery and curtain treatments, shades, and soft and hard furnishings (curtains and valences, blind and shades, shutters and screens).

Retail and Wholesale

Both retail and wholesale design involves the planning of boutiques, malls, department stores, outlets, showrooms, food retailing centers, service businesses, specialty retailers, temporary trade show exhibits, and wholesale showrooms. Designers also venture into owning their own retail or wholesale store, start a catalogue or work as a buyer. The following represents the subspecialties:

Catalogue

This includes everything from the nuts and bolts of owning an online or mail order catalogue to interior design and product consultant, merchandise buyer, layout designer, display designer, and writer.

Display

Designers who are well versed in the art of display can specialize in a variety of areas from retail, wholesale, trade show, specialty shops and museum exhibits. Many designers specialize in the area of tabletop display for china showrooms, department stores, restaurants, retail shops, and catalogues.

Furniture Designer

Talented furniture designers develop and design product and furniture lines for furniture manufacturers. Depending upon the size of the company, they can also be involved in sales, marketing, and showroom and gallery display.

Sales and Marketing

Designers work as a manufacturer's representative and/or sales representative

FIGURE 11.24 Interior designer turned furniture designer Thomas O'Brien has a collection for Hickory Chair. Seen here is the Bailey Chest.

and show product lines across a particular territory. They provide product and home furnishings information to interior designers, architects, and furniture stores. They need communication and organizational skills as the ability to present and sell is a must.

(See Chapter 14: The Designer in Hollywood for further description.)

Showroom: "To the Trade Only"

Manufacturers, vendors, furniture, fabric, and lighting showrooms make up this area. Jobs can range from sample librarian, salesperson, marketing, and promotion display designer to field sales representative and owner.

Set Decoration and Production Design

Known as the interior designer's glamorous counterpart, set decorators design and decorate finished sets for film, tele-vision, commercials, and theatre, turning a blank soundstage or space into a believable environment for the audience. "Dressing the set" includes the selection and installation of fabric, furniture, drapery, accessories, and the appropriate props.

Technical

This area includes the technical skills used in the design and presentation of interior and exterior spaces, products and furniture.

CAD and Drafting Specialist

Computer-aided design (CAD) (also known as computer-aided drafting) involves the use of computer technology to design and draft all types of products and interior and exterior structures.

FIGURE 11.25
Set decoration is an important element of the production design of films, television, theater, and commercials. Shown here on set is the cast of ABC Television's drama *Brothers and Sisters.*

Rendering

Designers with artistic talents can specialize in the design of renderings, a vital part of the overall design process. These artists are often hired by design firms to complete the visual presentation to the client.

Transportation

Popular forms of transportation utilize the need for interior designed spaces such as trains, buses, and motor homes as well as luxury market areas of private yachts and airplanes. Some of the sub-specialties include:

Airplane Design

From large commercial aircraft to small private passenger planes, many designers find this luxury market to be quite lucrative. Ergonomics, codes and safety standards and aviation technology are just a few of the many areas of expertise required for this unique field. The work might include refurbishing an interior, choosing colors, fabrics and leathers for cabin seats with lumbar supports, installing electric window shades or creating a multi-functioning airborne office.

FIGURE 11.26
Renderings are extremely useful in helping a client to visualize a project. Shown here are the designs for the Bejing Summer Palace resort.

Cruise Ships

Elegant staterooms, private small
cabins, meeting spaces, exercise rooms,
auditoriums, and lounges are just a few
of the spaces that integrate many of the
interior design specialties.

Houseboat Design

Whether it's a second home or a commercial one, houseboat design is another
unique area in the transportation field.
Virtually a structure on water, houseboats require a tremendous amount of

technology and safety requirements along with custom furnishings, woodwork, and the use of weather resistant materials.

Yacht Design

This area represents another luxury boat market, one that involves the technological knowledge of boating, use of materials and craftsmanship.

There are numerous specialties, sub-specialties and even further niche areas in the field of interior design. For one of the more comprehensive lists available, please refer to author Mary Knackstedt's book *The Interior Design Business Book* (Wiley, 2005) and see Chapter 1: The Domicile of Design.

REFERENCES

American Society of Interior Design (2007). About Interior Design. Retrieved on January 26, 2008 from www.asid.org.

Croix, Wendy. (June 30, 2006). Universal Design: Home Interior Design Jobs With Heart. *Interior Design School Review.* Retrieved January 10, 2007 from www.interior designschoolreview.com.

_____. Interior Design Careers: Healthcare Design. *Interior Design School Review.* Retrieved September 23, 2007 from www.interior designschoolreview.com.

_____. Designing Interiors: Careers in Facilities Management. *Interior Design School Review.* Retrieved September 12, 2007 from www. interiordesignschoolreview.com.

Graf, Stefan. *Importance of Using a Lighting Designer.* International Association of Lighting Designers. Retrieved January 27, 2008 from www. iald.org/design/importance.asp.

Johnson, Kathy A. Historical Preservation and Interior Design. *Interior Design School Review.* Retrieved January 26, 2008 from www.interior designschoolreview.com.

_____. Home Interior Redesign Growing in Popularity. *Interior Design School Review.* Retrieved January 26, 2008 from www.interior designschoolreview.com.

Marsa, Linda. (March 15, 2007). Design Psychologists Analyze Your Interior Psyche. *Los Angles Times.* Retrieved November 22, 2007 from www. latimes.com.

McIntyre, Kate. Home Staging: Interior Design on a Deadline. *Interior Design School Review.* Retrieved January 26, 2008 from www.interiordesign school.com.

Naversen, Nate. *Help! I Want to Be a Theme Park Designer. What Do I Do Now? 13 Guidelines For Your Success.* Retrieved January 27, 2008 from www.themedattraction.com/design. htm.

Zimmer, Robert. (February 13, 2006). Balancing Mind, Body and Spirit/ Why The Current Spa Explosion Is Still At The Tip Of The Iceberg. Retrieved January 13, 2008 from www.hospitalitynet.org.

PART 4

The Designer in the Media

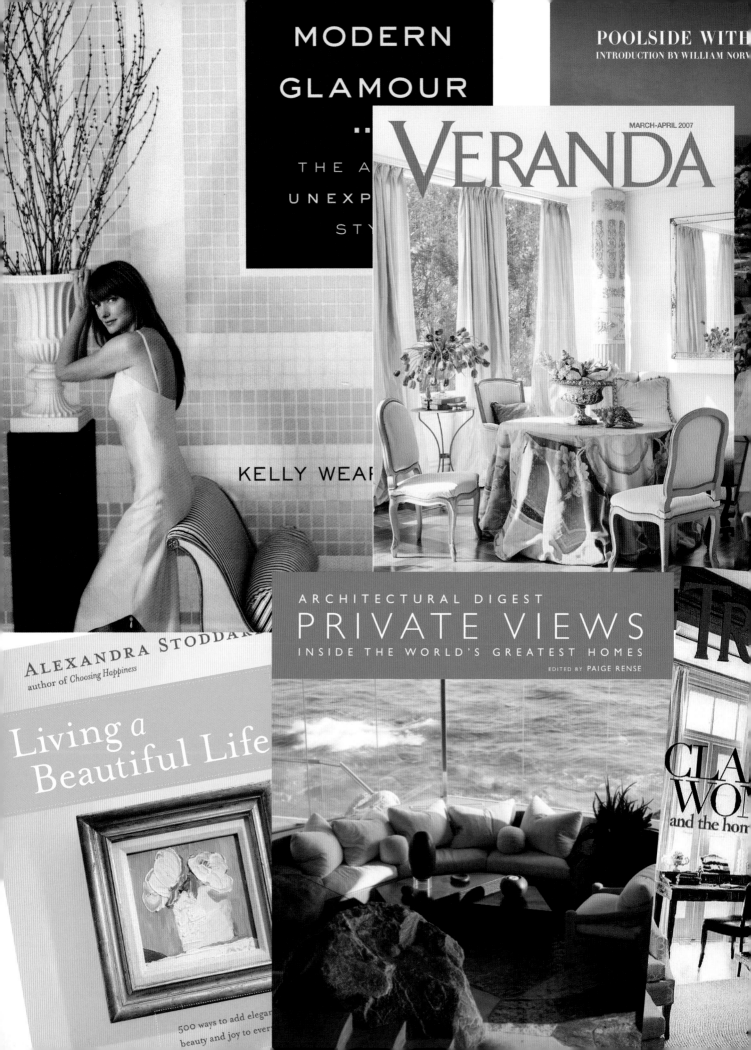

MODERN
GLAMOUR

THE A...
UNEXP...
STY...

KELLY WEAR...

POOLSIDE WITH
INTRODUCTION BY WILLIAM NORW...

MARCH–APRIL 2007

VERANDA

ARCHITECTURAL DIGEST
PRIVATE VIEWS
INSIDE THE WORLD'S GREATEST HOMES
EDITED BY PAIGE RENSE

ALEXANDRA STODDAR...
author of *Choosing Happiness*

Living a
Beautiful Life

500 ways to add elegan...
beauty and joy to ever...

TR

CLA
WO
and the hom...

"Writing has laws of perspective, of light and shade, just as painting does, or music. If you are born knowing them, fine. If not, learn them. Then rearrange the rules to suit yourself."
— TRUMAN CAPOTE, NOVELIST

The Designer in Print

OVERVIEW OF THE PROFESSION

The selections are staggering and the array of assorted publications offers something for every taste and interest. Glossy pictorials of luxury homes and exotic locations grace the pages of one magazine while another dispenses practical decorating tips for the apartment dweller. From *Country Living* to *Dwell* magazines to vanity designer tomes and style books of every category, shelter publications are alive and well.

To date, there are 195 magazines (regional and national) and book titles too numerous to count, all devoted to the beautification of the home. According to the National Directory of Magazines, the number of shelter magazines increased by 57 percent between 2002 and 2007, with over 13,653 pages of editorial content covering every type of living space. The term "shelter" was designated by the publishing trade to segment magazines that cover lifestyle topics—home, design, furnishings, and garden—of virtually every type of dwelling. While many of the glossies have been around for the past century (*House and Garden* just closed its doors after 106 years), they became increasingly popular during the advent of the "cocooning" trend as homeowners began to spend more time

FIGURE 12.1
A laptop computer
is the writer's best
friend.

at home. Increasing fortunes meant a rise in homeownership that translated into a thirst for knowledge and the need for design direction. Interior decoration became the topic du jour as home furnishings and fashion go hand in hand on the style horizon.

Like its monthly cousin, the ubiquitous coffee table book became a fashionable art form and a bible of design style. Perhaps aptly named as an ornament for the coffee table (legend has it the genre was to serve as a conversation starter), luxurious oversize books of heavy stock paper represent a visual luxury. And at $35.00 and up, they are an expensive treat as well. Visual works of art, these "look books" provide the perfect vehicle for a variety of subjects on interior design.

While these publications provide design inspiration, education and entertainment, as well as a vital list of resources, they signify another excellent career path for the designer who wants to expand their creativity. Aspiring journalists and those with a gift for words can put pen to paper for trade and consumer magazines, or write or edit books, a newspaper feature, or column.

THE PROCESS

A career in design journalism can venture down several avenues. For the interior designer who wants to supplement their income and/or increase their stature in the industry, writing books, magazine articles, and/or a newspaper column is a wonderful career move. The designer can apply an area of expertise to a new book project of timely interest, or invent a new approach.

Author Suzanne Slesin took a simple concept—style—and applied it to a

FIGURE 12.2
Traditional Home's annual classic women issue features women who give back and their homes.

FIGURE 12.3
Kelly Wearstler's best-selling book *Domicilium Decoratus* (Collins Design, 2006) showcases her family's home.

series of lifestyle books incorporating design, travel, and food from everything to *Caribbean Style* (Thames and Hudson, 2002) and *Greek Style* (Thames and Hudson, 1987) to *French Style* (Clarkson Potter, 1982) and many other countries.

Authors Kim Johnson Gross and Jeff Stone made a cottage industry out of the *Chic Simple* concept with a series of books on the home, paint, storage, and bed linens.

The subject of decoration in the home took on a conversational tone with the success of writers such as interior designers Alexandra Stoddard (author of twenty-five books which center around the home and well-being) and Bunny Williams (*An Affair With a House*, Stewart, Tabori and Chang, 2005). Stoddard studied under Eleanor McMillen Brown, founder of the legendary New York design firm McMillen, Inc. as a residential designer. Calling herself a "self acclaimed contemporary philosopher," she studies Aristotle everyday and was one of the first to apply philosophy and psychology to the home. "I had all these high-end clients who spent millions of dollars and they were just setting up their rooms like a still life and not living in them. I was intuitively fascinated with the meaning of life and what makes people do what they do," Stoddard notes.

Freelancing for shelter magazines is another viable option. A designer establishes relationships with editors and submits article ideas for consideration.

Story ideas can run the gamut and generally include features on residential and contract installations, interior design tips, how-to projects, profiles of notables in the industry, homeowners

FIGURE 12.4
Interior decorator and lifestyle author Alexandra Stoddard.

and celebrities, as well as lifestyle stories on antiquing, cooking, entertaining, travel, and gardening. Both magazines and books are an excellent platform for the designer to promote their business and educate the public.

For a designer seeking a more permanent career move, working at a magazine, newspaper, or publishing house in an editorial capacity is another career option.

Positions on the other side of the desk include working with writers, cultivating projects, and in many cases,

ALEXANDRA STODDARD
author of *Choosing Happiness*

Living *a* Beautiful Life

500 ways to add elegance, order,
beauty and joy to every day of your life

FIGURE 12.5
Living A Beautiful Life (Collins Design, 1988) is one of a series of twenty-five books by Stoddard.

MARCH–APRIL 2007

VERANDA

FIGURE 12.6
Veranda magazine went from a regional to one of the most successful shelter magazines to date.

writing. Interior designers should naturally seek publishing houses with lifestyle and design lists, shelter magazines, or the lifestyle section of the newspaper.

The Bureau of Labor statistics reports that the "Employment of writers and editors is expected to grow 10 percent, or about as fast as the average for all occupations, from 2006 to 2016. Employment of salaried writers and editors is expected to increase as demand grows for web-based publications." Writers can also look to the Internet as another avenue of communication, writing for online magazines, blogging, or technical writing. As with all types of businesses, market niche is the name of the game and print magazines are looking to reach readers via cyberspace with Internet-only content.

The home furnishings industry is relying increasingly on public rela-

tions, marketing, and special events to promote their products and reach new customers and writing plays a pivotal role. Designers with a flair for writing, business, and promotion are finding second careers working for independent public relations firms or on staff with a manufacturer, firm, or showroom.

THE PREPARATION

A mastery of the English language is not enough for a career in writing. Those who wish to move into this arena will need the following skill sets.

Requirements and Skills Needed

Communication Skills

Naturally, the ability to write and communicate is imperative. Writers must be able to creatively express and interpret ideas and organize thoughts and images. They should know their reader and market and write with a great deal of vision. For the editor and publicist, communication skills will be useful when dealing with authors and agents and vice versa for the writer. Research is also another important tool.

Time and Organization Skills

For the procrastinator, this can be a difficult profession as this is a business that depends upon meeting deadlines. Planning and organization can make or break a project. The ability to organize and structure material in a cohesive fashion is essential. A public relations campaign requires organizing people, places, and events in a timely manner.

FIGURE 12.7
Good communication skills are a necessity for an interior designer.

Technological Skills

Computer skills such as the use of Adobe Photoshop, InDesign, and Word programs are extremely important if not mandatory.

Business Skills

For the editor and publicist, negotiation is an important asset as this skill is utilized for everything from negotiating contracts to editorial content. Both professions will involve business expertise in dealing with the media or publishing budgets, marketing plans, and special events.

Education and Training

A bachelor of arts degree in journalism is generally required for a career in writing. For specialization in the area of design and architecture, a degree in interior design is strongly suggested. For a career in public relations, a bachelor's degree in communications is advised.

Creative writing classes, community newspapers and Internet blogs provide practical writing experience. Photography and digital imaging classes are relevant as well as a background in web design and computer graphics.

Design Curriculum

The curriculum for the journalism career consists of classes in communications, electronic and print journalism, research, reporting, and copywriting. Media law and ethics in journalism are also useful. Classes tailored to specific interests can include magazine writing and editing, feature and news writing, and writing for television. Public relations, public speaking, photography, and photojournalism are also excellent courses.

PROFESSIONAL ASSOCIATIONS

Design journalists can join the American Society of Journalists and Authors (ASJA), American Society of Magazine Editors (ASME), American Society of Newspaper Editors (ASNE), Society of Professional Journalists (SPJ), and the Association for Women in Communications, (AWC). Public relations specialists can become a member of the Public Relations Society of America (PRSA).

THE PATH

Publishing is widely considered an "apprenticeship industry," which translates to on the job training for most positions. It is also an industry that allows the opportunity to move back and forth between departments depending upon the level of interest and expertise.

Book Publishing

The following is a list of the types of positions available within the structure of a publishing house:

Internship/Editorial Assistant>Associate Editor>Editor>Senior Editor>Executive Editor (this position is not in every hierarchy)>Editorial Director or Editor-in-Chief (depending on the company)>Publisher

Internships

This is the perfect way to experience the inner-workings of the publishing industry. Some positions are paid or may offer college credit and provide invaluable knowledge and a much-needed foot in the door for a permanent job.

Many editors got their start as freelancers as well.

Editorial Assistant

This position covers a wide range of administrative duties in addition to working on editorial projects. Assistants may read and evaluate editorial submissions and write summary reports.

Editor/Senior Editor/Executive Editor

As one of the major positions within a publishing house, this job is involved in the acquisition of manuscripts and proposals and subsequent development of books. They will also develop and maintain relationships with authors, write copy for dust jackets, book catalogues, marketing materials, and coordinate publication schedules through completion. Participation in editorial, creative (art and design), production, sales and marketing meetings is also an important aspect of the job.

Editorial Director

The director oversees the entire editorial group and sets and implements the publishing program. They identify and develop new concepts, recruit new authors, and negotiate contract and subsidiary rights for domestic and international markets. Overseeing budgets along with the hiring and supervising of staff are also important duties.

Publisher

The publisher is responsible for the entire life cycle of a title from acquisition to production. They approve all titles and budgets and are responsible for the overall vision and initiatives of the company.

Magazines

Positions in magazine publishing are very similar to those in book publishing.

Entry-level positions are obtained via internship or hired at the assistant level.

Editorial assistants handle a multitude of activities, from tracking down a resource, assisting on a photo shoot to writing and editing material for trade (industry) and consumer magazines. An editor's responsibilities vary with the employer and type and level of editorial position held. Editors and publishers may assign topics to staff writers or review proposals from freelance writers.

"When I started it was really very simple," says Stephen Drucker, editor-in-chief of *House Beautiful*. "You started as an editorial assistant. You hoped your boss left, retired, or died and you stayed, stayed, and stayed, and the last person standing with luck got to be the editor-in-chief in their forties or fifties. It was really a very linear career path. It was about digging in, and one person rose to the top," he says.

Today's magazine environment is somewhat different as staffs have downsized from what they were decades ago. "It used to be that every assistant had an assistant, and jobs were incredibly specialized, and you started out writing one caption an issue, if you were lucky," explains Drucker. As staff size diminishes, look for assistants, editors and even stylists to do double duty.

Editors on a shelter publication are very segmented, depending upon the editorial focus. It is not unusual to have an editor for each department—design, garden, style, fine arts, travel, food, lifestyle, architecture, and arts and antiques.

ARCHITECTURAL DIGEST
PRIVATE VIEWS
INSIDE THE WORLD'S GREATEST HOMES

EDITED BY PAIGE RENSE

The editor-in-chief (EIC) is responsible for editorial content and the look of the magazine, often setting the aesthetic tone as Lisa Newsom, editor-in-chief of *Veranda* explains, "My taste is a good indicator of what our reader will appreciate." This position works closely with the art director on design, placement, and layout and the managing editor who deals with budgets, deadlines, and contracts.

Planning for an issue typically begins three month's prior to hitting the newsstands. Editors plan throughout the year, adhering to an editorial calendar and adding trends, special features and stories as they arise. Monthly meetings, photo shoots, writing, and editing feature stories, attending home furnishing markets and various promotional activities representing the magazine are all in a day's work.

FIGURE 12.9
There are a variety of opportunities for designers who can write.

As with book houses, the national shelter magazines are primarily located in New York, Los Angeles, and a fair number in Des Moines, Iowa with Meredith Publishing (*Better Homes and Gardens*, *Traditional Home* and *Renovation Style* are a few of their many titles). "At a national magazine you have the advantage of being able to recruit from other publications, even for the entry-level jobs," explains Drucker. "Very often we'll recruit from regional magazines, where we've seen people that show real talent. Or we'll recruit people from interior design offices, people looking to make a career switch. They started off as interior designers but decided they don't like being designers, although they do love the industry."

Newspapers

Writers with an interest for home and garden can work on local, national, and trade newspapers as a reporter, writer, correspondent, or editor. The industry is facing an evolution at the moment (primarily because of the Internet) but good writers are always in demand. Interior designers will be primarily marketable for the lifestyle section. (The nation's top newspapers—*Los Angeles Times*, *New York Times*, *Washington Post*, *Chicago Tribune*, and the *Miami Herald* have some of the most prominent coverage in this area.)

Major newspapers and newsmagazines have several types of editors on staff with a variety of duties. The executive editor will oversee assistant editors and have the last word on what stories will make the pages. Assistant editors have responsibility for particular subjects, such as home, garden, food, and general lifestyle. Smaller weekly newspapers usually hire a single editor to handle everything from writing copy to planning budgets.

Entry-level jobs are at the assistant level and many start as copy editors, reviewing text for grammatical errors, spelling, and fact checking.

Newspaper editors like to see experience in a candidate. Former newspaper features writer, *Southern Accents* magazine editor, and book author of *Urban Country Style* (Gibbs Smith, 2006), Elizabeth Betts Hickman advises designers to focus on learning good writing techniques and building a book of "clips" (i.e. writing samples). "While in college, write for the (student) paper to get some basic clips, anything lifestyle or personal profile-wise, and then try to get an internship at a newspaper or magazine; almost every magazine, from the majors to city magazines and regionals (Atlanta, Texas Monthly, etc.) hire interns, paid and/or not paid," she details, "Write as much for publication as possible! Find the story . . . the student artist who's making a product they want to sell at High Point, pitch it to the student paper, follow them there and do your story. Meet all the PR people along the way and have a good system of keeping up with contacts."

Large newspapers will want to see some experience at a smaller paper or magazine so either get experience or arrive with an impressive portfolio of articles. "Someone with a design background would do well to try to at least do an internship with a magazine in order to gain contacts and experience with photo styling; even the person doing only the filing and assisting gets

to see great photography and hear why editors chose what they did, and that kind of insider info is invaluable," details Hickman. "It will also give you the opportunity to know a lot of industry insiders, from shop owners to influential consumers, architects, and designers."

Unlike magazines, newspapers are for the general writer as opposed to a specialist and best to keep in mind that you are a journalist first, a design journalist second. As a result, writers might end up covering a local human-interest story in addition to the latest trends in local landscape design. Hickman advises designers "probably won't be hired unless they have an interest in the broad topic of design, from commercial construction to residential homes, historic buildings to garden design."

Freelance Writer

Writers with determination, drive and skill freelance for publishing houses, magazines, newspaper and the Internet. They become book authors, contributing editors and writers, and freelance newspaper columnists. The Internet also provides another outlet for the freelance writer, penning copy for websites, providing editorial content for online magazines or writing a blog.

It is important to build a reputation of talent and reliability to meet deadlines.

Experience will lead to long-term projects and often staff positions. For many designers, being a design journalist can provide freedom to work on other aspects of their business such as designing homes or developing a line of products.

URBAN
COUNTRY
STYLE

ELIZABETH BETTS HICKMAN and NANCY GENT

FIGURE 12.10
Elizabeth Betts Hickman is a newspaper, magazine, and book author (*Urban Country Style*, Gibbs Smith, 2007) and former newspaper and magazine editor.

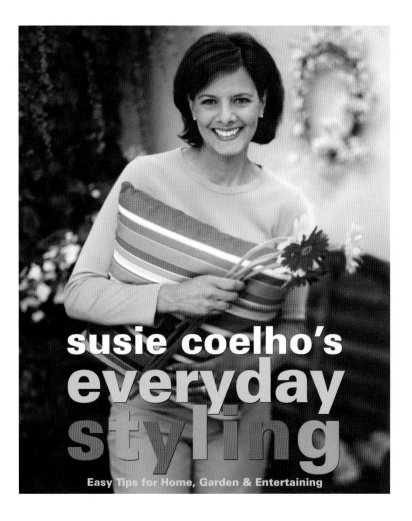

susie coelho's
everyday
styling
Easy Tips for Home, Garden & Entertaining

FIGURE 12.11
Lifestyle author
Susie Coelho
represents a new
breed of illustrated
book author.

(Note: Jobs with major book publishers, magazines and public relations firms are concentrated in New York, Chicago, Los Angeles, Boston, Philadelphia, and San Francisco.)

Public Relations

From a new product introduction to a residential interior design project, promotion and marketing play a viable part of business.

Public relations experts promote and publicize a product, service, or individual using a targeted campaign. The modus operandi includes writing press releases and press kits, arranging media appearances, and disseminating information to a variety of media outlets (broadcast and print). Press conferences, product launches, special events, media seminars, and working with advertising and marketing are common activities.

Public relations specialists (often known as publicists, managers, or directors) can work directly for the client or with an agency that specializes in home furnishings clients. They can start as interns or assistants and many come from newspapers or the promotional department of a magazine.

A former west coast editor of *House and Garden*, Karen Figilis started her own public relations and marketing firm, specializing in luxury lifestyle and

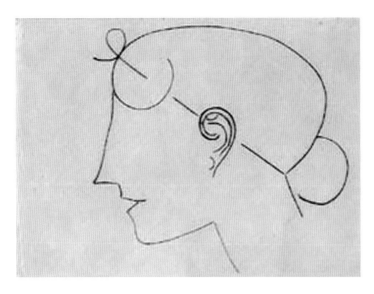

home furnishings clients such as Nancy Corzine, William Haines Designs, and Houles trims. "The whole industry is changing and we are seeing a seismic shift in the way people buy. We will continue to see how the design centers are challenged to bring in new customers, " she notes. Public relations and targeted marketing will play an important role in bridging the product and showroom with the interior designer and the ultimate end-user, the client.

THE PAY

According to the U.S. Bureau of Labor Statistics, the median annual earnings for editors' salaries ranged anywhere from $27,340 to $87,400 with the media annual earnings at $59,090.

Book Publishing: Publishing salaries are notoriously low and the profession is indeed a labor of love. According the *Publisher's Weekly 2007 Salary Survey*, salaries for entry-level positions range from $26–32,000. Editor positions generally run $55,000 to $65,000.

Senior and executive editors around $71,000 plus and editorial directors $85,000 plus and based on factors of experience, geography and the size of the publishing house.

Magazines: Editorial Assistants can expect to make $28,000 to $34,000 and upwards as a starting salary. Salary levels for editors are across the board. Editors pull down salaries from $51,000 to $64,000 while managing editors range from $54,446 to $62,094, executive editors earn $64,878 to $88,249, and editorial directors $77,637 to $92,916 (those with twenty years experience can warrant upwards of $185,000).

For high-profile national magazine editors, salaries are predominantly higher.

Editors-in-chief positions at industry giants Conde Nast and Hearst reportedly earn $300,000 to $400,000 plus bonuses, while Hachette Filipacchi and Rodale pay somewhat less at $175,000 to $200,000.

Newspapers: Entry-level positions range $30,000 to $35,000 and editors $43,000 to $66,000.

Freelance Writing: Magazine writers are paid by the article which varies widely depending upon the publication. Book writers receive an advance and royalties; financial success depends upon the book and many will supplement with speaking engagements (fees start at $1,000 and upwards depending upon notoriety), consulting work, and a line of ancillary products.

Public Relations: These salaries vary from in-house to agency. The average specialist salary runs $40,000 to $97,000 while assistants start from $28,000 to $53,000.

THE PROFILES

*"I fell in love with illustrated books—it
was the perfect marriage between my
skill with words and strong visual
instincts."*

—ANDREA DANESE

Ask any editor why they choose a career
in publishing and you will discover a
major love affair with books. Such is the
case of Andrea Danese, senior editor of
Harry N. Abrams, a prestigious publisher of beautifully illustrated high-
quality books. "I went into publishing
for the love of it, not the salary, and I
think that is the best approach," she says.

The Manhattan-based editor's career
took the more traditional route. Upon
the suggestion of her college English
professor, Danese obtained a postgradu-
ate program at the University of Denver
Publishing Institute, which proved to be
an invaluable experience. Work soon followed, first as an assistant to a small book
packager and next as an editorial assistant
at Stewart, Tabori and Chang, a small
book publisher known for their lifestyle
and design book titles. Eighteen years
later, she finds herself at the oldest illustrated book publisher in the United States.

The illustrated book market has
undergone an evolution, enjoying a
heyday in the nineties where a variety of
stunning volumes found their way from
bookstore shelves to coffee tables across
the country (hence the name coffee
table book).

"Today, it is much more brand
driven, commercially driven, bottom

line-oriented," Danese explains, "I'd say
the market is still alive, but harder to
find.

Knowing trends and diversification is crucial for survival these days."
She also notes they partner with major
luxury corporations such as Tiffany &
Company and *Architectural Digest* to
publish their books.

In terms of interior design and lifestyle titles, she is drawn to books that
are attached to a successful individual,
designer, brand or corporation. "If it's
an individual, it's best if they have a
successful television show, column in
a newspaper or magazine, or a shop or
chain of stores (or products that can
help promote and sell the book)," she
details. "This is what we call a platform.
We would also consider a familiar,
well-published topic as long as it offers a
new, innovative view and/or a very cool,
interesting package." *Project Runway* star
and fashion chair of Parson's School of
Design, Tim Gunn is an example of
their author with a platform.

For those interested in a publishing
career, Danese recommends "any one
of the publishing programs offered at
universities around the country, such as
Stanford, Radcliffe, or New York University." She advises students to peruse
books and magazines to obtain an idea
of their likes and dislikes that can help
determine what type of publishing they
would be interested in. Nonfiction illustrated is a popular area for those who
want to tie in their design interests as
the category will include architecture,
house and garden, and how-to books.
She also recommends freelancing as a
way to get a foot in the door. "I started
out at Abrams as a freelance editor for

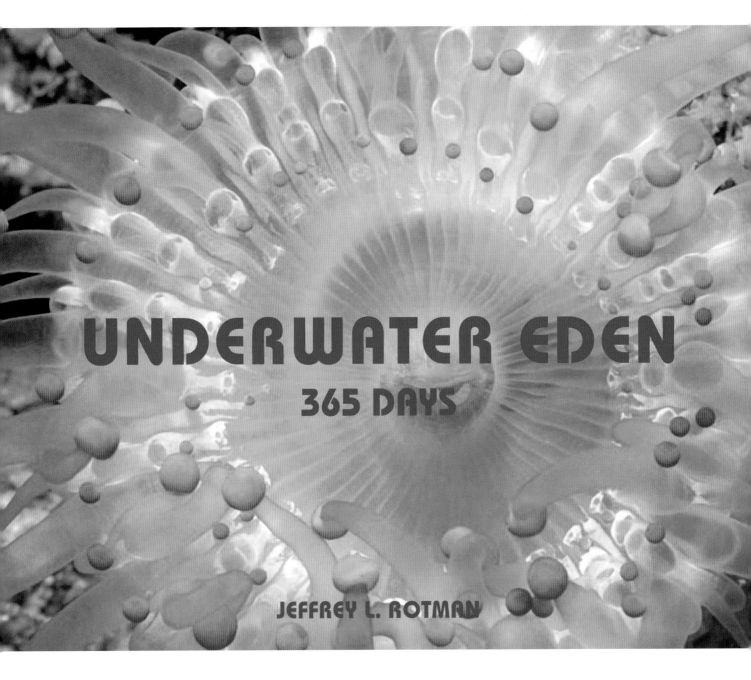

UNDERWATER EDEN

365 DAYS

JEFFREY L. ROTMAN

about a year before I became a full-time staff member," she explains.

While most of the editors at Abrams do not have specific design backgrounds, Danese notes, "Those of us who have stayed in illustrated book publishing have a very strong interest in the visual arts, whether the interest lies in graffiti art, Richard Avedon, (interior designer) Bunny Williams or the latest architect's work." In terms of hiring, "We look for someone who demonstrates a general interest in the visual arts in editorial type of work (editing, copyediting, proofreading; project management of a museum catalogue or any visual publication)" as well as those with backgrounds in architecture, popular culture, and art photography.

FIGURE 12.14
Poolside with Slim Aarons (Abrams Books, 2007).

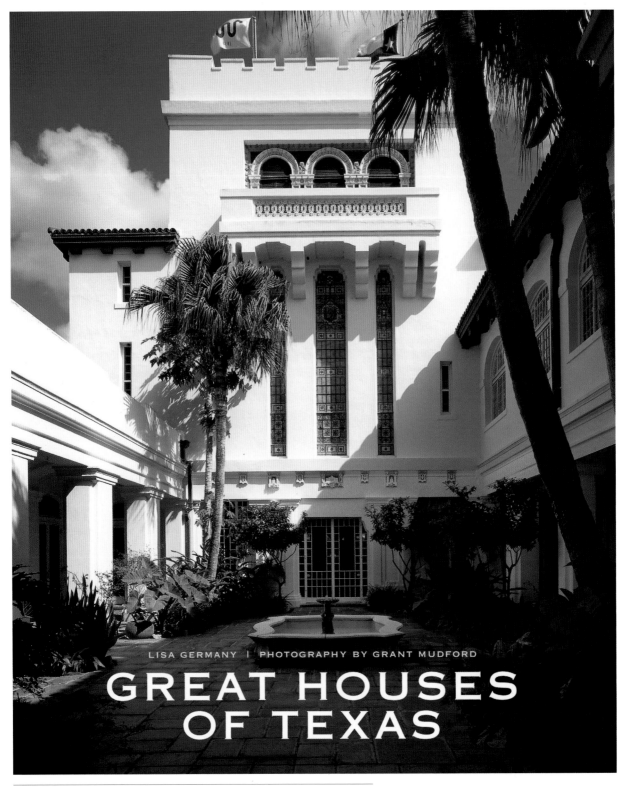

LISA GERMANY | PHOTOGRAPHY BY GRANT MUDFORD

GREAT HOUSES
OF TEXAS

FIGURE 12.15
Great Houses of Texas (Abrams Books, 2008) shows the diversity of interior design titles.

A BOOK EDITOR'S TO-DO LIST

This represents a week in the life of Andrea Danese, a senior editor of illustrated books at Harry N. Abrams:

1. Work on the development of a brand new project
2. Check the proofs of a book (or two or three!)
3. Attend weekly editorial meeting
4. Attend weekly publishing board meeting to review and approve new projects
5. Research writer to possibly hire to write preface for new book
6. Line edit a 60,000 word manuscript
7. Write jacket flap copy
8. Select and edit 200 photos from a collection of 800 for new book (which was whittled down from a treasure trove in the thousands!)
9. Write a book proposal for presentation to a corporation
10. Make an offer to an author.
11. Work with a designer on the layout of a book to shape its look and feel.
12. Take a favorite author to lunch to discuss the concept of a new book.

Candace Ord Manroe, Senior Design Editor, *Traditional Home Magazine*

"Everyone tells me the future is on the Internet. I don't believe it. People need hard copy with beautiful pictures to linger over in the tub and the bed. For me, the computer equals work. Books and magazines equal pleasure."

— CANDACE ORD MANROE

For Candace Ord Manroe, it all began with her first shelter publication assignment, "The Art of Framing" for *Dallas/ Fort Worth Home & Garden* magazine. While stints as the city editor of the *Arlington Daily News* and at a political public relations firm gave her valuable experience, this was the gig that launched her career.

The old adage of "success begets success" certainly applies to Manroe. *Texas Homes* magazine soon saw her work and called with assignments that led to every design writer's dream, a cover story for *Architectural Digest*. "It was cool receiving copies of my cover story printed in Japanese, German, French, and Italian," she says. A permanent position as senior design editor for *Country Home* followed and today she serves in the same position at *Traditional Home*.

The University of Texas journalism graduate is also the author of an astounding sixteen books ranging from *The Home Office* (Readers Digest, 1997) to *Storage Made Easy* (Readers Digest, 1995).

As senior design editor, she oversees the Des Moines-based design department and is responsible for all house locations that are published. Residential interiors are naturally one of the most important subjects of the magazine and culling through submissions, both solicited (from contributing editors and writers acting as "scouts") and unsolicited (from homeowners and designers) remain the most time consuming aspect of the job. "I am also responsible for cultivating and working with field editors to bring in material for publication and supervise front-of-book material," she says.

The Christmas holiday issue will be planned in the dead of the summer and thoughts of spring decorating seem inconceivable with snow on the ground. Each editor has a monthly issue meeting with editor-in-chief Ann Maine to plan and set deadlines for upcoming stories. Story proposal meetings also take place once a month along with staff meetings and conference calls with editors on both the East and West Coasts.

Her job is never dull and there is no typical day. In addition to editing, writing, and story planning duties, Manroe is the go-to woman representing the magazine in the media. "A couple of weeks ago, I did a radio program for the "Three Sisters" XM satellite show and prior to that, a newspaper interview on Feng Shui," she explains. "I also attend press events like the Mohawk carpet event at the Chelsea Art Museum in New York or the markets in High Point, Decorex in London, and Maison d'Objet in Paris."

Other duties include editorial roundtables, a service parent company Meredith offers its advertisers and represents an opportunity "for clients to pick the brains of design experts from all our magazines to get a big picture of the industry," she says. The occasional writing related requests come from other departments.

"Yesterday, it was drafting ideas for a Thomasville presentation for our national ad manager; the day before, it was selecting fifteen images for our research department that would illustrate all the different faces of traditional design," Manroe explains.

Manroe also works synergistically with New York editors Jenny Bradley, who handles the *Body and Soul* column, and Krissa Rossbund, whose monthly *Marketplace* feature showcases new product introductions. She also takes into consideration senior editor Amy Elbert's special kitchen and bath sections and house stories with a building/architectural angle.

The life of a magazine is rarely in present time as editors prepare three months in advance. Plans for an issue in November will be in full swing by July with a late August deadline.

FIGURE 12.17
Traditional Home magazine cover.

Her advice to students? "GET AN INTERNSHIP! The field has become very competitive and it's imperative to get a leg up," she exclaims. For the experienced job candidate, writing samples and clips are a must. "We don't look at job candidates unless they have heavy print experience. The more clips you can amass, the better your chances of getting an editorial position," Manroe says of the hiring process. Everything from independent design courses to a full-fledged interior design degree will sway a hiring decision. One editor took antique classes at Sotheby's while another studied interior design in London. Do anything you can to gain a competitive edge.

And Manroe's advice to fellow design journalists? "In our business, it's important to motivate and inspire readers without selling out to advertisers," she states. "I struggle with promoting consumerism, which I believe is a huge problem in our society. It is a fine line to walk, and design writers have a social responsibility to pay attention."

Lisa Newsom, Founder and Editor-in-Chief, *Veranda* Magazine

"Starting a magazine is all about perseverance and timing . . . and sticking to it through thick and thin."
—LISA NEWSOM

The story is an interesting and ironic bit of publishing history.

Thirty years ago, Lisa Newsom saw a brochure in an Atlanta antiques shop, a test magazine featuring Southern homes. Convinced the concept was a good one, she called the publisher to check the status and was told of its dismal response.

"At that time the South had very little coverage. Most people thought we lived in Tara or on the railroad tracks. There was no-in-between," Newsom reflects.

Sensing an opportunity, she devised a list of potential subscribers from her address book and took it to W.R.C. Smith Publishing in Atlanta. A second brochure was sent, the response was enormous, and *Southern Accents* magazine was born.

Newsom joined the editorial staff and eventually found her name on the masthead as editor-in-chief. She resigned from the magazine in 1985 and launched *Veranda* in 1987.

Today the luxury design magazine is one of the most successful shelter publications in the country—and a major competitor of *Southern Accents*.

Charles Ross, art director of rival icon *Architectural Digest*, came on board in the same position with *Veranda*. Fellow Junior League friends sold ad pages (the first issue had thirty paid ads in a 112 page book) and her children stuffed brochures in mailboxes for the initial launch. Totally financed by Newsom, the lean staff and budget gave new meaning to the term "shoestring."

The lush glossy pages of the quarterly read like that of an illustrated coffee table book, setting it apart from its competitors. Readers and advertisers soon responded and Newsom decided to go national with six issues. Their subscriber base extended past the South (California is one of their biggest markets) and Newsom expanded her editorial, gave it a more universal appeal, and eventually featured interiors all over the world. Today the readership extends to Italy, France, Australia, and South Africa.

The heart, soul, and voice of each issue, Newsom starts with the cover and its subsequent interior and then plans for a balanced issue. "We don't do themed issues," she says, " People want to see an entire house as a virtual tour. We use simple elegant rooms in larger photos so you can see the designs." The editorial is a healthy mix of cultural and historical features, interiors, lifestyle and exquisitely photographed floral arrangements that equal the work of famed photographer Irving Penn. "I try to balance each issue of *Veranda* with a mixture of periods, antiques, contemporary, ethnic, all white, color-filled," she explains.

Another important distinction that sets the publication apart from its competitors—there are no cover lines. "We feel they were not needed and the cover says visually what the magazine is all about," she notes. Caption credits throughout the magazine give credit to the manufacturers and designers, allowing the photographs to take center stage.

By 2001, the magazine reached a circulation of 400,000, representing the highest income demographic of any shelter publication. The ultimate validation of their success came that year as well when they joined the stable of titan Hearst Corporation's successful magazines (a list that includes *Town and Country*, *Cosmopolitan*, and *House Beautiful*).

FIGURE 12.18
Lisa Newsom, founder and editor-in-chief of *Veranda* magazine.

Newsom still runs the magazine in the original Atlanta offices where her children addressed correspondence.

While her main concern is maintaining the interest and loyalty of their readers, she credits *Veranda*'s long-time continued success to a loyal staff and advertiser support, as well as the integrity of the magazine's content. "We report on interior design. We don't focus on trends. And we present the most outstanding photography of many of the most beautiful homes in the world," she notes.

THE VIEW FROM VERANDA
SAVING HISTORY

FINE ANTIQUES REMIND US THAT GOOD DESIGN NEVER GOES OUT OF STYLE. THEY CONNECT US TO THE PAST, OFTEN THREADING FROM PARENT TO CHILD, GENERATION AFTER generation. In this issue, one of America's most admired antiquarian scholars and teachers, Wendell Garrett, is profiled in Visionary by Allison Ledes, editor of *The Magazine ANTIQUES*. For fifty years, he has shared his expert knowledge of our nation's antiques legacy, and for that we are eternally grateful. • Today's furnishings mix well with antiques, and an entire room can be built around one great piece. On the Portofino peninsula, Milanese architect Piero Castellini renovates a *casa padronale* to create large open spaces where antiques complement his refreshing interiors. With a refined taste and eye, Kay O'Toole fills her home with the same mix of antiques and curiosities she sells in her Houston shop. Designer Carole Weaks searches France for primarily eighteenth-century antique furniture for an Atlanta landmark home restored and expanded by architects Frederick Spitzmiller and Robert Norris. For a summerhouse on the coast of Maine, designers Jim Gauthier and Susan Stacy collaborate with architect Paul Gosselin to refine the interiors and add antiques and accessories for a relaxed, cozy ambience. Designer Suzanne Rheinstein understands the virtues of handhewn antiques and timeworn wood patinas and incorporates those elements with an Asian flair into a traditional back-east home in Southern California. Designer Charlotte Moss uses antiques for a "breath of history" in a show house billiard room. Designer Marie Triboulot juxtaposes fresh florals with exceptional objects in Et Caetera, Franck Delmarcelle's tony furnishings and antiques shop in Paris. • Also in this issue, designer Lori Weitzner, lustrous pearls, Italian furniture, tile and fabrics, luxurious sinks, species tulips, distinctive books, the Moscow World Fine Art Fair and exhibitions featuring the art of Pissarro and Antoine-Louis Barye. Enjoy.

Lisa Newsom

FIGURE 12.19
A monthly *Letter From the Editor* page is a standard feature in design magazines.

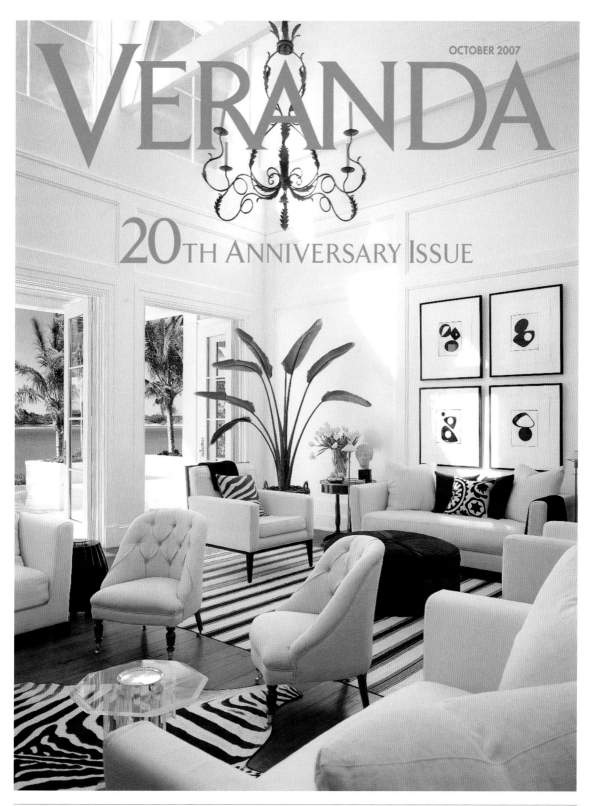

FIGURE 12.20
Veranda magazine cover.

FIGURE 12.21
Lemore Moses,
public relations
director, HBA/Hirsch
Bedner Associates.

Lemore Moses, Public Relations Director, HBA/Hirsch Bedner Associates

"You can't be a good publicist without being a good writer."

—LEMORE MOSES

Public relations represents yet another element of sales in the practice of interior design. Whether it's publicity for the design projects of a contract firm or promoting a line of hand-painted wallpaper, sales is an indirect part of the process.

According to Lemore Moses, public relations director of the international design firm HBA/Hirsch Bedner Associates, "A big component of PR is communications in general. It's not just about media relations and getting stories in the glossy pages. It's about creating unity and communication standards across all corporate entities."

Moses oversees the communications between twelve different offices all over the world and the exchange of information from office to office is crucial. The tools in her public relations arsenal include a corporate newsletter, blog, and a pod cast to aid in the task. She explains, "I work hard to make sure that the same corporate identity is alive in all twelve offices, part of that is by sharing that wealth of information with everyone. I oversee that all messaging and communication is consistent and reflects the appropriate company message . . . who we are, what we do, what we strive for."

Her days are spent in a variety of media related activities from writing press releases and replying to editorial requests to looking for new story ideas to pitch to the media. "I spend an hour walking around the design floor and studio to get a feel for what projects people are working on to see what's super exciting and what's about to get sent out and completed," she notes.

An effective publicist must love the product they are selling as well as the process. Moses found a happy medium with both architecture and design and public relations and marketing. She says, "I LOVE architecture and design and that helps to make my job easier, because I love to talk about it. That fervor largely came from my parents, who are both architects. However, I knew that I never wanted to be an

FIGURE 12.22 HBA/Hirsch Bedner Associates is an international design firm specializing in contract interiors. Shown here is The Cove Atlantis.

FIGURE 12.23
Pan Pacific interior
by HBA/Hirsch
Bedner Associates.

architect. I always wanted to do something that in my mind was more 'practical' or business oriented."

REFERENCES

Borod, Liz. (May 1, 2004). *Finally, A Little More In The Paycheck*. Retrieved March 2, 2008 from website www.mediabistro.com.

Bureau of Labor Statistics, U.S. Department of Labor, *Occupational Outlook Handbook, 2008–09 Edition*, Writers and Editors. Retrieved March 7, 2008 from website www.bls.gov/oco/ocos089.htm.

Bureau of Labor Statistics, U.S. Department of Labor, *Occupational Outlook Handbook, 2008–09 Edition*, Public Relations Specialists. Retrieved on March 8, 2008 from website www.bls.gov/oco/ocos.086.htm.

Eakins, Patricia. *Writing for Interior Design* (2005). New York: Fairchild Books.

Foote-Smith, Elizabeth. (1997). *Opportunities in Writing Careers*. Chicago: NTC Contemporary Publishing Group.

Kho, Nancy Davis. (January 16, 2008). Shelter Magazine Publishers Adjust to Changing House Market. *San Francisco Chronicle*. Retrieved March 6, 2008 from website www.sfgte.com.

Knackstedt, Mary V. (1995). *Interior Design & Beyond: Art-Science-Industry*. New York: Wiley.

Lindsay, Greg. (December 12, 2007). *So What Do You Do, Stephen Drucker, House Beautiful EIC?"* Retrieved March 1, 2008 from website www.mediabistro.com.

Lloyd, Carol. (March 23, 2004). Shelter-Shocked: Is the Proliferation of Home Mags About Post 9/11 Nesting or the Need to Fetishize Our Big Mortgages? *San Francisco Chronicle.* Retrieved March 16, 2007 from website www.sfgate.com.

Magazine Handbook 2007. Retrieved March 6, 2008 from Magazine Publishers of America website www.magazine.org/content/Files/magHandbook07_08.pdf.

Millot, Jim. (July 23, 2007). Measuring the Salary Divide. *Publisher's Weekly.* Retrieved on March 8, 2008 from website www.publishersweekly.com/article/CA6461981.html.

National Directory of Magazines, 2008; Oxbridge Communications. Retrieved March 5, 2008 from website www.magazine.org/editorial/editorial_trends_and_magazine_handbook/1145.cfm.

www.bookjobs.com.

www.payscale.com.

www.quoteland.com.

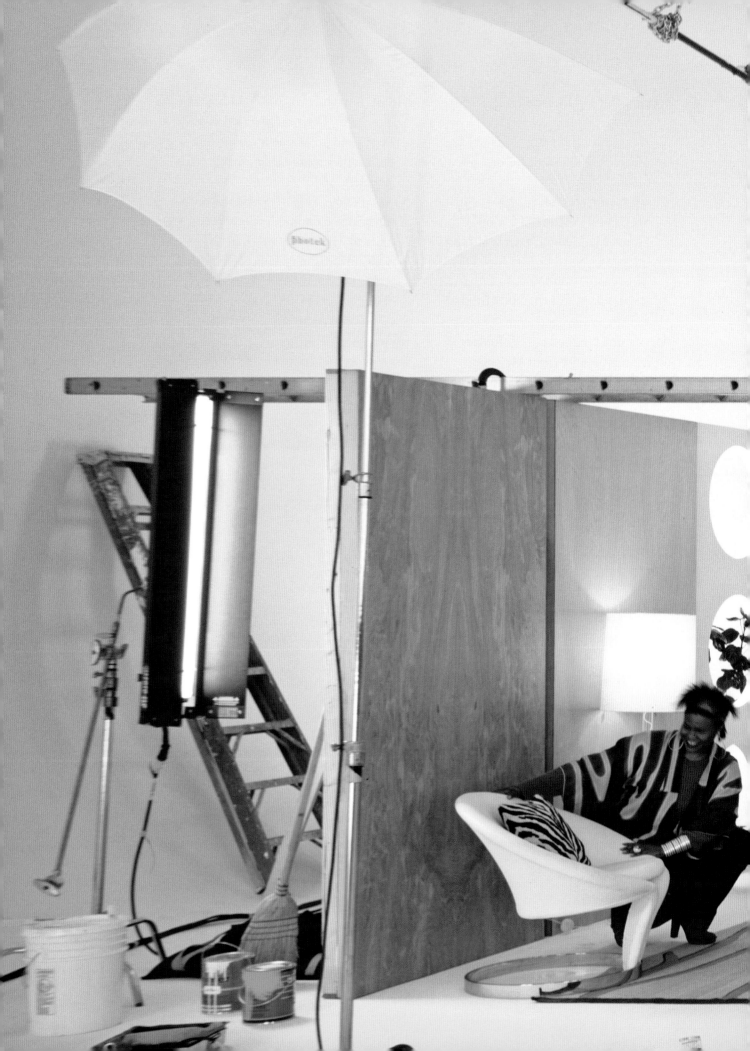

13

"Television is a powerful medium that has to be used for something better than sitcoms and police shows."
—ROONE ARLEDGE, PRESIDENT, ABC NEWS (1931–2002)

The Designer on Television

OVERVIEW OF THE PROFESSION

It is a literal plethora of topics, offering something for every viewer taste and interest. There are do-it-yourself shows that offer step-by-step instructions on the art of wallpapering to tiling a bathroom floor. Fighting with your spouse over where to place the sofa? Tune in to *Designing for the Sexes*. Need to get your home ready to sell? Turn on *Designed to Sell*. Wonder what color to paint the walls? *Color Correction* can guide you. Want an inside look at how a design firm works? Watch *Design Inc.*

From renovation and decoration to psychology and make-overs, the interior design profession is ready for its close-up, Mr. Demille.

The interior designer on television today has become a media star, establishing a platform as a television expert (known in the industry as "on-air personality" or "host"). With its roots based in the popular medium of reality television, home design, garden, do-it-yourself, and lifestyle programs inspire and inform up to 89 million households all over the globe.

The concept began in the early 1990s with the success of PBS show *This Old House* and Martha Stewart's *Martha*

Stewart Living. Finding a niche and filling a void, Home and Garden Television became the first network to devote programming solely to the topic in 1994. They have since added the Fine Living Channel and DIY (Do-It-Yourself) network to their stable. Similar outlets include PBS with their staple *This Old House* and The Learning Channel/Discovery Channel's popular *Trading Spaces*.

"The history of the United States is one big makeover show," notes Robert Thompson, director of the Center for the Study of Popular Television at Syracuse University in New York. "The pilgrims came here to annihilate their history, to create a new and improved life. That . . . theme hums loudly

under the surface of American life, and HGTV has managed to turn all the do-it-yourself stuff into entertainment, based on the theme of before and after."

In addition to design programming, designers also appear on short five- to ten-minute segments on local and national morning shows and news programs. They are guests on design and entertainment shows, afternoon programming, as well as home shopping channels such as QVC. Oprah has launched many a design star's career such as Nate Berkus (host of *Oprah's Big Give*) and Chris Casson Madden (*Interiors by Design*).

Design reality shows have made the world of interior design accessible to viewers of all ages, income levels, and cultures. For the charismatic and personable designer with a yen for the spotlight and a desire to teach and entertain the public, this is the career for you.

In the medium's pioneer days, hosts included Michael Payne (*Designing for the Sexes*), Kitty Bartholomew (*Kitty Bartholomew: You're Home*), Christopher Lowell (*Christopher Lowell Show*), and Chris Casson Madden (*Interiors by Design*). Today, design rock stars include Candice Olsen (*Divine Design*), Sheila Bridges (*Sheila Bridges Design Living*), and Constance Ramos (*Color Correction*) with new up and comers on the horizon.

Following the success of reality competition shows like *American Idol*, *Top Chef*, and *Project Runway*, the networks are giving viewers similar design fare with Bravo's *Top Design* and HGTV's *Design Star*. Contestants compete in various interior design challenges (such as designing a room using only materials from a landfill!) and are eliminated each week until a winner is chosen.

FIGURE 13.1
The cast of the hit show *Trading Spaces*. From left to right in back are Genevieve Gorder and Kia Steave-Dickerson, in middle are Hilda Santo-Tomas and Amy Wynn Pastor, and seated on the floor is Laurie Hickson-Smith.

From *Trading Spaces* to *Divine Design*, the interior design industry can thank television for elevating and shining a light on the practice.

Today the interior design host as television star is in demand. Jim Samples, president of *Home and Garden Television* says, "It's about better hosts. In the past HGTV viewers could feel like they were getting trusted information, and that was the star. And while that certainly hasn't changed, since our core value is the takeaway, we're not afraid of finding the stars to deliver that information and then using the stars across the network." Many are doing double duty such as Vern Yip, who made his debut as a judge on HGTV's *Design Star, and* also hosts *Deserving Design.* Due to the proliferation of cable channels and globalization, there will be an increase in programming and design talent will be needed as a result.

THE PROCESS

While the work may appear glamorous, looks can be deceiving. And like a snowflake, there are no identical days in the life of a design show host.

The workday can begin with an early morning start when the host arrives on set. Pre-shooting activities occur as the host goes over the various tasks to be performed on camera that can range from a how-to demonstration on making a lampshade to interviewing the head of a major furniture company. A run-through with camera, lighting, and script adjustments are made and it's off to make-up, hair, and wardrobe. Next, it's "lights, camera, and action" as taping

begins. An introduction to the feature is made, cue cards are referred to, and the segment begins . . . hopefully without a hitch.

Several shows might be taped in a single day and the work and hours can be grueling. When Constance Ramos starred on ABC's *Extreme Makeover: Home Edition*, she taped a demanding forty-two-week schedule of ten- to sixteen-hour days. Depending upon the show's budget, the host does everything from helping construct the set to simply showing up to a finished one. The work lends itself to odd hours, location shoots, holidays, weekends, long days, and often short-term employment.

For Sarah Richardson, multidimensional host of Fine Living's *Design Inc.*, her workday is somewhat different as a camera follows the designer and her team of six as they work on actual residential, hotel, and restaurant installations. She begins the day at 8:00 AM and her activities include meeting with the crew, sourcing materials, purchasing

FIGURE 13.2
The emergence of design television in the past ten years represents new career options for the interior designer.

FIGURE 13.3
Cast and designers
of *Design Star*.

accessories, and meeting with manufacturers and clients up until 6:00 PM for four days (day five is spent on the paperwork!). Her design office is the virtual studio and her staff act as co-hosts.

THE PREPARATION

There is no clear cut path to a career in this highly sought after area of the design field. Many have arrived from the more traditional areas to winning a contest on reality television. Having great communication skills and an on-camera presence, in addition to a working foundation of design knowledge will increase your chances of success.

Requirements and Skills Needed
Communications

The ability to perform, communicate, resonate, and connect with an audience through the lens of a camera is extremely important for the on-air host. While this is one of those intangible skills that people either possess or do not, in some cases it can be learned. Charm, confidence, being articulate, being able to think and speak quickly, and a sense of humor and a comfort on camera are also essential.

Acting and Performing

The ability to perform demonstrations, read cue cards, manage on-air time, and tell a story will be critical as a television show host. Joel Rizor, executive producer and president of Screen Door Entertainment (*Outer Spaces* and *Real Estate Confidential*) looks for two essential ingredients—charisma and expertise. "Susie Coelho (host of *Outer Spaces*) is a good example of a host who is attractive and personable, but also has design exper-

tise and can communicate that to an audience," he says.

Interior Design
It is crucial for the host to understand the show's subject. Depending upon the type of show (construction, crafts, design, and documentary), a well-rounded degree in interior design and broad knowledge of both theory and application will make a host more marketable.

Education and Training
This is an industry where no formal education is required, but it is always best to have one. An ASID article on the subject notes, "The professional design talent would be the first to tell you that the magical world of television, with its strategic editing and instant gratification, is far different from the real world

of interior design where good results require careful planning, patience, and expectations." In addition to a Bachelor's Degree or courses in interior design, a degree in communications, particularly broadcasting, is advisable. Classes in acting, voice, movement, and speech are recommended.

FIGURE 13.4
Set design for all-American family of the hit CBS show *Everybody Loves Raymond.*

FIGURE 13.5
Designers need to be able to conduct demonstrations on camera for "how to" television shows.

THE PATH

As in the world of Hollywood, there are no direct routes on the path of an interior design talent and they arrive from all walks of life. Many designers will act as spokespersons for the industry, promoting products as guests on a design show or on a segment for a news or women's lifestyle show. Other design personalities are recognized through books, published commissions, and popular product lines and receive their own show.

For Constance Ramos, her career started when she entered and won HGTV's *Designer's Challenge* that led to *Extreme Makeover* and *Color Correction*.

Chris Casson Madden wrote a series of interior design books that turned into one of HGTV's very first design shows, *Interiors by Design*. Interior designer Rachel Ashwell's successful Shabby Chic line moved to the screen with her own show on the *E! Channel* and *Style* network.

For those seeking the spotlight, contact the various networks to see if they are hiring hosts. Get a headshot, make a videotape or DVD showcasing your talents on camera. If you have not had any experience, try taping your own segments or pitch a design segment to your local television or cable provider. Take acting or broadcasting class and perfect your technique. Read the television trade and casting publications and check websites of the various networks for casting information.

Producers look for that inimitable "It" factor as well as design knowledge and skills. Joel Rizor, executive producer and president of Screen Door Entertainment (*Outer Spaces* and *Real Estate Confidential*) says "there will always be a need and demand for design and "how-to" videos, whether its delivered on TV, Internet, or podcast." He also recommends another avenue for the aspiring design host, "on demand" videos on cable television. He notes that they are "one of the best resources because you can watch what appeals most to you, when you want, and as many times as you need to."

Richardson advises, "this is a very tricky career path" composed of many other elements besides just design. Be prepared and arrive armed with as many skills as possible.

FIGURE 13.6
Twelve aspiring interior designers competed weekly for the top prize on Bravo's reality show *Top Design.*

THE PAY

Salaries are very hard to determine and can range from a nominal fee in very small markets to an average of $1800 per show in larger ones. Depending upon the level of experience, notoriety, and participation (producer or co-producer), contracts literally run the gamut. While Martha Stewart makes approximately $8 million for her television show *The Martha Stewart Show*, this is definitely not the norm. Hosts will supplement their design shows with books, a line of related merchandise, and product endorsements.

Many on-air hosts will join unions such as the American Federation of Television and Radio Artists (AFTRA) and often the Screen Actors Guild (SAG). Check sources for contact information.

THE PROFILES

Constance Ramos—The Star, Host, *Color Correction*, Home and Garden Television
"You need to be a performer. Understand what every actor knows about what the camera sees."
—CONSTANCE RAMOS

Talk about being at the right place at the right time.

After winning the competition on HGTV's *Designers Challenge*, Constance Ramos was told that ABC was looking for a designer for *Extreme Makeover: Home Edition*. Drinking coffee one Saturday morning, she read about the listing on Craigslist and made the call. By Friday, the former Kansas City Chief cheerleader got the job.

Ramos was not just another novice with a pretty face. The attractive

FIGURE 13.7
This Old House **was one of the first home improvement shows on television.**

graduate of Kansas State University came armed with a degree in architecture plus a theater background, which was quite the winning combination for design television. Her credentials are impressive—she interned at Walt Disney Imagineering and worked on themed retail buildings, coordinating drawings with German engineers, Japanese HVAC engineers, and California designers. Through her company Constance Ramos Designs, she has worked on a variety of residential and contract projects and with giants such as Sony Entertainment and I.M. Pei Partners.

A former actress, her credits included bit parts in *Mr. and Mrs. Bridge* (Merchant Ivory, 1990) and *The Truman Show* (Paramount, 1998) as well as commercials for

FIGURE 13.8
Constance Ramos, HGTV host.

FIGURE 13.9
Extreme Makeover: Home Edition is one of ABC's highest rated prime time shows.

Wal-Mart and Hallmark Cards that prepared her for life in front of the camera.

The premise of *Extreme Makeover: Home Edition* is to rebuild an entire house (interior, exterior, and landscaping) in seven days—a process that would normally take four to six months. Lucky and deserving families are selected as recipients and their lives are dramatically changed as a result.

Each person has a certain area of expertise and Ramos was the building/planning designer for the show. "I could literally 'speak contractor' which gave me a leg up. There was a great difference between those with architecture and those with design experience on the show," she says. Days were long and it was not unusual for the star to be on set for the delivery of a bathtub at 2:00 AM, "It was construc-

tion on the fast track," she says of the shoot. In addition to fabulous exposure and training, Ramos received another perk—she met her husband J.J. Carrell while on set.

Ramos is now host of her own show, *Color Correction* on HGTV. The show comes to the aid of homeowners and their color dilemmas, tackling one room per episode. "Color is so universal," the host explains, "and can be an extremely emotional experience."

A typical day on the set will find her installing wall molding for a Parisian style room with her "crack team of carpenters" or go on location to hotels, clubs and spas all over Los Angeles. Shooting a staggering 50 weeks out of the year, Ramos maintains, "I get to do fun work and have a beautiful emotional experience."

FIGURE 13.10 Constance Ramos helps viewers out of color dilemmas on HGTV's *Color Correction* television show.

Joel Rizor—The Producer, Executive Producer and President, Screen Door Entertainment

"I think television from MTV to HGTV has caused people to become more aware of their home and living spaces. This kind of programming also lets people be voyeuristic and see how other people live."

—JOEL RIZOR

It takes a special breed of producer to do reality, lifestyle, and how-to programming, a genre that has become extremely popular television fare in the past decade.

Joel Rizor, producer/director/writer of Screen Door Entertainment, opened his company in 2001 with *The Seasoned Gardener*, *Outer Spaces* with Susie Coelho, and the award-winning *Insider's*

Garden. He has produced over hundreds of hours for HGTV, A&E, Disney, Fine Living, and the DIY Channel.

Rizor cut his teeth on the ABC program *The Home Show* in the late 1980s. "*The Home Show* covered a number of topics, but regularly featured guests and segments that dealt with design, décor, and home improvement," he explains. "Although it was never a huge hit, I really believe that it was *The Home Show* that launched the current genre of home improvement and design television programs."

A television veteran of over twenty years, he relates "Do-it-yourself TV appeals to people on many levels. There is the obvious money saving issue of doing something that you would have had to pay someone else to do, but I think greater than that is the satisfaction of accomplishment that comes from doing something from a simple repair to a

FIGURE 13.11 Screen Door Entertainment specializes in lifestyle and how-to programming.

FIGURE 13.12
Outer Spaces was one of HGTV's most successful garden shows.

major project." The studios soon discovered viewers were completing projects not out of a monetary reasons, but sheer enjoyment.

Reality television is enjoying popularity like never before. "Because of the pressure to get higher ratings, networks, channels, and programmers want the next break out hit show like *Trading Spaces, Extreme Makeover Home Edition*, or *Queer Eye*," Rizor explains. "Design and decorating shows have evolved from just giving straight information to either incorporating and entertainment twist or being shot like docu-soaps or docu-reality." He notes that the challenge in producing design shows is finding the right balance, "that magic mix of information and entertainment and hoping a network gives the show a chance to find an audience."

For the designer or design student who wants to have their own show, Rizor suggests they discover a unique quality and capitalize on it. "Pinpoint whatever it is that is going to make them stand out from all the others, personality, style, etc. Get on a local news show, pitch a story to a local newspaper, or magazine, contact a production company and present a concept."

"There is no substitute for pounding the pavement and knocking on as many doors as possible," he concludes.

Sarah Richardson—The Producer and Star, Sarah Richardson Design

"Every day it's a healthy dose of grit, stress, and a little bit of glamour thrown in."

— SARAH RICHARDSON

Combine talent, skill, endless enthusiasm and being at the right place at the right time and you have the career of Sarah Richardson.

Host of Fine Living Channel's *Room Service* and *Design Inc.*, Richardson began her career in decorative arts and

FIGURE 13.13
Sarah Richardson, host of *Room Service* and *Design Inc.*

as a prop stylist. Called upon by a Canadian television show to demonstrate the mechanics of making a floorcloth on camera, good fortune placed a network executive in the control booth who liked what he saw. One appearance turned into fifty, and the rest as they say was history.

As one of the young, fresh faces in lifestyle design television, Richardson soon teamed up with producer Michael Prini and added co-producer to her resume. Both of her television creations grew out of a need to offer content that was empowering, educational, and not just how-to programming. *Room Service* deals with the transformation of a single room from inspiration to final installation while *Design Inc.* is a day in the life of a design project, offering an inside view of a realistic portrayal of a design firm. "We are like storm trackers and go where the action is," the mother of two explains. "We tell the story of a room coming to life and deal with long-term solutions, prioritize spending, and offer great deals and big splurges." Clients range from university students to those with multimillion dollar budgets.

While her career may have begun in her words as a "total fluke," she has received incredible on-the-job training. She credits her success to the fact that "No successful project happens without great design team. Even Martha Stewart has many people (behind the scenes) helping her." As creator of an impressive ninety television shows, her duties include on-camera work, content, and location. She credits a positive attitude and allowing the "camera to be my friend" as the keys to her television success.

THE HOME AND GARDEN TELEVISION REVOLUTION

As with most inventions, Home and Garden Television Network began from a need for lifestyle programming. The year was 1994 and no such channel existed.

The network was founded by Ken Lowe, now president and CEO of parent company E. W. Scripps. He pitched the idea by "drawing a house in which every room from attic to wine cellar was its own television show." Moving up the corporate ladder involved many changes in residence and subsequent house renovation which gave Lowe an appreciation for "do-it-yourself." Six-and-a-half million households received the show and today 98 million do-it-yourselfers and design aficionados are watching a variety of shows on seven continents.

Programming centers naturally on the home and primarily showcases in a reality and instructional format. In addition to television, HGTV boasts a website, which attracts an average of 5 million design-crazed consumers a month and supplies an eager audience with product information and newsletters.

The Knoxville, Tennessee based company has since added five cable channels—The Food Network, DIY, Fine Living, Shop at Home, and Great American Country (country music channel). DIY Network reaches 47.5 million homes and Fine Living Network is now available in 49.8 million across the United States. They are also cross branding their hosts with products to sell on Shop at Home, such as craft expert Carol Duvall.

Following in the steps of the lifestyle designer, Richardson has a national newspaper column, is a contributing editor for *Canadian House and Home* magazine, and has a line of both interior and exterior furniture sold in retail stores throughout Canada.

"I do what I do with conviction and I'm fortunate enough to be involved in all aspects of the business," she concludes. "It's about a lot of things other than design. You don't have to be on camera to be a good designer!"

REFERENCES

Ascher-Walsh, Rebecca. (December 10, 2007). Welcome to the Good Life. *Hollywood Reporter*.

Finney, Robert G. Unions/Guilds. Retrieved March 10, 2008 from website www.museum.tv/archives/etv/U/htmlU/unionsguilds/unionsguilds.htm.

Lights, Camera, Action . . . Design? Retrieved from the ASID website March 11, 2008 at www.asid.org/designservices/asseen/lightscameraaction.htm.

Lubenski, Cathy. (May 8, 2005). *The Age of HGTV*. Received March 21, 2008 from website www.signonsandiego.com/uniontrib/20050508/news_mz1hs08hgtv.html.

Scarbrough, Marsha. (July 1, 2002). *Pitching Home & Garden Television*. Retrieved March 22, 2008 from website http://digitalcontentproducer.com/coverstory/video_pitching_home_garden.

www.fineliving.com.

www.hgtv.com.

14

"It was a world you created, it was not a world you went out and found."

— RICHARD SYLBERT (1928–2002),
ACADEMY AWARD WINNING PRODUCTION DESIGNER

The Designer in Hollywood

OVERVIEW OF THE PROFESSION

Imagine *Gone with the Wind* (MGM, 1939) without Tara or *Casablanca* (Warner Brothers, 1943) without Rick's Place. Picture *Grey's Anatomy* (ABC) without Seattle Grace or *CSI* (CBS) without its crime lab.

All of these iconic yet seemingly realistic places can be attributed to the work of the unsung heroes of the film industry, the production designer and set decorator.

Even the most infrequent filmgoer can tell you what a director, actor, and even a cinematographer does, but when the film credits roll and production designer and set decorator grace the screen, the audience is puzzled. In layman's terms, production design is the art of creating the overall visual look of a film, television program, commercial, or music video. Collaborating with the director and cinematographer, they literally set the tone, mood, and visual look for the story's locations and characters.

The set decorator is in charge of decorating and dressing the set. That includes all the accoutrements from furniture, drapery, and wall coverings to lighting fixtures and accessories. They work with a variety of artisans, set dressers, and the prop department to provide items needed for a particular

scene that can range from a matchbook on a table to a tombstone in a graveyard.

While both fields apply many of the same disciplines and business practices as interior design, the two industries could not be any more different. Far from glamorous, the hours are long, the work is hard and very stressful. It involves a lot of planning, flexibility, and unexpected problems arise constantly. The old Hollywood adage of "hurry up and wait" is the order of the day as a set is quickly constructed for a scene that may take hours (and even days) to shoot —and then is immediately dismantled.

Jobs are very hard to come by and it is estimated that less than 10 percent of the industry is employed. Governed by unions, the industry is prone to strikes, is extremely competitive, and only a handful find themselves in demand.

However, there are many rewards. Designs are immortalized on the silver screen or in television re-runs for decades and even centuries to come. The satisfaction, camaraderie, and stimulation of working in such a highly creative field is immeasurable. Collaborating with gifted actors, cinematographers, writers and directors is often gratifying. Working on location for long periods can feed the gypsy in a designer's soul.

And there is nothing like the possibility of an Emmy or Oscar on the mantle as the ultimate reward for your efforts.

THE PROCESS

As the interior design process begins with a client and a project, film design starts with a producer, director, and a script.

Designs for the contemporary comedy *Something's Gotta Give* (Columbia, 2003) started when production designer Jon Hutman received the script from the film's director and writer Nancy Myers (a huge interior design aficionado). Primarily set in a Hamptons beach house (via soundstage), the story centers around an aging music executive lothario (Jack Nicholson) who falls for his young girlfriend's mother (Diane Keaton), a successful Broadway playwright who nurses him back to health after a heart attack.

Hutman and set decorator Beth Rubino broke down the script scene by scene according to individual settings and themes. The pair knew one of the main characters of the film would be the beach house, designed to portray the success, passion, and discipline of the character. They devised a design scheme right out of the pages of *Architectural Digest* which became one of the most copied film looks in the past decade. Budgets were devised and drawings, storyboards, and blueprints were prepared by the art department.

They say "God is in the details"—a bowl of all white seashells indicates an anal retentiveness while a desk with stacks of paper, reading glasses and a computer gives the viewer a glimpse of a writer.

Rubino set the scene with Tony and Drama Desk awards, Playbills, and even things the viewer might not

FIGURE 14.3
The sets for the romantic comedy *Something's Gotta Give* (Columbia, 2003) were some of the decade's most widely copied by homeowners.

FIGURE 14.4
The kitchen is the
nucleus of activity
for the Walker family
household in the hit
ABC television series
Brothers and Sisters.

see such as a Filofax filled with agents'
names and a drawer of personal items
(which actually help the actors get in
character). The Academy Award nomi-
nated set decorator notes, "The details
you don't see had intrinsic value for the
actors." Other factors contribute to not
only the overall look, but also the mood
of the film—both on and off screen.
Rubino sprayed sunscreen on the set,
noting "The fragrance of sunscreen
is so specific, it immediately puts you
in that place," she explained. "Music
and scent do that. I often use music
to enhance the mood. The idea is to
create an entire environment—the set
decorator's job goes far beyond choosing furniture."

Episodic television can be quite different. Unlike film, the work is steady
and the sets can last for months as noted
by production designer Denny Dugally

and set decorator Bryan Scott Venegas
of ABC's *Brothers and Sisters.*

Their methodology and workday is
somewhat different. "We get a script that
is fifty-five pages, and shooting occurs
in nine days and we have two sets a day,"
says Venegas of the marathon method
of design. He and Dugally will pull tear
sheets of design ideas and do a concept
board for the central house where the
family dramas take place. "We don't
want it to look too perfect, we want a
family to look like they live there with
clutter, mail, books, etc.," he details.

Whether in film or television, production designers and set decorators
perform many of the same functions.
The production designer is responsible
for budgets and extensive research
(often working with specialist researchers). They deliver technical drawings to
the construction department as Rome

must literally be built in a day. In the case of *Brothers and Sisters*, their season typically lasts eleven months with eight months of shooting and the remaining three spent prepping the show (with a bit of a vacation hiatus worked in).

For the set decorator, a typical day can involve locating and purchasing furnishings from prop shops, antique markets, and vendors, and working with prop masters or the leadman who is in charge of the set dressers. They prepare a detailed prop breakdown and are often involved in product placement arrangements with vendors and advertisers. Reporting to the production designer, they are also responsible for maintaining a budget for furnishings and props.

The actual shooting day for the design crew begins early and ends late as teams assemble to dress the set, obtain final approval, and then work on the next scene detailed on the schedule. Last minute changes can mean replacing a lampshade that clashes with the color of an actor's costume or rearranging a floor plan to accommodate a fight scene.

Months of planning, weeks of shopping, days of preparation, and hours of shooting occur. The actors take their mark, the scene is shot and the set is taken down. It's all in a day's work on a Hollywood film set.

THE PREPARATION

This area represents uncharted waters for many designers and specialized courses, knowledge of the film and television industry, contacts, and luck will certainly make a difference in getting a job in this highly competitive field.

Requirements and Skills Needed

Communications

Working behind the scenes, designers should be able to effectively communicate and explain their design plans as they will have to present ideas to producers and directors as well as members of the design team for execution.

Interior Design

All skill sets and application of design theory will apply. Knowledge of lighting, space, sketching, architecture, color theory, and design and decoration, as well as the ability to read and draw blueprints and floor plans are required. Due to the variety and scope of projects, designers can be called upon to create sets from an historical eighteenth century period piece (*Marie Antoinette*) to futuristic "galaxies far, far away" (*Star Wars*). Art and furniture history are also important subjects.

As with the practice of interior design, a well-stocked rolodex can be a set decorator's best friend. It is useful to have resources for prop houses, workrooms, and eclectic off-the-wall items. Being able to locate a vintage Art Deco fabric or track down a specialty artisan to age a city for an ancient Greece set is all in a day's work.

Research and Analytical Skills

The ability to read a script, analyze the characters, and create what is known as a "back-story" (the history behind the narrative which determines the environment of the characters and their lifestyle) is important. Designers are required to research each period and style and be very detailed, as a forties kitchen set will need to have the appropriate appliances. Such was the case with the film *The Godfather* (Paramount, 1972) as production designer Dean Tavoularis created labels for olive oil cans from the period for a cooking scene.

FIGURE 14.6
Psychiatrist Frasier Crane's Seattle living room for the long-running television show *Frasier*.

Set decorator Cloudia Rebar advises students should "study all the design styles so they are automatically part of your creative vocabulary so you can be fully present in the design 'moment' without the distraction of second guessing yourself."

Organizational Skills

Organization is essential, as the script will have to be broken down into various sets and locations. Being able to prioritize and meet deadlines is crucial.

Supervision

The production designer oversees not only the set decorator, but is responsible for the work of the art director, teams of artisans, and the construction department to ensure deadlines are met. Set decorators will supervise set dressers, buyers, drapery persons, and furniture

FIGURE 14.7
Production designer Mark Friedberg's rendering for the film *Far from Heaven* (Focus Features, 2002).

makers to complete the overall decoration of each set.

Technological Skills

AutoCAD and the ability to work with a variety of special effects software programs will be useful. Knowledge of the requirements of health and safety codes is also important. Production designers must have expert knowledge in drafting, technical drawing, cinematography, and building and construction.

Education and Training

Few universities and interior design schools offer a degree in the field; look for more specialized film schools or organizations such as the American Film Institute, the Savannah College of Art, and the Tisch School of the Arts at New York University for courses in production and set decoration.

FIGURE 14.8
Fifties style designs for the film *Far From Heaven* (Focus Features, 2002) is a classic example of a period interior.

Professionals in both disciplines often have architecture, interior design, or art degrees and some may complete graduate courses in film and/or theater design.

A strong interest in the medium helps. Venegas advises would-be set decorators "A large part of the job requires organization, good management skills, a grasp on budgetary issues, and most importantly the ability to tell a story through the characters eyes, with the decor. I watch a lot of films and suggest anyone interested in my craft, to do the same. By watching films and television you can get valuable information on how lighting and depth of field compliments the decor and sets a mood which assists in telling a story."

Design Curriculum

Lighting, drafting, AutoCAD, color theory, and basic interior design curriculum will be covered. Specialized courses in film, television, and theatre production, costume, art history, set illustration, rendering, storyboarding, model building, accounting, film theory and criticism and other specialized digital classes will be beneficial.

PROFESSIONAL ASSOCIATIONS

Several organizations are available for interior designers in the entertainment area. Production designers can join the Art Directors Guild (see www.

artdirector.org for membership requirements) and set decorators can become members of the Set Decorators Society of America (SDSA) (www.setdecorator.org). Founded in 1993, the SDSA is the only national nonprofit group for set decorators and allied members who supply furnishings to the trade.

Student memberships are available and provide an excellent entrée to the industry. Both organizations publish outstanding industry publications, *Perspectives* and *Set Décor*, respectively.

Many designers who meet the requirements have also benefited from joining the American Institute of Architects (www.aia.org). All practices require joining a union (see resources for contact information).

FIGURE 14.9
Set Décor magazine is the publication for the Set Decorators Society of America and showcases the latest work of its members.

THE PATH

Since the film and television industries are a completely different medium and unlike any other, there are no sure paths to employment (or success for that matter).

Getting a foot in the door is the first step of the process. Many have entered through work on an independent film, internships, and as assistants on a film crew. Contacts, being at the right place at the right time, and persistence have been never more important. Rebar recommends, "scanning the trade papers (Hollywood Reporter and Daily Variety) to see what films are going into production. Call and try to get an appointment with the production designer or set decorator to work as their buyer or assistant."

Rebar also reiterates "Your portfolio is your passport. I suggest students design a set, create drawings and presentation boards for their portfolio. This shows the uniqueness you can bring to any job and your special way of seeing things as well as your eye for design, understanding, and creativity."

Venegas advises those interested in television should "gain some practical experience by either interning in the department, assisting another set decorator, working on the crew if you get the opportunity, gaining the knowledge on how the department works."

He also recommends that if you are not a union member, work as an intern for the job experience on a non-union show. "If someone wants to get into the union, you have to be lucky enough to be on a non-union show that happens to turn union," he says. "After a show turns, thirty union days is needed to be allowed to join the union."

Production designers often rise through the ranks of the art department working as junior draftsmen, assistant art director to art director and production designer. They may also come from the theatre or work on commercials and music videos.

Set decorators arrive from interior design schools, working as assistants, set dressers, and other various jobs on a film crew. Many start their careers as assistants in the art department before working in set decoration (assistants will work on lead crews, set dressing props, and serve as shoppers). Depending on the size of the films they have worked on, and the levels of experience acquired, assistants may work in this role for several years before becoming set decorators.

Joining the SDSA is a good career start as they offer fellowships and networking opportunities that can lead to work. Working without pay as a production assistant will open doors as well. The roads to success in Hollywood are paved with stories of those at the right place at the right time.

THE PAY

Salaries are varied in the industry as to whether a show is union or nonunion. For union work, set decorators make anywhere from $2,800 to $3,500 (based on a flat rate for a twelve-hour day). No information for production designers was available at this time. Overtime is rare.

THE PROFILES

Glenda Rovello—The Production Designer, *Will and Grace*

"Pay attention (with your eyes) to the world around . . . it will help inform the work on stage."
—GLENDA ROVELLO

He's a gay corporate lawyer who likes his interiors tailored, sophisticated, and with an immaculate flair. She is a straight interior designer and favors eclectic and trendy designs with a bold touch of color. Together and unlucky in love, they share an apartment on Manhattan's Upper West Side . . . by way of the CBS soundstages in Studio City, California.

This was the world of the enormously entertaining hit television show *Will and Grace*. Responsible for creating the memorable interiors (nightly emblazoned to our memory thanks to syndication) is three-time Emmy Award–winning production designer Glenda Rovello.

Rovello comes to the field of production design by means of a masters

FIGURE 14.10
Glenda Rovello, Emmy Award–winning production designer of NBC's *Will and Grace*.

degree in architecture (University of Texas-Austin). She feels her education served her well, explaining "The skills required in production design and architecture are similar as you need to understand space and of course you must be able to communicate your design visually."

She admits her design process for an architectural job is similar to that of a hit television show, "without the benefit of script," she notes. "My process for production design tends to be this:

I read the script
Dream
Read the script
Sketch plan
Hardline a plan
Build a model
Dream

FIGURE 14.11
Rovello designed the Emmy Award winning sets for *Will and Grace* for twelve years.

Revise model
Do final drawings
Build color boards with material samples
Meet with the decorator
Stand back and let everyone work"

Like many situations in Tinseltown, Rovello landed her job by being at the right place at the right time. A chance luncheon with two producers triggered talk of a possible job—only she was ineligible and not a member of the union. "By the time I arrived home there was a message on my phone machine from a non-union production designer stating he was my ticket to success in Hollywood. After that fateful lunch, one of the producers called and told him about me. And he was right—I worked on his shows for twelve years," she details.

Along with luck, the former art director recommends a top-notch portfolio as the best tool for job hunting. "For set decorators, I want to see a portfolio that shows me the person's design work, i.e., how complete are the spaces, layers of details, etc." she says. "In the interview I want to discuss their thought process and how they made certain decisions . . . this is very subjective!"

Cloudia Rebar—The Set Decorator, 24

The life and career of interior designer and set decorator Cloudia Rebar are as varied as her film credits.

Career number one is her Los Angeles interior design practice, CBR Interiors International where the ASID member specializes in Feng Shui. Career number two encompasses set decoration for over forty major motion pictures including *Vanilla Sky* (Paramount, 2001), *Doc Hollywood* (Warner Brothers, 2001) and director Brian De Palma's *Body Double* (Columbia, 1984).

Inspired by the Fellini film *La Strada*, Rebar moved to Rome after graduation (having already mastered the basic elements of theatrical design through her studies and classes at Hunter College and London's Slade School of Fine Art). Her portfolio landed her a coveted spot at the Government Film School in Italy and an eventual job with her lifelong mentor, the legendary John DeCuir, Sr. (his credits include the films *Cleopatra* and *The King and I*). "One of the most important things he taught me was to see

FIGURE 14.12
Grace Adler (Deborah Messing) portrayed a Manhattan interior designer on the hit show *Will and Grace*.

the finished set in my mind and work backwards from there, organizing all the tasks and elements needed in order to let others see it," she details.

A year later, she signed her first contract and in true Hollywood fashion, bumped into Fellini himself.

Presently, she is the set decorator of the groundbreaking (and heart stopping) television show *24* (Fox). She notes, "Unlike my design projects as an interior designer in Beverly Hills (with sometimes months to complete a project), the reality of television and film time frames is quite unique."

The work is daunting. Last season she and production designer Joseph Hodges put together from scratch a 15,000-square-foot business complex for the CTU Headquarters, six formal presidential reception spaces and another thirty sets in three weeks time. She notes

of the "sheer logistics of handling scores of design tasks at high speed" along with the "level of activity goes on at the start of a new season on most shows and requires nerves of steel, amazing stamina and a definite sense of humor to get through it all and still be smiling."

Much like designing a house or an office, acquiring and installing furnishings is a large part of the process. Rebar comments, "Each time I set out on a project like this, I ask myself the same questions: Will I really be able to find the perfect green sofa? Can thirty linear feet of elaborate drapes really be manufactured in two days? Can a custom carpet be created and delivered to the set in four days? Of course, in the film industry, there is no such word as "No."

A typical day for her can start at 3:30 AM when she travels to location, dresses sets until noon and then might drive forty miles to another location and repeat the process. "I might look for furniture for other sets, start a budget for two more episodes while dressing two more sets," she says. Her eighteen-hour plus day ends at 9:15 PM only to realize she starts the entire process over the next day.

The following day brings several four-hour production meetings that are scheduled for each eight-day episode, along with eight to ten hour location scouts. "This can really cut into a set decorator's prepping time," Rebar says. "I've found that this seems to be a compelling factor or thread throughout most set decorators' experiences. I have to believe it's the daily adrenaline rush that bonds filmmakers together and fuels us throughout our grueling weeks. Where else does one get such a variety

FIGURE 14.14
The main hub of activity for Fox's show *24* sets is CTU.

FIGURE 14.15
Set decorator Cloudia Rebar employed her contract interior design skills for this White House interior on the television show *24*.

of challenges in which to excel, so often, and every day?"

(Note: Rebar is one of the founding officers of the Set Decorators Society of America (SDSA) and a member of the Academy of Motion Picture Arts and Sciences.)

Andrew Baseman—Interior Designer and Set Decorator, *The Nanny Diaries*

Design inspiration can arrive in the most obscure ways.

Andrew Baseman found his calling at an early age as he "was drawn to room recreations in museums and historical buildings, making my own interpretations using Lincoln Logs and Tinker Toys." Legos were used for his first contemporary model home, furnished with Cracker Jack prizes. Influenced by the television shows *The Munsters* and *Addams Family*, he constructed haunted house dioramas in shoeboxes and the die was cast for a career in set decoration.

Armed with a background in theatre design, he apprenticed as a set designer at the Berkshire Theatre Festival in Cambridge and majored in set and costume design at Carnegie Mellon University. The school proved to be an excellent training ground as he was exposed to all design periods, designing sets and costumes for varied projects such as Eugene O'Neill's *Long Days Journey Into Night*, the operetta *Die Fledermaus*, and Genet's *The Blacks*.

Baseman got his start as PA (production assistant) and eventually worked

his way up to set decorator on television's *Spin City* series and films such as *Kinsey* (Fox Searchlight Pictures, 2004) and *The Nanny Diaries* (The Weinstein Company, 2007). He explains working as a PA "is a great way to observe what each member of the design team does, as well as get an overview of film production."

For those starting out in the business, he advises to "be as well rounded as possible. Travel as much as budget

and work permits. Take photos of things that inspire you, including details of colors and textures. Go to museums and wander into galleries you may not initially be drawn to. The better educated you are in art and design, the better you will be able to communicate with your clients."

He also stresses the importance of a portfolio and strongly advises, "take pictures of your work. I am still surprised at how many set decorators do not take the time to archive their work. If you are unable to show visual examples of your color sense and taste to production designers and productions, the next candidate with a more complete presentation may get the job before you do."

Many set decorators will supplement their work with an interior design practice as well. Baseman does double duty with a successful practice of high-end clients in Manhattan, designing interiors from a Chelsea garden apartment to the Ars Nova Theater.

As for the differences in the two practices, Baseman comments, "Most of my clients have been wonderful to work with and really appreciate what I do for them. I enjoy knowing that they are living in the environments I create for them, as opposed to the ephemeral settings used in film, which eventually end up in a dumpster. I also like the luxury of longer prep periods and higher budgets to work with."

REFERENCES

Heisner, Beverly. (1997). *Production Design in the Contemporary American Film*. Jefferson, North Carolina: McFarland & Company.

Howard, Jason. (Winter 2003/2004) Cloudia Rebar: "A Singing Heart and a Ongoing Education." *Set Décor* Magazine.

Jackman, Ann. (January, 2003). *How to Be . . . a Production Designer*. Retrieved March 11, 2008 from website www.newenglandfilm.com.

"On the Set of *24* with Cloudia Rebar." *Beyond AD*. Retrieved December 15, 2007 from the website www. beyondad.com.

"Something's Gotta Give." (Winter 2003/2004) *Set Décor* Magazine.

www.setdecorator.org.

www.skillset.org.

FIGURE 14.19 Andrew Baseman, set decorator and interior designer.

FIGURES 14.20, 14.21 Baseman does double duty as a residential interior designer. Shown here are his designs for a New York garden apartment.

Resources

CONSULTING

Fred Berns
Business By Design Inc.
656 Wildrose Way
Louisville, CO 80027-1081
303-665-6688
888-665-5505
Fax: 303-665-5599
www.fredberns.com

Sherri Donghia
CEO
SD International
sherridonghia@mac.com

Keith Granet
Granet & Associates
4151 Redwood Avenue, Suite 405
Los Angeles, CA 90066
310-306-8100
www.granet.net

Steve Nobel
Nobelinks
61 East 77th Street
New York, NY 10021
917-648-4993
www.nobelinks.com

EMPLOYMENT

Archipro
80 SW 8 Street, Suite 2000
Miami, FL 33130
305-571-9727
www.archipro.com

Interior Talent Inc.
1430 Lake Baldwin Lane, Suite A
Orlando, FL 32814
800-915-3012
400 North Wells, Suite 304
Chicago, IL 60610
800-915-3035
Fax: 800-915-3032
www.interiortalent.com

Rita Sue Siegel
162 Fifth Avenue, Floor 11
New York, NY 10010
212-682-2100
Fax: 212-682-2946
www.ritasue.com

INTERIOR DESIGNERS

Albert Hadley
Albert Hadley, Inc.
24 East 64th Street
New York, NY 10021
212-888-7979

Alexa Hampton
Mark Hampton LLC
654 Madison Avenue
New York, NY 10021
212-753-4110
212-758-2079
www.markhampton.com

Alexandra Stoddard
87 Water Street
Stonington, CT 06378
www.alexandrastoddard.com

Andrew Baseman
Andrew Baseman Design
131 Varick Street, Suite 904
New York, NY 10013
212-989-2940
Fax: 212-989-2941
www.andrewbaseman.com

Angelo Donghia (1935–1985)

Betty Sherrill
McMillen Inc.
155 East 56th Street
New York, NY 10022
212-759-7563

Billy Baldwin (1903–1984)

Callison
1420 Fifth Avenue, Suite 2400
Seattle, WA 98191-2343
206-623-4646
Fax: 206-623-4625
www.callison.com

Celerie Kemble
Kemble Interiors Inc.
224 West 30th Street
New York, NY 10001
212-675-9576
Fax: 646-638-4573
www.kembleinteriors.com

Charles Basant-Percier
(1764–1838)

Chris Madden Inc.
181 Westchester Avenue, Suite 408
Port Chester, NY 10573
www.chrismadden.com
914-939-3937

Clodagh Design
670 Broadway, 4th Floor
New York, NY 10012
212-542-5069
www.clodagh.com

David Hicks (1928–1998)

Dorothy Draper & Co. Inc.
60 East 56th Street
New York, NY 10022
212-758-2810

Dotty Travis
Travis Interiors
425 Peachtree Hills Avenue, NE
Atlanta, GA 30305
404-233-7207

Eleanor McMillen Brown
(1891–1991)

Elsie de Wolfe (1865–1950)

HBA/Hirsch Bedner
3216 Nebraska Avenue
Santa Monica, CA 90404
310-829-9087
Fax: 310-453-1182
www.hbadesign.com

John Black
J. Black Designs
www.jblackdesigns.com

John Fowler (1906–1977)

Jonathan Adler
333 Hudson Street, 7th Floor
New York, NY 10013
212-645-2802
Fax: 212-645-3072
www.jonathanadler.com

Kelly Wearstler
Kwid
317 North Kings Road
Los Angeles, CA 90048
323-951-7454
Fax: 923-951-7455
www.kwid.com

Mark Hampton
(1940–1998)

Mario Buatta (1935–)

Martha Stewart
Martha Stewart Omnimedia
20 West 43rd Street
New York, NY 10036
212-827-8000
www.marthastewart.com

Michael Graves
Michael Graves & Associates
31 Nassau Street
Princeton, NJ 08540
609-924-6409
Fax: 609-924-1795
www.michaelgraves.com

Mimi McMakin
Brooke Hutig
Kemble Interiors
294 Hibiscus Avenue
Palm Beach, FL 33480
561-659-5556
www.kembleinteriors.com

Nancy Lancaster (1897–1994)

Nina Campbell
318-326 Wandsworth Bridge Road
London SW6 2TZ
0207-471-4270
Fax: 0207-471-4299
www.ninacampbell.com

Pierre Francois-Leonard Fontaine
(1752–1853)

Rick Roseman
Director
RWR Designs Ltd
5760 Daniel Road, Suite 7304
Plano, TX 75024
214-520-6341
Fax: 972-596-1434
www.rwrdesigns.com

Robert Adam (1728–1792)

Ruby Ross Wood (1881–1950)

Ruthie Sommers
Chapman Radcliff
517 North LaCienega Boulevard
West Hollywood, CA 90048
310-659-8062
http://chapmanradcliffhome.com

Sally Sirken Lewis
J. Robert Scott
500 North Oak Street
Inglewood, CA 90302
310-680-4380
Fax: 310-680-4323
www.jrobertscott.com

Sister Parish (1910–1994)
www.sisterparishdesign.com

Soucie Horner
208 West Kinzie, 2nd Floor
Chicago, IL 60610
312-755-0202
Fax: 312-755-0404
www.souciehorner.com

Susie Coelho Enterprises
www.susiecoelho.com

Sybil Colefax (1874–1954)

Syrie Maugham (1879–1955)

Tracy Bross
Decorator & Stylist
220 East 72nd Street
New York, NY 10021
917-690-2761

Trisha Wilson
Wilson Associates
3811 Turtle Creek Boulevard
Dallas, TX 75219
214-521-6753
Fax: 214-521-0207
www.wilsonassoc.com

Van Day Truex (1904–1979)

Vicente Wolf
Vicente Wolf Associates, Inc.
333 West 39th Street, 10th Floor
New York, NY 10018
212-465-0590
Fax: 212-465-0639
www.vicentewolf.com

William Haines (1900–1973)

William Kent (1685–1748)

LICENSING
The Beanstalk Group
28 East 28th Street
New York, NY 10016
212-303-1142
Fax: 212-421-6388
www.beanstalk.com

LAN Partners Inc.
875 North Michigan Avenue, 31st Floor
Chicago, IL 60611
312-253-4123
Fax: 312-268-6123
www.lanpartnerslicensing.com

MAGAZINES

Architectural Digest
6300 Wilshire Boulevard
Los Angeles, CA 90048
www.architecturaldigest.com

Elle Décor
1633 Broadway
New York, NY 10019
212-767-5800
www.elledecor.com

House Beautiful
1700 Broadway
New York, NY 10018
212-649-2000
www.housebeautiful.com

Interior Design
360 Park Avenue South
New York, NY 10010
646-746-6400
www.interiordesign.net

Martha Stewart Living
226 West 26th Street
New York, NY 10001
212-741-4927
www.marthastewart.com

Metropolitan Home
www.methome.com

Traditional Home
1716 Locust Street
Des Moines, IA 50309-3023
515-284-3000
www.traditionalhome.com

Veranda
455 East Paces Ferry Road
Atlanta, GA 30305
404-975-5300
www.veranda.com

PROFESSIONAL ORGANIZATIONS

American Academy of Healthcare
Interior Designers (AAHID)
111 West Spring Valley Road, Suite 200
Richardson, TX 75081
972-759-0721
www.aahid.org

American Furniture Manufacturers
Association (AFMA)
P.O. Box HP-7
High Point, NC 27261
336-884-5000
Fax: 336-884-5303

American Home Furnishings Alliance
(AHFA)
317 West High Avenue, 10th Floor
High Point, NC 27260
336-884-5000
Fax: 336-884-5303
www.ahfa.us

American Institute of Architects (AIA)
1735 New York Avenue, NW
Washington, DC 20006-5292
800-AIA-3837
202-626-7300
Fax: 202-626-7547
www.aia.org

American Resort Development
Association (ARDA)
1201 15th Street NW, Suite 400
Washington, D.C. 20005-2842
202-371-6700
Fax: 202-289-8544
www.arda.org

American Society of Furniture
Designers (ASFD)
519 West Cornwallis Drive
Greensboro, NC 27408
336-617-3209
Fax: 274-9553
www.asfd.com

American Society of Interior Designers
(ASID)
608 Massachusetts Avenue, NE
Washington, DC 20002-6006
202-546-3480
Fax: 202-546-3240
www.asid.org

American Society of Journalists and
Authors (ASJA)
1501 Broadway, Suite 302
New York, NY 10036
212-997-0947
Fax: 212-937-2315
www.asja.org

American Society of Magazine Editors
(ASME)
asme@magazine.org

American Society of Newspaper Editors
(ASNE)
11609B Sunrise Valley Drive
Reston, VA 20191-1409
703-453-1122
Fax: 703-453-1133
www.asne.org

Art Director's Guild (ADG)
11969 Ventura Boulevard, Suite 200
Studio City, CA 91604
818-762-9995
Fax: 818-762-9997
www.artdirectors.org

Association for Contract Textiles (ACT)
Headquarters
P.O. Box 101981
Fort Worth, TX 76185
817-924-8048
Fax: 817-924-8050
www.contracttextiles.org

Association for Retail Environments (ARE)
4651 Sheridan Street, Suite 470
Hollywood, FL 33021
954-893-7300
Fax: 954-893-7500
www.nasfm.org

Association for Women in
Communications (AWC)
3337 Duke Street
Alexandria, VA 22314
703-370-7436
Fax: 703-370-7437
www.womcom.org

Center For Health Design
1850 Gateway Boulevard, Suite 1083
Concord, CA 94520
925-521-9404
Fax: 925-521-9405
www.healthdesign.org

Direct Marketing Association (DMA)
1120 Avenue of the Americas
New York, NY 10036-6700
Telephone: 212-768-7277
Fax: 212-302-6714
www.the-dma.org

Furniture Marketing Group (FMG)
www.fmgbuiyinggroup.com

High Point Showroom Association
High Point Design Center
P.O. Box 175
High Point, NC 27261
www.highpointshowroomassociation.
com

Hospitality Industry Network
NEWH, Inc.
P.O. Box 322
Shawano, WI 54166
800-593-NEWH
Fax: 800-693-NEWH
www.newh.org

International Association of Home
Staging Professionals (IAHSP)
4807 Clayton Road, Suite #200
Concord, CA 94521
925-686-2413
Fax: 925-686-6386
www.iahsp.com

International Furnishings and Design
Association (IFDA)
150 South Warner Road, Suite 156
King of Prussia, PA 19406
610-535-6422
Fax: 610-535-6423
www.ifda.com

International Hotel & Restaurant
Association (IH-RA)
48, Boulevard de Sebastopol 75003
Paris, France
331-4488-9220
Fax: 331-4488-9230
www.ih-ra.com

International Interior Design
Association (IIDA)
222 Merchandise Mart, Suite 567
Chicago, IL 60654
888-799-4432
Fax: 312-467-0779
www.iida.org

Interior Design Educators Council (IDEC)
7150 Winton Drive, Suite 300
Indianapolis, IN 46268
317-328-4437
Fax: 317-280-8527
www.idec.org

Interior Design Society (IDS)
3910 Tinsley Drive, Suite 101
High Point, NC 27265
800-888-9590
Fax: 336-801-6110
www.interiordesignsociety.org

Interior Designs of Canada (IDC)
717 Church Street
Toronto, Ontario, M4W 2M5
Canada
416-594-9310
Fax: 416-921-3660
www.interiordesigncanada.org

Interior Redesign Industry Specialist, Inc.
(IRID)
8 South Michigan Avenue, Suite 1000
Chicago, IL 60603
866-388-5208
Fax: 312-580-0165
www.weredesign.com

Institute of Store Planners (ISPO)
25 North Broadway
Tarrytown, NY 10590
914-332-0040
Fax: 914-332-1541
www.ispo.org

National Association of the Remodeling
Industry (NARI)
780 Lee Street, Suite 200
Des Plaines, IL 60016
847-298-9200
Fax: 847-298-9225
www.nari.org

National Council of Interior Design
Qualification (NCIDQ)
1200 18th Street, NW, Suite 1001
Washington, DC 20036-2506
202-721-0220
Fax: 202-721-0221
www.ncidq.org

National Kitchen & Bath Association
(NKBA)
687 Willow Grove Street
Hackettstown, NJ 07840
800-THE-NKBA
www.nkba.org

National Retail Federation (NRF)
325 7th Street, NW, Suite 1100
Washington, DC 20004
202-783-7971 or 800-673-4692
Fax: 202-737-2849
www.nrf.com

Organization of Black Designers (OBD)
300 M Street Southwest
Washington, DC 20024
202-659-3918
www.obd.org

Public Relations Society of America
(PRSA)
33 Maiden Lane, 11th Floor
New York, NY 10038-5150
212-460-1400
Fax: 212-995-0757
www.prsa.org

Set Decorators Society of America
(SDSA)
1646 North Cherokee Avenue
Hollywood, CA 90028
323-462-3060
Fax: 323-462-3099
www.sdsa.org

Society of Professional Journalists (SPJ)
3909 N. Meridian Street
Indianapolis, IN 46208
317-927-8000
Fax: 317-920-4789
www.spj.org

Themed Entertainment Organization
(TEA)
175 East Olive Avenue, Suite 100
Burbank, CA 91502-0126
818-843-8497
Fax: 818-843-8477
www.themeit.com

PUBLIC RELATIONS

KFWB Consulting Design Marketing
& Public Relations
8946 Appian Way
Los Angeles, CA 90046
323-650-4914
212-772-8171
www.kfwbdesign.com

PUBLISHING

Clarkson Potter
Random House, Inc.
1745 Broadway
New York, NY 10019
212-782-9000
www.randomhouse.com/crown/
clarksonpotter.html

Gibbs Smith
P.O. Box 667
Layton, UT 84041
800-748-5439
Fax: 800-213-3023
www.gibbs-smith.com

Harper Collins/Collins Design
10 East 53rd Street
New York, NY 10022
212-207-7000
www.harpercollins.com

Harry N. Abrams/Abrams Books
115 West 18th Street
New York, NY 10011
212-206-7715
Fax: 212-519-1210
www.hnabooks.com

Pointed Leaf Press
Suzanne Slesin
1100 Madison Avenue
New York, NY 10028
212- 535-1086
www.pointedleafpress.com

Rizzoli
300 Park Avenue South, 3rd Floor
New York, NY 10010
212-387-3400
www.rizzoliusa.com

Stewart, Tabori and Chang
c/o Harry N. Abrams
115 West 18th Street
New York, NY 10011
212- 206-7715
Fax: 212-519-1210
www.hnabooks.com

RETAILERS
Ballard Designs
800-536-7551
www.ballarddesigns.com

Bella Linea
2210 Crestmoor Road
Nashville, TN 37215
615-352-4041
www.bellalinea.com

Charlotte Moss
20 East 63rd Street
New York, NY 10021
212-308-7088
Fax: 212-308-7888
www.charlottemoss.com

Crate & Barrel
800-967-6696
www.crateandbarrel.com

Environment Furniture, Inc.
7257 Beverly Boulevard, Suite 108
Los Angeles, CA 90036
323-935-1330
www.environmentfurniture.com

Grandin Road
866-668-5962
www.grandinroad.com

JC Penney
www.jcpenney.com

Kmart
www.kmart.com

Mitchell Gold + Bob Williams
135 One Comfortable Place
Taylorsville, NC 28681
Fax: 828-632-2693
www.mitchellgold.com

Nina Griscom Inc.
958 Lexington Avenue
New York, NY 10021
212-771-7373
Fax: 212-717-7375
www.ninagriscom.com

Sue Fisher King
3067 Sacramento St,
San Francisco, CA 94115
415-922-7276
Fax: 415-922-9241
www.suefisherking.com

Target
800-440-0680
www.target.com

Williams Sonoma Home
888-922-4108
www.wshome.com

SHOWROOMS AND MANUFACTURERS
Baker, Knapp and Tubbs
www.kohlerinteriors.com

Beacon Hill
800-333-3777
www.robertallendesign.com

Brunschwig and Fils
75 Virginia Road
North White Plains, NY 10603
914-684-5800
Fax: 914-684-5842
www.brunschwig.com

California Closets
1000 Fourth Street, Suite 800
San Rafael, CA 94901
415-256-8500
Fax: 415-256-8501
www.californiaclosets.com

Designer's Gallery
3205 B Powell Avenue
Nashville, TN 37204
615-279-5600
Fax: 615-279-5603
www.designersgallery.biz

Donghia, Inc.
256 Washington Street
Mt. Vernon, NY 10553
914-665-0800
www.donghia.com

F. Schumacher & Co.
79 Madison Avenue, 15th Floor
New York, NY 10016
800-523-1300
www.fschumacher.com

Haworth
www.haworth.com

Hickory Chair
www.hickorychair.com

Merillat
www.merillat.com

Ralph Pucci International
www.ralphpucci.net

Thomas Lavin
8687 Melrose Avenue, Suite B310
West Hollywood, CA 90069
310-278-2456
Fax: 310-278-2469
www.thomaslavin.com

Todd Oldham for La-Z-Boy Furniture
www.la-z-boy.com

Travis & Company
351 Peachtree Hills Avenue NE
Atlanta, GA 30305
800-258-2214
Fax: 404-233-0192
www.travisandcompany.com

Tui Pranich
1855 Griffin Road, Suite B-318
Dania Beach, FL 33004
954-925-6801
Fax: 954-925-6884
www.tuipranich.com

William Haines Collection
www.williamhaines.com

TELEVISION

ABC (*Extreme Makeover* Series)
500 S. Buena Vista Street
Burbank, CA 91521-4551
http://abc.go.com

Bravo TV (*Top Design*)
NBC/Universal
3000 W. Alameda Ave., Suite 250
Burbank, CA 91523
www.bravotv.com

DIY Network
www.diynetwork.com

Fine Living Channel
www.fineliving.com

Home and Garden Television (HGTV)
9721 Sherrill Boulevard
Knoxville, TN 37932
865-694-2700
Fax: 865-531-1588
www.hgtv.com

PBS (*This Old House*)
www.pbs.org

TLC/Discovery Channel
(*Trading Spaces*)
www.tlc.discovery.com

UNIONS/GUILDS

American Federation of Television and
Radio Artists (AFTRA)
5757 Wilshire Boulevard, 9th Floor
Los Angeles, California 90036-3689
323-634-8100
Fax: 323-634-8194
www.aftra.org

Screen Actors Guild (SAG)
5757 Wilshire Boulevard, 7th Floor
Los Angeles, CA 90036-3600
323-954-1600
www.sag.org

Bibliography

BUSINESS AND CAREER

Allen, Lloyd. (2006). *Being Martha: The Inside Story of Martha Stewart and Her Amazing Life.* New York: Wiley.

Byron, Christopher M. (2002). *Martha Inc.: The Incredible Story of Martha Stewart Living Omnimedia.* New York: Wiley.

Forest, Sara D. *Vault Guide to Interior Design Careers* (2006*).* New York: Vault, Inc.

Goulet, Tag and Catherine. *Fabjob Guide to Become an Interior Decorator* (2005). Fabjob.com.

Knackstedt, Mary V. (1995). *Interior Design & Beyond: Art-Science-Industry.* New York: Wiley.

Piotrowski, Christine M. (2003). *Becoming an Interior Designer (A Guide to Careers in Design).* New York: Wiley.

Popcorn, Faith and Marigold, Lys. (1996). *Clicking: 16 Trends to Future Fit Your Life, Your Work, and Your Business.* New York: Harper Collins.

Stearns, David. (2001). *Opportunities in Interior Design and Decorating Careers.* New York: McGraw-Hill.

U.S. Department of Labor (2006). *Occupational Outlook Handbook, 2006–07 Edition.* JIST Works.

Znoy, Jason A. and ASID Illinois (2004)**.** *Professional Interior Design: A Career Guide.* iUniverse, Inc, NewYork.

COMMUNICATIONS

Eakins, Patricia. *Writing for Interior Design* (2005). New York: Fairchild Books.

Foote-Smith, Elizabeth. (1997). *Opportunities in Writing Careers.* Chicago: NTC Contemporary Publishing Group.

Hamilton, Nancy M. (2004). *Uncovering the Secrets of Magazine Writing: A Step-by-Step Guide to Writing Creative Nonfiction for Print and Internet Publication.* Allyn and Bacon.

Kliment, Stephen W. (2006). *Writing for Design Professionals: A Guide to Writing Successful Proposals, Letters, Brochures,*

Portfolios, Reports, Presentations and Job Applications, Second Edition. New York: W. W. Norton.

Ruberg, Michelle (2005). *Writer's Digest Handbook of Magazine Article Writing: Handbook of Article Writing.* Writer's Digest Books.

Wray, Cheryl Sloan (2004). *Writing for Magazines: A Beginner's Guide.* New York: McGraw Hill.

CONTRACT DESIGN

Alves, Alison (1996). *Commercial (Interior Design Library Series).* Rockport, MA.

Caywood, Douglas (2003). *The Designers Workspace: Ultimate Office Design.* Architectural Press.

Chueca, Pilar (2005). *Office and Corporate Interiors.* Links International.

Farren, Carol (1999). *Planning and Managing Interior Projects.* Kingston, MA: R. S. Means.

Harmon, Sharon Koomen (2005). *The Codes Guidebook for Interiors.* New York: Wiley.

Lawson, Fred (1995). *Hotels and Resorts: Planning and Design (Butterworth Architecture Design and Development Guides).* Architectural Press.

Leach, Robin and Wilson, Trisha. (2007). *Spectacular Hotels: The Most Remarkable Places On Earth.* Panache Publishing.

Mays, Vernon (1999). *Office and Work Spaces: International Portfolio of 43 Designers.* Rockport Publishers.

Piotrowski, Christen. *Designing Commercial Interiors.* New York: Wiley, 1999.

Rayfield, Julie K (1997). *The Office Interior Design Guide: An Introduction for Facility and Design Professionals.* New York: Wiley Professional.

Reznikoff, S. (1989). *Specifications for Commercial Interiors.* New York: Watson Guptill.

Rutes, Walter (2001). *Hotel Design, Planning and Development, New Edition.* New York: W. W. Norton and Company.

Yee, Roger (2005). *Corporate Interiors, Volume 6.* Visual Reference Publications.

EDUCATION

American Society of Interior Designers (2007). *The Interior Design Profession: Facts and Figures.* Washington, D.C.: American Society of Interior Designers.

Ballast, Kent (2006). *Interior Design Reference Manual: A Guide to the NCIDQ Exam (3rd Edition).* California: Professional Publications.

Barron, Cynthia (2003). *Designing a Digital Portfolio.* New Riders Press.

Cramer, James P. (2007). *America's Best Architecture & Design Schools.* Greenway Communications.

Doyle, Michael E. (2002). *Color Drawing: Design Drawing Skills and Techniques for Architects, Landscape Architects, and Interior Designers, 2nd Edition.* New York: Wiley.

Eisenman, Sara (2006). *Building Design Portfolios: Innovative Concepts for Presenting Your Work (Design Field Guides).* Rockport Publishers.

Gilliatt, Mary (1985). *Interior Design Course.* New York: Watson Guptill, 2001.

Henley, Pamela E. B. (2002). *Interior Design Practicum Exam Workbook, Second Edition.* California: Professional Publications.

Lin, Mike W. *Architectural Rendering Techniques: A Color Reference.* New York: Wiley.

Linton, Harold and Rost Steven (2004). *Portfolio Design, Third Edition*. New York: W.W. Norton & Company.

Market Probe International (2006). *2006 Universe Study of the Interior Design Profession*.

Mills, Criss B. (2005). *Designing with Models: A Studio Guide to Making and Using Architectural Design Models*. New York: Wiley.

Mitton, Maureen (2003). *Interior Design Visual Presentation: A Guide to Graphics, Models and Presentation Techniques, Second Edition*. New York.

Pile, John (2000). *A History of Interior Design*. New York: Wiley.

_____. (2003). *Interior Design (3rd Edition)*. New York: Prentice Hall.

Piotrowski, Christine (2003). *Becoming an Interior Designer*. New York: Wiley & Sons.

Ray, Katerina Ruedi (2004). *The Portfolio: An Architectural Student's Handbook (Architectural Students Handbook)*. New York: W. W. Norton & Company.

Slotkis, Susan (2005). *Foundations of Interior Design*. New York: Fairchild Publications.

Sparke, Penny (1998). *A Century of Design: Design Pioneers of the 20th Century*. New York: Barron's.

Sutherland, Martha (1999). *Model Making: A Basic Guide*. New York: W.W. Norton and Company.

Tangaz, Tomris (2003). *Interior Design Course: Principles, Practices and Techniques for the Aspiring Designer*. New York: Wiley.

INTERIOR DESIGN

Abercrombie, Stanley and Whiton, Sherill (2006). *Interior Design and Decoration*. Prentice Hall Art: New York.

Abercrombie, Stanley (1991). *A Philosophy of Interior Design (Icon Editions)*. Westview Press.

_____. (2003). Century of *Interior Design 1900–2000: The Designers, the Products, and the Profession*. Rizzoli International Publications: New York.

Adler, Jonathan (2005). *My Prescription for Anti-Depressive Living*. Collins Design: New York.

Baldwin, Billy. (2008) *Billy Baldwin Decorates*. New York: Rizzoli.

Banks-Oye, Roger (1987). *Colefax and Fowler Interior Inspirations*. Ryland, Peters and Small.

Blakemore, Robbie G. (1997). *The History of Interior Design and Furniture: From Ancient Egypt to Nineteenth-Century Europe*. New York: Wiley.

Brown, Erica. (1980) *Interior Views: Design at Its Best*. New York: Viking Studio.

_____. (1982). *Sixty Years of Interior Design: The World Of McMillen*. New York: Viking Studio.

Campbell, Nina (1996). *Art of Decoration*. New York: Clarkson Potter.

_____. (2004). *Nina Campbell's Decorating Notebook: Insider Secrets and Decorating Ideas For Your Home*. New York: Clarkson Potter.

Campbell, Nina (2000). *Decorating Secrets*. New York: Clarkson Potter.

Campbell, Nina and Parsons, Alexandra. (2007) *Elements of Design: Elegant Wisdom That Works In Every Room of Your Home*. Cico.

Clodagh. (2001). *Total Design: Contemplate, Cleanse, Clarify and Create Your Personal Space*. New York: Clarkson Potter.

Coelho, Susie. (2002). *Susie Coelho's Everyday Styling: Easy Tips for Home,*

Garden, and Entertaining. New York. Simon & Schuster.

—————. (2003). *Susie Coelho's Styling for Entertaining: 8 Simple Steps, 12 Miracle Makeovers.* New York. Simon & Schuster.

—————. (2006). *Secrets of a Style Diva: A Get-Inspired Guide to Your Creative Side.* Nashville: Thomas Nelson.

Dampierre, Florence (1989). *The Decorator.* New York: Rizzoli.

De Wolfe, Elsie (2004). *The House in Good Taste.* New York: Rizzoli. Originally published in l913.

Diamonstein, Barbara Lee. (1982). *Interior Design.* New York: Rizzoli.

Donghia, Sherri and Lehrman, Karen (2006). *Donghia: The Artistry of Living in Style.* New York: Bulfinch.

Frankel, Candie; Litcheield, Michael and Manroe, Candace Ord. (2002). *Design and Details: Creative Ideas for Styling Your Home.* Metrobooks.

Gross, Kim Johnson and Stone, Jeff. (1993) *Chic Simple Home.* New York: Alfred A. Knopf.

Hampton, Mark (1989). *Mark Hampton on Decorating.* New York: Random House.

—————. (1992). *Legendary Decorators of the 20th Century.* London: Robert Hale.

Hicks, Ashley. (2002). *David Hicks: Designer.* Scriptum Editions.

Hicks, David. *Style and Design (1988).* Boston: Little, Brown.

Jeffrey, Noel. *Design Diary (2001).* New York: Rizzoli.

Jeffrey, Noel. *Interior Details.* (1994). New York: PBC.

Jones, Chester (1989). Colefax and Fowler. New York: Bulfinch.

Kemble, Celerie (2008). *Celerie Kemble: To Your Taste: Creating Modern Rooms with a Traditional Twist.* New York: Clarkson Potter.

Lewis, Adam (2001). *Van Day Truex, The Man Who Defined Twentieth Century Taste and Style.* New York: Penguin.

—————. (2004). *Albert Hadley: The Story of America's Preeminent Interior Designer.* New York: Rizzoli.

Madden, Chris (1997). *A Room of Her Own: Women's Personal Spaces.* New York: Clarkson Potter.

Manroe, Candace. (1997) *Home Office.* Reader's Digest.

—————. (2003). *Uncluttered: Storage Room by Room.* New York: Freidman/ Fairfax.

Martha Stewart Living Magazine. (1996). *How to Decorate: The Best of Martha Stewart Living.* New York: Clarkson Potter.

Parish, Sister; Hadley, Albert and Petankas, Christopher. (1995). *Parish Hadley: Sixty Years of American Design.* Boston: Little, Brown.

Patton, Phil. (2004). *Michael Graves Designs the Art of the Everyday Object.* New York: Melcher Media.

Russell, Margaret (2001). *Designing Women: Interiors by Leading Style Makers.* New York: Stewart, Tabori and Chang.

Sparke, Penny (1998). *A Century of Design: Design Pioneers of the 20th Century.* New York: Barron's.

Tappert, Annette and Edkins, Diana. (1994). *The Power of Style.* New York: Crown.

Varney, Carleton (1980). *There's No Place Like Home: Confessions of an Interior Designer.* New York: Bobbs Merrill.

—————. (2006). *In the Pink: Dorothy Draper, America's Most Fabu-*

lous Decorator. New York: Pointed Leaf Press.

Wearstler, Kelly (2004). *Modern Glamour: The Art of Unexpected Style.* New York: Collins Design.

_____. (2006). *Domicilium Decoratus.* New York: Collins Design.

Wolf, Vicente (2002). *Learning to See: Bringing the World Around You Into Your Home.* New York: Artisan.

_____. (2006). *Crossing the Boundaries: A Global Vision of Design.* Monacelli Press.

INTERIOR DESIGN PRACTICE

Ballast, Kent (2005). *Interior Construction and Detailing for Designers and Architects, Third Edition.* California: Professional Publications.

Coleman, Cindy and *Interior Design Magazine* (2001). *Interior Design Handbook of Professional Practice.* New York: McGraw-Hill Professional.

Crawford, Tad (2001). *Business and Legal Forms for Interior Designers.* New York: Allworth Press.

Downey, Joel (1995). *Successful Interior Projects Through Effective Contract Documents.* R. S. Means.

Gibbs, Jenny (1995). *A Handbook for Interior Designers.* London: Ward Lock.

Kendall, Gordon T. (2005). *Designing Your Business.* New York: Fairchild.

Knackstedt, Mary. (1992). *Marketing and Selling Design Services: The Designer Client Relationship.* Van Nostrand Reinhold.

_____. (2006). *The Interior Design Business Handbook: A Complete Guide to Profitability.* New York: Wiley.

Onstott. Scott (2005). *Enhancing CAD Drawings with Photoshop.* Sybex.

Sampson, Carol (2001). *Estimating for Interior Designers.* New York: Watson-Guptill.

Siegel, Harry (1982). *A Guide to Business Principles and Practices for Interior Designers, Revised Edition.* New York: Watson Guptill.

Williams, Theo Stephan (2005). *The Interior Designers Guide to Pricing, Estimating and Budgeting.* New York: Allworth Press.

INTERNET

www.accessorymerchandising.com
www.artdirectors.org
www.asid.org
www.careersininteriordesign.com
www.contractmagazine.com
www.designtrade.net
www.dezignare.com
www.furnituretoday.com
www.homeaccentstoday.com
www.iida.com
www.interiordesignjobs.com
www.interiordesign.net
www.setdecorators.org

MAGAZINES

Architectural Digest
Architectural Record
Array
ASID Icon
Better Homes and Gardens
Beautiful Homes
British House and Garden
Coastal Living
County Living
Dwell
Elle Décor
Home
House Beautiful
Interior Design
Martha Stewart Living

Metropolis
Metropolitan Home
Renovation Style
Set Décor
Southern Accents
Traditional Home
Unique Homes
Veranda
Vogue Living
Wallpaper
Western Interiors
World of Décor

PRODUCTION DESIGN AND SET DECORATION

Albrecht, Donald (2000). *Designing Dreams: Modern Architecture in the Movies.* Santa Monica: Hennessey + Ingalls.

Bellantoni, Patti (2005). *If It's Purple, Someone's Gonna Die: The Power of Color in Visual Storytelling.* Focal Press.

Heisner, Beverly (1997). *Production Design in the Contemporary American Film.*

————. (2002). *Film Guide to Production Design.* New York: Allworth Press.

Jefferson, North Carolina: McFarland & Company.

Lamster, Mark (2000). *Architecture and Film.* New York: Princeton Architectural Press.

Lo Brutto, Vincent (2002). *The Filmmaker's Guide to Production Design.* New York: Allworth Press.

Neumann, Dietrich (1999). *Film Architecture: From Metropolis to Blade Runner.* Munich: Prestel.

Preston, Ward (1994). *What an Art Director Does: An Introduction to Motion Picture Production Design.* Los Angeles: Silman-James Press.

Sennett, Robert S. (1994). *Setting the Scene: The Great Hollywood Art Directors.* New York: Abrams, Inc.

Set Décor Magazine, Set Decorator's Society of America. www.setdecorators. org.

Woodbridge, Patricia (2000). *Designer Drafting for the Entertainment World.* Focal Press.

RETAILING

Cerver, Francisco (1997). *Boutiques.* New York: Watson Guptill.

Dennis, Charles (2004). *E-Retailing.* New York: Routledge E-Business.

Edwards, Clive (2005). *Turning Houses into Homes: A History of Retailing and Consumption of Domestic Furnishings.* Ashgate.

Edwards, Diana (2003). *Catalog Design: The Art of Creating Desire.* Rockport, MA.

Floor, Ko (2006). *Branding a Store: How to Build Successful Retail Brands in a Changing Marketplace.* Kogan Page.

Muldoon, Katie (1995). *How to Profit Through Catalog Marketing.* NTC.

Richards, Kristen (2002). *Retail and Restaurant Spaces: An International Portfolio of 41 Designers.* Rockport, MA.

Schroeder, Carol O. (2002). *Specialty Shop Retailing; How to Run Your Own Store Revised.* New York: Wiley.

Varley, R. (2001) *Retail Product Management, Buying and Merchandising.* Routledge.

Worsley, Tim (2001). *Building a Website.* New York: DK Publishing.

SPECIALTY DESIGN

Cheng, Kelley and Yabuka, Narelle (2005). *Hip Interiors: Shops and Showrooms: Style Shopping*. Rockport Publishers.

Delgado, Llorenc Bonet (2005). Ultimate Shop Design. Te Neues Publishing.

Fischer, Joachim (2004). *Lounge Design*. Daab.

Huffadine, Margaret (1999). *Resort Design: Planning, Architecture and Interiors*. New York: McGraw Hill Professional.

Kibert, Charles J. (2005). *Sustainable Construction: Green Building Design and Delivery*. New York: Wiley.

Mendler, Sandra F. (2005). *The HOK Guidebook to Sustainable Design*. New York: Wiley.

Pegler, Martin (2001). *Gourmet and Specialty Shops*. Visual Reference Publications.

Ryder, Bethan (2005). *New Bar and Club Design*. New York: Abbeville Press.

Credits

OPENER. © Branko Miokovic/iStock Photo

FIGURE 3.1. University of Cincinnati

FIGURE 3.2. Somos Images/Corbis

FIGURE 3.3. University of Cincinnati

FIGURE 3.4. RISD/© 2007 John Horner

FIGURE 3.5. University of Cincinnati

FIGURE 3.6. Copyright 2008 by Greenway Communications, L.L.C. Used with permission. All rights reserved.

FIGURE 3.7. © www.imagesource.com

FIGURE 3.8. RISD/© 2007 Alice Engel/MFA Textiles

FIGURE 3.9. RISD/© 2007 Mark Johnston

FIGURE 3.10. Valtekz/Katherine Slinghuff

FIGURE 3.11. Branko Miokovic/iStock Photo

FIGURE 3.12. Copyright 2008 American Society of Interior Designers

FIGURE 3.13. Copyright 2008 American Society of Interior Designers

FIGURE 3.14. Courtesy of IIDA

FIGURE 3.15. Copyright 2008 American Society of Interior Designers

OPENER. © Radius Images/Corbis

FIGURE 4.1. Patrik Giardino/Corbis

FIGURE 4.5. © Amanda Rohde/iStockPhoto

FIGURE 4.6. iStockPhoto

FIGURE 4.7. iStockPhoto

FIGURE 4.10. © Dieter K. Henke/iStockPhoto

FIGURE 4.12. iStockPhoto

OPENER. Jan Baldwin/*Nina Campbell's Decorating Notebook*/Published by CICO Books

FIGURE 5.1. Courtesy of Hickory Chair

FIGURE 5.2. Design and Photography by Vicente Wolf

FIGURE 5.3. Sean Justice/Corbis

FIGURE 5.4. Courtesy of Han Yoon Lee; Shelby Bogaard; Tracy Franson

FIGURE 5.5. Chris Carroll/Corbis

FIGURE 5.6. © Branko Miokovic/iStockPhoto

FIGURE 5.7. Copyright Peter Manganelli

FIGURE 5.8. © Silvia Jansen/iStockPhoto

FIGURE 5.9. © Frank van Haalen/iStockPhoto

FIGURE 5.10. Photography by Vicente Wolf

FIGURE 5.11. Courtesy of Hickory Chair

FIGURE 5.12. Courtesy of Hickory Chair

FIGURE 5.13. Courtesy of Hickory Chair

FIGURE 5.14. Alexa Hampton/Courtesy of Visual Comfort

FIGURE 5.15. Courtesy of Nina Campbell

FIGURE 5.16. *Nina Campbell's Decorating Notebook*/Published by CICO Books

FIGURE 5.17. Courtesy of Nina Campbell

FIGURE 5.18. *Nina Campbell's Decorating Notebook*/Published by CICO Books

FIGURE 5.19. Courtesy of Nina Campbell

FIGURE 5.20. Photography by Vicente Wolf

FIGURE 5.21. Photography by Vicente Wolf

FIGURE 5.22. Vicente Wolf/Ralph Pucci International

FIGURE 5.23. Design and Photography by Vicente Wolf

OPENER. Wilson & Associates/Photography by Robert Miller

FIGURE 6.1. Wilson & Associates/Michael Wilson

FIGURE 6.2. KWID/Photography by Annie Schlechter

FIGURE 6.3. Clodagh/Copyright Daniel Aubrey

FIGURE 6.4. KWID/Photography by Grey Crawford

FIGURE 6.5. Courtesy of Gensler

FIGURE 6.6. iStockPhoto

FIGURE 6.7. From the archives of Dorothy Draper & Company, Inc. (New York)/The Carleton Varney Design Group

FIGURE 6.8. Luxury Brands

FIGURE 6.9. Gensler/Nlc Lehoux

FIGURE 6.10. Wilson Associates/Andrew Cerino

FIGURE 6.11. Wilson Associates/Michael Wilson

FIGURE 6.12. Wilson Associates/Photography by Peter Vitale

FIGURE 6.13. Wilson Associates/Photography by Peter Malinowski

FIGURE 6.14. Collins Design

FIGURE 6.15. KWID/Photography by Annie Schlechter

FIGURE 6.16. KWID/Photography by Grey Crawford

OPENER. Jonathan Adler/Photography by Annie Schlechter

FIGURE 7.1. Photo provided by Crate & Barrel

FIGURE 7.2. Branca/Thibault Jeanson

FIGURE 7.3. Branca/Thibault Jeanson

FIGURE 7.4. Mitchell Gold + Bob Williams

FIGURE 7.5. Mitchell Gold + Bob Williams

FIGURE 7.6. Nina Griscom

FIGURE 7.7. Nina Griscom

FIGURE 7.8. Courtesy of Chapman Radcliffe

FIGURE 7.9. KWID Designs/Photography by Annie Schlechter

FIGURE 7.10. Benny Chan © Environment Furniture

FIGURE 7.11. Bella Linea

FIGURE 7.12. Mitchell Gold + Bob Williams

FIGURE 7.13. Mitchell Gold + Bob Williams

FIGURE 7.14. Mitchell Gold + Bob Williams

FIGURE 7.15. Mitchell Gold + Bob Williams

FIGURE 7.16. Courtesy of Ballard Designs

FIGURE 7.17. Courtesy of Ballard Designs

FIGURE 7.18. Courtesy of Ballard Designs

FIGURE 7.19. Courtesy of Ballard Designs

FIGURE 7.20. Sue Fisher King

OPENER. J. Robert Scott/Photography by Tim Street-Porter

FIGURE 8.1. Brunschwig and Fils

FIGURE 8.2. Charles Cohen/D&D Building All right s Reserved

FIGURE 8.3. Thomas Lavin Inc.

FIGURE 8.4. J. Robert Scott/Photography by Tim Street-Porter

FIGURE 8.5. Brunschwig and Fils

FIGURE 8.6. Brunschwig and Fils

FIGURE 8.7. © 2008 F. Schumacher & Co.

FIGURE 8.8. Clodagh/Copyright Daniel Aubry

FIGURE 8.9. © 2008 F. Schumacher & Co.

FIGURE 8.10. J. Robert Scott/Photography by Jim McHugh

FIGURE 8.11. Courtesy of J. Robert Scott

FIGURE 8.12. Courtesy of J. Robert Scott

FIGURE 8.13. J. Robert Scott/Photography by Tim Street-Porter

FIGURE 8.14. Travis & Company/Paper City

FIGURE 8.15. Travis & Company/Paper City

FIGURE 8.16. Travis & Company/Paper City

FIGURE 8.17. Travis & Company/Paper City

FIGURE 8.18. Travis & Company/Paper City

FIGURE 8.19. Courtesy of Hickory Chair

FIGURE 8.20. Courtesy of Hickory Chair

FIGURE 8.21. Courtesy of Hickory Chair

OPENER. © William Haines Design

FIGURE 9.1. Jonathan Adler/Photography by Annie Schlechter

FIGURE 9.2. © William Haines Design

FIGURE 9.3. Clodagh

FIGURE 9.4. Sanctuary Collection™/Clodagh by Oakworks®

FIGURE 9.5. Laneventure

FIGURE 9.6. Courtesy of Hickory Chair

FIGURE 9.7. Michael Graves/Courtesy of Michael Graves Design Group

FIGURE 9.8. Michael Graves/Courtesy of Alessi

FIGURE 9.9. Michael Graves/Courtesy of David Edward Company

FIGURE 9.10. Michael Graves/Courtesy of Michael Graves Design Group

FIGURE 9.11. John Black

FIGURE 9.12. John Black

FIGURE 9.13. John Black

FIGURE 9.14. Jonathan Adler/Photography by Annie Schlechter

FIGURE 9.15. Jonathan Adler/Photography by Annie Schlechter

FIGURE 9.16. Jonathan Adler/Photography by Annie Schlechter

FIGURE 9.17. Jonathan Adler/Photography by Annie Schlechter

FIGURE 9.18. Jonathan Adler/Photography by Annie Schlechter

PAGE 189. Courtesy of J. Robert Scott

OPENER. AP

FIGURE 10.1. Courtesy of Susie Coelho Enterprises

FIGURE 10.2. © Fernando Bengoechea/Beateworks/Corbis

FIGURE 10.3. © Fernando Bengoechea/Beateworks/Corbis

FIGURE 10.4. Courtesy of Celerie Kimble

FIGURE 10.5. Valtekz/Katherine Slingluff

FIGURE 10.6. Courtesy of Everett Collection

FIGURE 10.7. © Davis Factor/Corbis

FIGURE 10.8. Laneveture

FIGURE 10.9. Photography by Scott Duncan

FIGURE 10.10. Photofest

FIGURE 10.11. Photofest

FIGURE 10.12. Copyright © 2008 by Martha Stewart Living Omnimedia Inc. Cover photo by Hugh Stewart

FIGURE 10.13. © Najlah Feanny/Corbis

FIGURE 10.14. Courtesy of Susie Coelho Enterprises

FIGURE 10.15. Courtesy of Susie Coelho Enterprises

FIGURE 10.16. Chris Casson Madden/Copyright Charles Maraia

FIGURE 10.17. Chris Casson Madden/Copyright Jennifer Levy

FIGURE 10.18. Chris Casson Madden/Copyright Matt Johnson

FIGURE 10.19. Chris Casson Madden/Copyright Matt Johnson/ Photography by Scott Duncan

PAGE 210. Beanstalk Group/© 2008 The Beanstalk Group LLC. All rights reserved.

OPENER. Hirsch Bedner Associates/Photography by Durston Saylor

FIGURE 11.1. Hirsch Bedner Associates/Photography by Corey Weiner

FIGURE 11.2. Hirsch Bedner Associates/Photography by Corey Weiner

FIGURE 11.3. Hirsch Bedner Associates/Photography by Durson Saylor

FIGURE 11.4. Wilson Associates/Photography by Michael Wilson

FIGURE 11.5. Hirsch Bedner Associates/Photography by Stephen Allard

FIGURE 11.6. Hirsch Bedner Associates/Photography by Peter Mealin

FIGURE 11.7. Gensler

FIGURE 11.8. Red Cover

FIGURE 11.9. Courtesy of Susie Coelho Enterprises

FIGURE 11.10. Brian Gassel/TVSA

FIGURE 11.11. Hirsch Bedner Associates/Photography by Peter Mealin

FIGURE 11.12. M.A. Meagher Design and Biltmore Estate

FIGURE 11.13. Callison, Chris Eden

FIGURE 11.14. Callison, Chris Eden

FIGURE 11.15. Design and Photography by Vicente Wolf

FIGURE 11.16. Courtesy of Nina Campbell

FIGURE 11.17. Michael Graves/Courtesy Delta Faucet

FIGURE 11.18. Michael Graves/Photography by Richard Payne/ Courtesy of Michael Graves and Associates

FIGURE 11.19. © 2008 California Closet, Inc. All rights reserved.

FIGURE 11.20. Haworth

FIGURE 11.21. Soucie Horner

FIGURE 11.22. Soucie Horner

FIGURE 11.23. © 2008 Califnornia Closet, Inc. All rights reserved.

FIGURE 11.24. Courtesy of Hickory Chair

FIGURE 11.25. ABC

FIGURE 11.26. Hirsch Bedner Associates

FIGURE 11.27. © 2006/RWR Designs Ltd./Dallas/ *www.rwrdesigns.com*

FIGURE 11.28. Holland America Line's MS Prinsendam-Superior Verandah Suite

OPENER. Collins Design; Harry N Abrams; Photography by Tria Giovan/Courtesy of *Traditional Home*; Photography by Tria Giovan/Courtesy of *Veranda*

FIGURE 12.1. © IPS Co., Ltd./Beateworks/Corbis

FIGURE 12.2. Photogrpahy by Tria Giovan, Courtesy of Traditional Home

FIGURE 12.3. KWID Designs

FIGURE 12.4. Harper Collins

FIGURE 12.5. Collins Design

FIGURE 12.6. Photography by Tria Giovan/Courtesy of *Veranda*

FIGURE 12.7. © Smart Creatives/Corbis

FIGURE 12.8. *Architectural Digest Private Views: Inside the World's Greatest Homes* © 2007 Condé Nast Publications/Courtesy of Harry N. Abrams, Inc.

FIGURE 12.9. © Serge Kozak/zefa/Corbis

FIGURE 12.10. Gibbs Smith

FIGURE 12.11. Courtesy of Susie Coelho Enterprises

FIGURE 12.12. Karen Figilis

FIGURE 12.13. Undewater Eden © 2007 Jeffre L. Rotman. Courtesy of Harry N. Abrams, Inc.

FIGURE 12.14. *Poolside with Slim Aarons* © 2007 Getty Images. Courtesy of Harry N. Abrams, Inc.

FIGURE 12.15. *Great Houses of Texas* © 2008 Lisa Germany. Courtesy of Harry N. Abrams, Inc.

FIGURE 12.16. Candace Ord Manroe

FIGURE 12.17. Photography by Tria Giovan/Courtesy of *Traditional Home*

FIGURE 12.18. Photograpy by Deborah Whitlaw Llewellyn

FIGURE 12.19. Copyright 2007 *Veranda*

FIGURE 12.20. Photography by Tria Giovan/Courtesy of *Veranda*

FIGURE 12.21. Hirsch Bedner/Photogaphy by Vladon Elakovic

FIGURE 12.22. Hirsch Bedner/Photography by Corey Weiner

FIGURE 12.23. Hirsch Bedner/Photography by Stephen Allard

OPENER. © Fernando Bengoechea/Beateworks/Corbis

FIGURE 13.1. © Thaddeus Harden/Corbis

FIGURE 13.2. iStockPhoto

FIGURE 13.3. HGTV

FIGURE 13.4. CBS/Ron Tom/Landov

FIGURE 13.5. Photofest

FIGURE 13.6. Photofest

FIGURE 13.7. Photofest

FIGURE 13.8. Courtesy Constance Ramos

FIGURE 13.9. Photofest

FIGURE 13.10. Photofest

FIGURE 13.11. Photofest

FIGURE 13.12. Photofest

FIGURE 13.13. Sarah Richardson

OPENER. © Joseph Sohm/Visions of America/Corbis

FIGURE 14.1. Landov

FIGURE 14.2. Photofest

FIGURE 14.3. Courtesy of Everett Collection

FIGURE 14.4. ABC

FIGURE 14.5. ABC

FIGURE 14.6. NBC Photobank

FIGURE 14.7. Mark Friedberg/Focus Features

FIGURE 14.8. Mark Friedberg/Focus Features

FIGURE 14.9. Courtesy of NBC/*Set Decor* Magazine/ Ken Haber Photography

FIGURE 14.10. Glenda Rovello

FIGURE 14.11. Photofest

FIGURE 14.12. NBC Photobank

FIGURE 14.13. Courtesy of Cloudia Rebar

FIGURE 14.14. Courtesy of Cloudia Rebar

FIGURE 14.15. Courtesy of Cloudia Rebar

FIGURE 14.16. Courtesy of Cloudia Rebar

FIGURE 14.17. Weinstein Company

FIGURE 14.18. Weinstein Company

FIGURE 14.19. Andrew Baseman/Kelly Campbell

FIGURE 14.20. Andrew Baseman/Joshua McHugh

FIGURE 14.21. Andrew Baseman/Joshua McHugh

Index

About the Author

Author and interior designer Cathy Whitlock's work has appeared in books, magazines, homes, and businesses across the country. Author of the upcoming book *A Century of Hollywood Art Direction* (HarperCollins, 2009), Cathy is a contributing writer for *Traditional Home* and her articles have appeared in *Architectural Digest*, *Array*, *ASID Icon*, *Veranda*, *British Glamour*, and *Four Seasons* magazines. She has also been profiled in the *Wall Street Journal* and *The Fine Living Channel* and appeared as a frequent on-air personality on Home and Garden Television's highest rated daytime show *Decorating with Style*. She is a graduate of Parsons the New School for Design in New York and a member of ASID.